THE COMPLETE UPMANSHIP

THE COMPLETE UPMANSHIP

Stephen Potter

Including

GAMESMANSHIP
LIFEMANSHIP
ONE-UPMANSHIP
SUPERMANSHIP

Illustrated by Lt-Col. Frank Wilson

Holt, Rinehart and Winston

New York   Chicago   San Francisco

First published in United States in January 1971

Library of Congress Catalog Card Number:
73-121642

SBN:03-064045-8

Printed in the United States of America

CONTENTS

The Theory and Practice of

GAMESMANSHIP

OR
THE ART OF WINNING GAMES
WITHOUT ACTUALLY CHEATING

Exterior of Lord Plummer's Fives-Court Adjoining 'Hoses'

1

INTRODUCTORY

IF I HAVE been urged by my friends to take up my pen, for once, to write of this subject – so difficult in detail yet so simple in all its fundamental aspects – I do so on one condition. That I may be allowed to say as strongly as possible that although my name has been associated with this queer word 'gamesmanship', yet talk of priority in this kind of context is almost meaningless.

It is true that in the twenties certain notes passed between H. Farjeon and myself. But equally notes passed between H. Farjeon and F.Meynell. It is true that in March 1933 I conceived and wrote down the word 'gamesmanship' in a letter to Meynell. Speaking of a forth-coming lawn tennis match against two difficult opponents, I said '. . . we must employ gamesmanship'.

It is true also that I was the most regular visitor – 'chairman' would imply a formality which scarcely existed in those early days of argle-bargle and friendly disagreement – at the meetings which took place in pub parlour or empty billiard hall between G. Odoreida, Meynell, 'Wayfarer' and myself. It is true that it was in these dis-cussions that we evolved a basis of tactic and even plotted out a first

rough field of stratagem which determined the *centres of development*
from which the new technique spread in ever-widening circles.
Small beginnings, indeed, for a movement which has spread so far
from the confines of the country, and has shown itself too big to be
contained by the World of Games for which it was fashioned.

But after the first formulation the spade-work was certainly done as
much by Meynell and a few other devoted collaborators as by myself.
And how well – wise after the event – we realize, now, from his
practice and example, that Farjeon had the gist of the thing under
his nose – the essential factors, the actions and reactions of the whole
problem, without having the luck to see the patterning alignment, the
overall theory, which made them make sense.

And yet had it not been for the dogged spadework of Farjeon in
the middle twenties, we should none of us now be enjoying the
advantages of a theory which devolves as naturally from those meti-
culously collected data of his as Rutherford's enunciation of atomic
structure derived from the experiments of that once obscure chemist
Mierff.

Origins

What is gamesmanship? Most difficult of questions to answer
briefly. 'The Art of Winning Games Without Actually Cheating' –
that is my personal 'working definition'. What is its object? There have
been five hundred books written on the subject of games. Five hundred books on play and the tactics of play. Not one on the art of
winning.

I well remember the gritty floor and the damp roller-towels of the
changing-room where the idea of writing this book came to me. Yet
my approach to the thing had been gradual.

There had been much that had puzzled me – I am speaking now of
1928 – in the tension of our games of ping-pong at the Meynells'.
Before that there had been the ardours and endurances of friendly lawn
tennis at the Farjeons' house near Forest Hill, where Farjeon had
wrought such havoc among so many visitors, by his careful construc-
tion of a 'home court', by the use he made of the net with the unilateral
sag, or with a back line at the hawthorn end so nearly, yet not exactly,
six inches wider than the back line at the sticky end. There had been a
great deal of hard thinking on both sides during the wavering tide of
battle, ending slightly in my favour, of the prolonged series of golf
games between E. Lansbury and myself.

June 8th 1931

But it was in that changing-room after a certain game of lawn tennis in 1931 that the curtain was lifted, and I began to see. In those days I used to play lawn tennis for a small but progressive London College – Birkbeck, where I lectured. It happened that my partner at that time was C. Joad, the celebrated gamesman, who in his own sphere is known as metaphysician and educationist. Our opponents were usually young men from the larger colleges, competing against us not only with the advantage of age but also with a decisive advantage in style. They would throw the service ball very high in the modern manner: the back-hands, instead of being played from the navel, were played, in fact, on the back-hand, weight on right foot, in the exaggerated copy-book style of the time – a method of play which tends to reduce all games, as I believe, to a barrack-square drill by numbers; but, nevertheless, of acknowledged effectiveness.

In one match we found ourselves opposite a couple of particularly tall and athletic young men of this type from University College. We will call them Smith and Brown. The knock-up showed that, so far as play was concerned, Joad and I, playing for Birkbeck, had no chance. UC won the toss. It was Smith's service, and he cracked down a cannonball to Joad which moved so fast that Joad, while making some effort to suggest by his attitude that he had thought the ball was going to be a fault, nevertheless was unable to get near with his racket, which he did not even attempt to move. Score: fifteen-love. Service to me. I had had time to gauge the speed of this serve, and the next one did, in fact, graze the edge of my racket-frame. Thirty-love. Now Smith was serving again to Joad – who this time, as the ball came straight towards him, was able, by grasping the racket firmly with both hands, to receive the ball on the strings, whereupon the ball shot back to the other side and volleyed into the stop-netting near the ground behind Brown's feet.

Now here comes the moment on which not only this match, but so much of the future of British sport was to turn. Score: forty-love. Smith at S^1 (see p. 12) is about to cross over to serve to me (at P). When Smith gets to a point (K) *not less than one foot and not more than two feet* beyond the centre of the court (I know now what I only felt then – that timing is everything in this gambit), Joad (standing at J^2) called across the net, in an even tone:

'Kindly say clearly, please, whether the ball was in or out.'

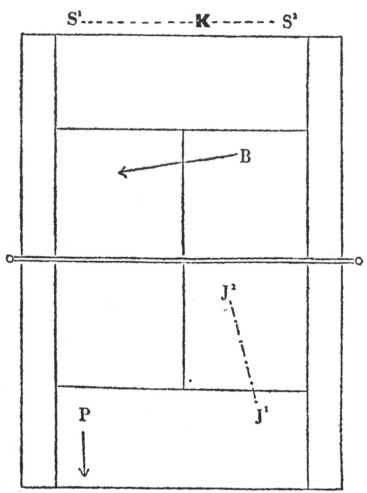

Key: P = Potter, J = Joad, S = Smith, B = Brown. The dotted line represents Smith's path from S[1] to S[2]. K represents the point he has reached on the cross-over when Joad has moved along the line (dot and dash) J[1] (where he had tried to return Smith's service) to J[2]. Smith having arrived at, but not further than, the point K on the line S[1]–S[2], J (Joad) speaks.

Crude to our ears, perhaps. A Stone-Age implement. But beautifully accurate gamesmanship for 1931. For the student must realize that these two young men were both in the highest degree charming, well-mannered young men, perfect in their sportsmanship and behaviour. Smith (at point K) stopped dead.

SMITH: I'm so sorry – I *thought* it was out. (*The ball had hit the back netting twelve feet behind him before touching the ground.*) But what did you think, Brown?

BROWN: I *thought* it was out – but do let's have it again.

JOAD: No, I don't want to have it again. I only want you to say clearly, if you will, whether the ball is in or out.

There is nothing more putting off to young university players than a slight suggestion that their etiquette or sportsmanship is in question. How well we know this fact, yet how often we forget to make use of it. Smith sent a double fault to me, and another double fault to Joad. He did not get in another ace service till halfway through the third set of a match which incidentally we won.

That night I thought hard and long. Could not this simple gambit of Joad's be extended to include other aspects of the game – to include all games? For me, it was the birth of gamesmanship.

2

THE PRE-GAME

'And now they smile at Paradine,
Who but would smile at Paradine?
(That man of games, called Paradine)
For the Gamesman came his way.'

Paradine

FOR THE EVOLUTION of gamesmanship I must refer the reader to my larger work on origins and history (see Appendix III). But I do not propose to enlarge on the historical aspects here.

Let us start with a few simple exercises for beginners: and let us begin with the pre-game, for much of the most important gamesmanship play takes place before the game has started. Yet if mistakes are made, there is plenty of time to recover.

The great second axiom of gamesmanship is now worded as follows: THE FIRST MUSCLE STIFFENED (in his opponent by the Gamesman) IS THE FIRST POINT GAINED. Let us consider some of the processes of Defeat by Tension.

The standard method is known as the 'flurry'.

The 'flurry' is for use when changing in the locker-room before a rackets match, perhaps, or leaving home in your opponent's car for, say, a game of lawn tennis. The object is to create a state of anxiety, to build up an atmosphere of muddled fluster.

Supposing, for instance, that your opponent has a small car. He kindly comes along to pick you up before the game. Your procedure should be as follows: (1) Be late in answering the bell. (2) Don't have your things ready. Appearing at last, (3) call *in an anxious or 'rattled' voice* to wife (who need not, of course, be there at all) some taut last-minute questions about dinner. Walk down path and (4) realize you have forgotten shoes. Return with shoes; then just before getting into car pause (5) *a certain length of time* (see any threepenny edition of Bohn's *Tables*) and wonder (*i*) whether racket is at the club or (*ii*) whether you have left it 'in the bath-room at top of the house'.

Like the first hint of paralysis, a scarcely observable fixing of your

Sketch plan to show specimen Wrong Route from Maida Vale to Dulwich
Covered Courts.

opponent's expression should now be visible. Now is the time to redouble the attack. Map-play can be brought to bear. On the journey let it be known that you 'think you know a better way', *which should turn out, when followed, to be incorrect and should if possible lead to a blind alley.* (See p. 15.)

Meanwhile, time is getting on. Opponent's tension should have increased. Psychological tendency, if not temporal necessity, will cause him to drive faster, and – behold! now the gamesman can widen his field and bring in carmanship by suggesting, with the minutest stiffening of the legs at corners, an unconscious tendency to put on the brakes, indicating an unexpressed desire to tell his opponent that he is driving not very well, and cornering rather too fast.

NOTE I. – The 'flurry' is best used before still-ball games, especially golf, croquet or snooker. Anxious car-driving may actually improve opponent's execution in fast games, such as rackets or ping-pong.

NOTE II. – Beginners must not rush things. The smooth working of a 'flurry' sequence depends on practice. The motions of pausing on the doorstep ('Have I got my gym shoes?'), hesitating on the running-board, etc., are exercises which I give my own students; but I always recommend that they practise the motions for at least six weeks, *positions only*, before trying it out with the car, suitcase and shoes.

Clothesmanship

The 'flurry' is a simple example. Simpler still, but leading to the most important subdivision of our subject, is the question of clothes-manship, or the 'Togman', as he used to be called.

The keen observer of the tennis-court incident described above would have noticed a marked disparity in clothes. The trousers of the young under-graduate players were well creased and clean, with flannel of correct colour, etc., etc. C. Joad, on the other hand, wore a shirt of deep yellow, an orange scarf to hold up his crumpled trousers, and – standing out very strongly, as I remember, in the hot June sun-light – socks of deep black.

Instinctively, Joad had demonstrated in action what was to become the famous 'Second Rule' of gamesmanship, now formulated as follows:

IF THE OPPONENT WEARS, OR ATTEMPTS TO WEAR, CLOTHES CORRECT AND SUITABLE FOR THE GAME, BY AS MUCH AS HIS CLOTHES SUCCEED IN THIS FUNCTION, BY SO MUCH SHOULD THE GAMESMAN'S CLOTHES FAIL.

Clothesmanship: wrong clothes in which Miss
E. Watson beat Mrs de Greim in the Finals of
the Waterloo Cup Croquet Tourney, August 18th,
1902.

Corollary: Conversely, if the opponent wears the wrong clothes, the gamesman should wear the right.

'If you can't volley, wear velvet socks,' we Old Gamesmen used to say. The good-looking young athlete, perfectly dressed, is made to feel a fool if his bad shot is returned by a man who looks as if he has never been on a tennis-court before. His good clothes become a handicap by virtue of their very suitability.

It is true that against the new golf-club member, inclined to be modest and nervous, a professional turn-out can be effective. A well-worn but well-cut golf jacket and a good pair of mackintosh trousers can, in this situation, be of real value. (My own tip here is to take an ordinary left-hand glove, cut the thumb off, make a diamond-shaped hole on the back, and say, 'Henry Cotton made this for me – he never plays with any other.')

Counter-Gamesmanship

But the average gamesman must beware, at this point, of counter-gamesmanship. He may find himself up against an experienced hand, such as J. K. C. Dalziel, who, when going out to golf, used to keep two changes in the dickey of his car – one correct and the other in-correct. One golf-bag covered in zips and with five woods, twelve irons and a left-handed cleek; a second bag containing only three irons and one wood, each with an appearance of string-ends tied round their necks. I always remember Jimmy Dalziel's 'bent pin' outfit, as he used to call it. ('The little boy with the bent pin always catches more than the professional angler.') Many is the time I have scoured London with him to find a pair of odd shoe-laces. His plan was simple. If he found, at the club-house, that his opponent was rather humbly dressed, he would wear the smart outfit. If the conditions were re-versed, out would come the frayed pin-stripe trousers, the stringy clubs and the fair-isle sweater.

'And I don't want a caddie,' he would say.

Of course, in his correct clothes, he would automatically order a caddie, calling for 'Bob', and mumbling something about 'Must have Bob. He knows my game. Caddied for me in the Northern Amateur.'

3

THE GAME ITSELF

'East wind dhu blëow
En-tout-cas dhu gëow.'

Essex Saying

SOME BASIC PLAYS

'HOW TO WIN Games Without Being Able to Play Them.' Reduced to
the simplest terms, that is the formula, and the student must not at
first try flights too far away from this basic thought.

To begin with, let him, say, carry on the 'flurry' motive. Let him
aim at tension. Let him, for instance, invent some 'train which he
would rather like to catch if the game was over by then', but 'doesn't
want to hurry'.

Sportsmanship Play

Remember the slogan: 'THE GOOD GAMESMAN IS THE GOOD SPORTS-
MAN.' The use of sportsmanship is, of course, most important. In
general, with the athletic but stupid player, ex-rowing or ex-boxing,
perhaps, who is going to take it out of you, by God, if he suspects you
of being unsporting, extreme sportingness is the thing, and the
instant waiving of any rule which works in your favour is the procedure.

On the other hand, playing against the introvert crusty cynical
type, remember that sportingness will be wasted on him. There must
be no unsportingness on your part, of course; but a keen knowledge
of little-known rules and penalties will cause him to feel he is being
beaten at his own game. (See under 'Croquet, rulesmanship in'.)

When questioned about the etiquette of gamesmanship – so important for the young player – I talk about Fidgets. If your adver-
sary is nervy, and put off by the mannerisms of his opponent, it is
unsporting, and therefore not gamesmanship, to go in, e.g., for a
loud noseblow, say, at billiards, or to chalk your cue squeakingly,
when he is either making or considering a shot.

On the other hand, a basic play, in perfect order, can be achieved by, say, whistling fidgetingly *while playing yourself*. And I once converted two down into two up when playing golf against P. Beard, known also as the leader of an orchestra, by constantly whistling a phrase from the Dorabella Variation with one note – always the same note – wrong.[1]

A good general attack can be made by talking to your opponent about his own job, in the character of the kind of man who always tries to know more about your own profession than you know yourself.

Playing-for-Fun Play

The good gamesman, like the good sportsman, never plays for large sums of money. But something can usually be made out of the situation if your opponent expresses a wish to play for the 'usual half crown', or a wish not to do so. It is obviously easy for the gamesman to make his opponent feel awkward by countering his suggestion that they should play for stakes with a frank 'Come, let's play for the fun of the game'. Alternatively, if your opponent refuses your offer to play for half a crown here is a neat counter:

LAYMAN: Half a crown on it? No, I'm not particularly anxious to play for money. What *is* the point? If one starts worrying about the pennies . . .

GAMESMAN: Exactly. If money is important to you, much better not.

LAYMAN: But I meant—

GAMESMAN: (*Friendly*). Of course.

[1] It may be worth recalling that Elgar himself, when playing croquet against fellow-musicians, made use of the Horn *motiv* from the *Ring*:

He would whistle this correctly except for the second note, substituting for A some inappropriate variant, often a slightly flattened D sharp, *sliding* up to it, from the opening note of the phrase:

A voice from the past indeed. Yet have any of our modern experts in the music ploy really improved on this phrase, devised before Gamesmanship was formulated or even described?

Nice Chapmanship

A bigger subject which may be introduced here revolves round the huge question of nice chapmanship and its uses. (I refuse to use the hideous neologism 'nicemanship' which I see much in evidence lately.)

Here is the general principle: that Being a Nice Chap *in certain circumstances* is valuable when playing against extremely young, public schooly players who are genuinely nice. A train of thought can be started in their minds to the effect that 'it would be rather a rotten trick to beat old G. by too much'. Thereby that fatal 'letting up' is inaugurated which can be the undoing of so many fine players. R. Lodge, at sixty-five, always said that he had never been beaten, in a key match, by any decently brought up boy under twenty-five, and that he could always 'feel 'em out by their phizzes'.

Audience Play

Nice chapmanship is, of course, closely associated with sportsmanship, especially in its relation to the question of playing or not playing to the audience. There is obviously some value in a good hearty 'Have it again' early in the game (of darts, for instance), or the lawn tennis ball slammed into the net after the doubtful decision, especially if this is done so that your opponent can see through the ploy[1] but the onlookers cannot.

But the experienced gamesman knows that if he is playing to a small audience he must make up his mind whether he is going to play *to* the audience, or whether he is going to retire behind an impersonal mask of modesty.

In general, the rule holds – LET YOUR ATTITUDE BE THE ANTITHESIS OF YOUR OPPONENT'S; and let your manner of emphasizing this different attitude put him in the wrong.

For example, if your opponent is a great showman, assume (e.g., at snooker) an air of modest anonymity; be appreciative, even, of his antics; then quietly play your shot, so that the audience begins to say, 'I prefer G.'s game. He gets on with it, anyhow.'

Per contra, when in play against a dour opponent, who studiously avoids all reaction to the audience, implying that 'this is a match' – *then*, by all means be the 'chap who doesn't care a damn' ... though

---

[1] Sub-plays, or individual manoeuvres of a gambit, are usually referred to as 'ploys'. It is not known why this is.

'Of course – sh! – old L. is taking this devilish seriously so I must keep a straight face.'

(There is some danger of counter-gamesmanship here. The layman, if he is wise, will pursue his poker-faced policy and you may find your assumption of ill-suppressed gaiety wearing thin. I have myself experienced a partial paralysis in this situation.)

So much for some of the principal general ploys. Now for some common technical phrases.

Ruggership and Ruggership Counter-play

Under the heading of 'Ruggership' comes all that great interplay of suggestion summarized in the phrase 'Of course, this isn't my game', with the implication that 'this game is rather an amusing game, but not grand, dangerous and classical like my game . . . '. If 'my game' is rugger or polo or tennis (see under 'Tennis players, how to press home advantage of, over lawn tennis players'), then very good work can be done with this gambit.

But it has severe weaknesses, and a promising gamesman in his second year may be able to counter with some such simple enquiry as this:

COUNTER-GAMESMAN (*with interest*): When did you *last play* rugger?

GAMESMAN: Oh! How long since actually playing? I wonder . . . I was talking to Leggers the other day—

COUNTER-GAMESMAN: Yes, but how long is it since you played yourself? I mean what date, roughly, was it when you last held a ball in your hand?

GAMESMAN (*hard-pressed*): 1913.

COUNTER-GAMESMAN: A bit of a time. But that, I imagine, is one of the grand things about rugger. If you've ever kicked a rugger ball, at a prep school or home club, you feel that you're a rugger player for the rest of your life.

Much exaggerated praise has been churned out in honour of gamesmanship and its part in the building of the British character. Still, if we study the records, they do reveal not a little of courage in the overcoming of apparently hopeless odds. I am thinking, of course, of G. Tearle – not the actor, but the croquet-player. And, indeed, some of the prettiest effects of gamesmanship are to be seen when an expert in, say, croquet, plays golf, it may be, off the same handicap, against a real expert in, say, rugger – a man who really has played rugger, twice capped for England. The rugger man certainly starts with a tremendous advantage. His name is a legend, his game is glorious. Croquet is considered, by the lay world, to be piddling. The two meet on the common ground of golf; and even golf, to the rugger man, is considered fairly piddling. Yet I have seen Tearle not only break down this view *but reverse it*, so that in the end the Rugger international would sometimes even be heard claiming that he came from croquet people, but that his character 'was not suited to the game'.

Tearle by long practice actually made capital out of croquet. And let me add that Tearle's triumph demonstrates once again that it is in these long-drawn-out reversal tactics that training and the proper diet stand you in such good stead.

Counterpoint

This phrase, now used exclusively in music, originally stood for Number Three of the general Principles of Gamesmanship. 'PLAY AGAINST YOUR OPPONENT'S TEMPO.' This is one of the oldest of gambits and is now almost entirely used in the form 'My Slow to your Fast'. E.g., at billiards, or snooker, or golf especially, against a player who makes a great deal of 'wanting to get on with the game', the technique is (1) to agree (Jeffreys always adds here 'as long as we don't hurry on the shot'); (2) to hold things up by fifteen to twenty disguised pauses. Peg-top tees for golf were introduced by Samuel in '33 for this use. The technique is to tee the ball, frame up for the shot, and then at the last moment stop, pretend to push the peg a little further in or pull it a little further out, and then start all over again. At the next hole vary this with Samuel's 'Golden Perfecto' peg tee, made in such a way that the ball, after sitting still in the cup for two to three seconds, rolls off. (P. 24.)

Through the green, the usual procedure is to frame up for the shot and then decide on another club at the last moment.

NOTE.– *Do not attempt to irritate partner by spending too long looking for your lost ball.* This is unsporting. But good gamesmanship which is also very good sportsmanship can be practised if the gamesman makes a great and irritatingly prolonged parade of spending extra time looking for his *opponent's* ball.

At billiards, the custom of arranging to be summoned to the telephone on fake calls, so as to break your opponent's concentration, is out of date now and interesting only as a reminder of the days when 'couriers' were paid to gallop up to the old billiard halls for the same purpose. In snooker, the equal practice is to walk quickly up to the table, squat half down on the haunches to look at sight-lines, move to

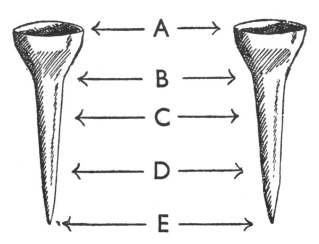

Samuel's 'Championship' (2d.) and 'Golden Perfecto' (4/6) golf tees. A = 'Cup', B = 'Neck', C = 'Upper Shaft', D = 'Lower Shaft', E = Point or 'Plungebill'.

the other end of the table to look at sight-lines of balls which may come in to play later on in the break which you are supposed to be planning. Decide on the shot. Frame up for it, and then at the last moment see some obvious red shot which you had 'missed', and which your opponent and everybody else will have noticed before you moved to the table, and which they know is the shot you are going to play in the end anyhow.

For chess tempos see 'Chess, tempi'.

'My Tomorrow's Match'

In a Key Friendly, or any individual match which you are particularly anxious to win, the best general approach (Rule IV) is the expression of *anxiety to play today, because of the match tomorrow.* Construct a story that you are playing A. J. du C. Masterman.[1] Or perhaps the name should be A. C. Swinburne (your opponent will feel he has vaguely heard of this name). Go on to say (if the game is golf)

[1] 'Names impress according to the square of their initials.'

– 'Do you mind if I practise using my Number One iron today?' – (no
need to use it or even have one) – 'as I want to know whether to take
it tomorrow'. Take one practice shot after having picked up your
ball, at a lost hole. Seek the advice of opponent. Ask him 'What *he*
would do if he found himself playing against a *really* long driver, like
A. C. Swinburne'.

Game Leg (also known as 'Crocked Ankle Play', or 'Gamesman's
   Leg'[1])

'Limpmanship', as it used to be called, or the exact use of minor injury, not only for the purpose of getting out of, but for actually
winning difficult contests, is certainly as old as the mediaeval tour-
neys, the knightly combats, of ancient chivalry. Yet, nowadays, no device is more clumsily used, no gambit more often muffed. 'I hope I
shall be able to give you a game,' says the middle-aged golfer to his
young opponent, turning his head from side to side and hunching up
his shoulders. 'My back was a bit seized up yesterday . . . this wind.'
How wretchedly weak. 'OK. My youth *versus* your age,' says the
young counter-gamesman to himself, and rubs this thought in with
a variety of subsequent slanting references: 'You ought to take it easy
for a week or two,' etc. No, if use the hackneyed ankle gambit you
must, let the injury be the result of a campaign in one of the wars, or a
quixotic attempt to stop a runaway horse, at least.

But, here as so often, it is the *reply*, the counter, wherein the ploy
of the gamesman can be used to best effect. Indeed, there is nothing
prettier than the right use of an opponent's injury. There is the
refusal to be put off even if the injury is genuine. There is the adop-
tion of a game which, though apparently ignoring and indeed even
favouring your opponent's disability, will yet benefit you in the end.
In their own different ways, the 'Two F's', Frier and Frith-Morteroy,
were the greatest masters of the art of 'Countering the Crock'. No one
who heard them will ever forget their apologies for sending a short
one to the man with the twisted ankle, their excuses for the accidental
lob in the sun against an opponent with sensitive eyes. But the
Frith-Morteroy counter, though not for beginners, has more of grace,
and needs more of explanation. Let it be lawn tennis – Frith's game.
Frith against 'Novice Gamesman', we will call him.

Novice Gamesman is limping slightly. 'Hopes he can give F.-M. a
game, but his rugger knee has just been prodded back into place by

[1] Usually shortened now into 'Game Leg'.

old Coutts of Welbeck Street.' Right. F.-M. is full of sympathy. F.-M. sends not a single short one. In fact he does nothing whatever. His supporters become anxious – and then – during, say, the *first* game of the *second* set, while they are changing sides Frith is heard to say (on arriving at point K – see p. 27) 'Ooo!' sharply.

NOVICE GAMESMAN: What's that?
FRITH-MORTEROY: Nothing. Nothing. I thought—
N.G.: (*further away*): What did you say?
F.-M.: Nothing.

The game continues. But at that next cross over, Frith says 'Ow!' (point S, p. 27). He pauses a minute, and stands as if lost in thought.

N.G.: What's up?
F.-M.: Nothing. Half a moment.
N.G.: Something's wrong?
F.-M.: (*rubs his chest with his knuckles*): No. No. It's only the old pump.
N.G.: Pump?
F.-M.: Yes. The ancient ticker.
N.G.: What – heart?
F.-M.: I'm supposed not to be using it full out at the moment. Only a temporary thing.
N.G.: Good Lord.
F.-M.: It's all right now!
N.G.: Good.
F.-M.: Couple of crocks!
N.G.: Well. Shall we get on?

'*Couple* of crocks.' Observe the triple thrust against the Novice Gamesman. (1) Frith establishes the fact that he, also, labours under a handicap; (2) the atmosphere which Novice Gamesman has built up with so much restraint, but so much labour – the suggestion of silent suffering – is the precise climate in which Frith is now going to prosper, and (3) – most important of all – Frith has won the gamesmanship part of the contest already, set and match, by sportingly waiting, say twenty-five minutes, before revealing his own somewhat worse disability. Novice Gamesman having mentioned his rugger knee – a stale type of infliction anyhow – is made to look a fool and a fusser. More, he is made to look unsporting.

I believe it is true to say that once Frith-Morteroy had achieved this position, he was never known to lose a game. He made a special

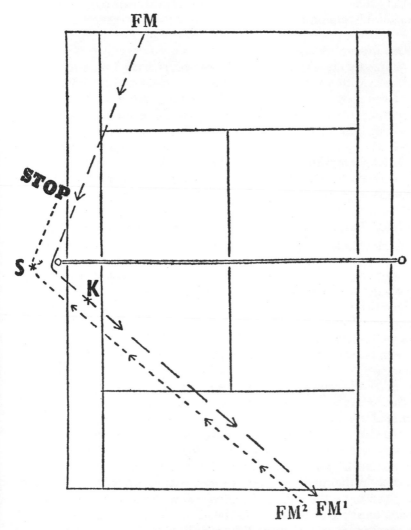

Diagram of tennis court to show Frith-Morteroy's path of changing, and the position S from which he makes his 'echo' attack, in Morteroy Counter Game Leg play. Point K on the line F M–F M¹ is the position from which the demi-cry is made (see text). At point S, on the line F M², the full cry is made (see text). 'STOP' marks the usual position for the actual verbal interchange or 'Parlette'.

study of it – and I believe much of his spare time was spent reading the medical books on the subject of minor cardiac weaknesses.

Jack Rivers Opening

After this most successful of basic plays, may I dare to end this chapter with a very simple but favourite gambit of my own?

I call it the Jack Rivers Opening. I have written elsewhere of the sporting–unsporting approach, always to be revered as the parent of modern gamesman play. But if sporting–unsporting is vaguely regarded as a thing of the past, the gamesman knows that it is a habit of thought still rooted in many British players.

Perhaps the most difficult type for the gamesman to beat is the man who indulges in pure play. He gets down to it, he gets on with it, he plays each shot according to its merits, and his own powers, without a trace of exhibitionism, and no by-play whatever. In golf, croquet or ping-pong – golf especially – he is liable to wear you down by playing the 'old aunty' type of game.

My only counter to this, which some have praised, is to invent, early in the game or before it has started, an imaginary character called 'Jack Rivers'. I speak of his charm, his good looks, his fine war record and his talent for games – and, 'by the way, he is a first-class pianist as well'. Then, a little later: 'I like Jack Rivers's game,' I say. 'He doesn't care a damn whether he wins or loses so long as he has a good match.'

Some such rubbish as this, although at first it may not be effective, often wears down the most successfully cautious opponent, *if the method is given time to soak in*. Allow your opponent to achieve a small lead, perhaps, by his stone-walling methods; and the chances are that – even if he has only been hearing about Jack Rivers for thirty minutes – he will begin to think: 'Well, perhaps I am being a bit of a stick-in-the-mud.' He feels an irrational desire to play up to what appears to be your ideal of a good fellow. After all, he remembers, hadn't he been once chaffed for breaking a window with a cricket-ball when he was on holiday at Whitby? He himself was a bit mad once. Soon he is throwing away point after point by adopting a happy-go-lucky, hit-or-miss method which doesn't suit his game in the least.

Meanwhile *you* begin to play with pawky steadiness, and screen this fact by redoubling your references to Jack Rivers. You talk of the way in which Jack, too, loved to open his shoulders for a mighty smite, landing him in trouble as often as not; but the glorious thing about him was that he didn't care two hoots for that . . . and so long as he had a good smack, and a good game . . ., etc.

So much for the Principal Plays, in gamesmanship. Now for the other gambits which must be brought into play as the game progresses.

4

WINMANSHIP

'. . . for the love of winning . . .'
Life and Laughter 'Mongst the People of North-Western Assam, by P. V. Chitterje; *trans.* Evadne Butterfield.

THIS IS A short chapter. The assiduous student of gamesmanship has little time for the *minutiae* of the game itself – little opportunity for learning how to play the shots, for instance. His skill in stroke-making may indeed be almost non-existent. So that the gamesman who finds himself winning in the early stages of the match is sometimes at a loss. Therefore although I am aware that this book must stand or fall by its all-important Chapter 6 on 'Losemanship', yet this seems to me the place to set down a few words of help and friendly advice to the winning gamesman, to help him keep his lead; to assist him to maintain his advantage, and rub his opponent's face in the dirt.

A Note on Concentration

Very often the opponent will show signs, just as he is beginning to lose, of being irritated by distractions. At golf, 'somebody has moved'. At billiards, 'somebody talked'. Take this opportunity of making him feel that he is not really a player at all by talking on these lines:

'Somebody yelling, did you say? Do you know, I didn't notice it. I'm a fool at games. Don't seem to be able to be aware of anything outside them, when I'm playing the shot. I remember, once, Joyce Wethered was putting. 18th green – semi-final. An express train went by within fifteen feet of her nose.

' "How did you manage to sink that putt – with that train . . .?"

' "What train?" she said.'

Always tell the same story to the same man, for your example. (See under 'Story, constant repetition of, to the same person'.)

When to Give Advice

In my own view (but compare Motherwell) there is only one correct

time when the gamesman can give advice : and that is when the gamesman has achieved a *useful* though not necessarily a *winning* lead. Say
three up and nine to play at golf, or, in billiards, sixty-five to his
opponent's thirty. Most of the accepted methods are effective. E.g.
in billiards, the old phrase serves. It runs like this :

GAMESMAN: Look . . . may I say something?
LAYMAN: What?
GAMESMAN: *Take it easy.*
LAYMAN: What do you mean?
GAMESMAN: I mean – you know how to make the strokes, but you're
stretching yourself on the rack all the time. Look. Walk up to the ball. Look
at the line. And make your stroke. Comfortable. Easy. It's as simple as that.

In other words, the advice *must be vague*, to make certain it is not
helpful. But, in general, if properly managed, the mere giving of
advice is sufficient to place the gamesman in a practically invincible
position.

NOTE. – According to some authorities the advice should be quite
genuine and perfectly practical.

When to be Lucky
The uses of the last of the three basic plays for winmanship are,
I think, no less obvious, though I believe this gambit is less used than
the other, no doubt because a certain real skill in play is involved,
making it a little out of place in the gamesman world. I have worded
the rule as follows. LET THE GAMESMAN'S ADVANTAGE OVER AN OPPO-
NENT APPEAR TO BE THE RESULT OF LUCK, NEVER OF PLAY. Always
sporting, the good gamesman will say :

'I'm afraid I was a bit lucky there . . . the balls are running my way. It's
extraordinary, isn't it, once they start running one way, they go on running
one way, all through an entire game. I know it's impossible according to the
law of averages . . .'

and so on, till your opponent is forced to break in with a reply.
Unless he sees through the gambit and counter-games, he is likely
to feel an ebbing of confidence if he can be made to believe that it is
not your play (which he knows is liable to collapse) but Fate, which is
against him.
Yet in spite of the ease with which most gamesplayers can be

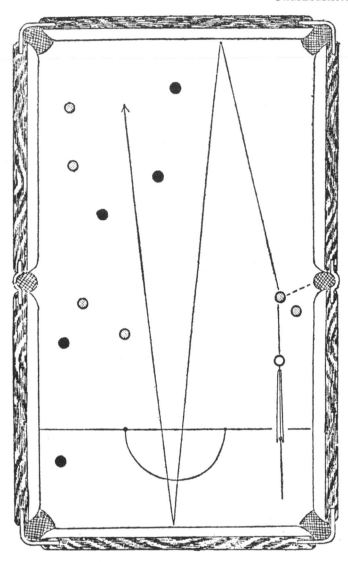

Diagram of billiards table to show Disguised Fluke play. Key: Black balls
= red balls; shaded balls = coloured balls; white ball = white ball; end of
cue = end of cue. Player has framed up as if to hit blue (on extreme right)
but actually pots black (ball on extreme right but one). Straight line = path
of white ball after impact (leaving an easy red). Dotted line = path of black
into middle pocket.

persuaded that they are unlucky, I know the difficulties of this gambit: and as I have had many complaining letters from all parts of the country from gamesmen saying: 'They can't do it', 'What's the point?', 'No good', etc., I will end this chapter with a few notes:

NOTE I. – The best shot to practise with cue and ivories is undoubtedly the Imitation Fluke. E.g. in billiards, play for an in-off the red top left of a kind which will give colour to your apology that you meant to pot the red top right. A. Boult (the snooker player, not the conductor) demonstrates a shot, suitable for volunteer only, in which he pots the black while apparently framing up to hit a ball of inferior scoring value (e.g. the blue). (See p. 32.)

A good tip, says Boult, is to chalk the end of the cue ostentatiously, while apologizing after making the shot.

NOTE II. – In my pamphlet for the British Council I listed eighteen ways of saying 'Bad luck'. I do not believe there are more.

NOTE III (For advanced students only). – Different from fluke play, though sometimes confused with it, is the demonstration of another kind of advantage over an opponent in which the gamesman tries to prove that he is favoured not by good luck but by *a fortunate choice of instruments*. To get away from text-book formulae, let me explain this by example.

In golf, for instance. You find yourself two up at the fifth hole. You wish to make certain of your advantage.

Supposing, for whatever reason, you hit your drive; and supposing you hit it five or preferably ten yards farther than your opponent. Procedure: walk off the tee *with* opponent, in the normal method of the two-up walk-off, conversing, and listening rather charmingly to what he says, etc. (See Number Twelve in my *Twenty-five Methods of Tee-leaving*: Scribners, August 1935.) As you approach the balls on the fairway, but before parting company (see below) say, 'Much of a muchness.' Opponent will then say over his shoulder:

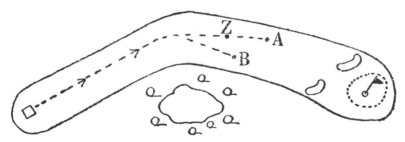

Diagram of golf hole. A = point by Gamesman's drive. B = opponent's drive. Z = point on arrival at which Gamesman commences Gamesplay or 'Parlette'.

'You're ten yards farther at least.'

'So I am,' you say.

Nearing the green you start thinking aloud in his presence.

'Funny. I thought those drives were level. It's that ball of mine.'

'What are you using? Ordinary two-dot, isn't it?'

'Oh, no – no – that's how it's been repainted. Underneath it's a Madfly.

'Madfly?'

'Madfly. Pre-war only. It goes like sin. Really does put ten yards on to your shot. I'll see if I can get you one. Honestly, I hardly feel it's fair of me to play with it.'

With proper management the gamesman can wreak far more havoc by suggesting that he has the advantage of a better ball, than by demonstrating that he has a better swing.

Tennis rackets strung with a special gut giving out a particularly high 'ping', suggesting a tigerish resilience, are made by dealers who cater for this sort of thing. G. Odoreida, on his first appearance at St Ives, brought with him a racket in which a stretch of piano wire, tuned to high G, was substituted for one of the ordinary strings. When 'testing his racket' before play, he plucked the piano wire, adding smilingly: 'I like something you can hit with.'

A propos of this, an amusing correspondence followed with 'Wagger' – WAGA, the West Australian Gamesmen's Association – which august body considered this action ungamesmanlike.

5

LUNCHEONSHIP

'For gamesmen work i' th' playtime,
To pledge their souls away.'
Plainsong of Perkins, Gent.

THE WAY OF the gamesman is hard, his training strict, his progress slow, his disappointments many. If he is to succeed, he must, for instance, read our next chapter, on 'Losemanship', with something more than concentration. He must *believe* that the precepts it contains are effective, and *trust* that they make sense, and *want* to put them into action.

So let us, as they say, 'take a breather'. Let us turn for a moment to what I always consider to be the lighter side of the subject, even if in all earnest many a match is won by a knowledge of what to say during the meal interval, and how to say it.

In golf, in the all-day lawn tennis or badminton tournament, in cricket or bowls, the luncheon interval is the ideal time in which to make up lost ground.

Drinkmanship

This huge subject, the notes for which I have been collecting for so many years that they threaten already to overstep the bounds of a single volume, can scarcely even be defined within the limits of a chapter. Put in the simplest possible words, the art of drinkmanship is the art of imparting uneasiness to your opponent by making a show of (1) readiness or (2) reluctance to 'go shares' in the hire of a court, payment for taxi, payment for meal, but above all in the matter of 'standing your round' of alcoholic drink; the art, moreover, of inseminating in the mind of your opponent, by this action, that he has paid more than his share, or, more rarely, less than his share; the whole gambit to be played with the object of setting up (by this action) a train of uneasiness in the mind, with subsequent bewilderment at the commencement or resumption of the game.

The rarer form ('Counter-drink Play') is for use *only in the following situation*, where, however, it is a gambit of the first value.

Take a young opponent (optimum age: twenty-two). He must be pleasant, shy and genuinely sporting. (The Fischer Test will tell you whether his apparent character is real or assumed – see 'Nice Chapmanship', p. 21.) Then (1) Place him by the bar and stand him a drink. (2) When he suggests 'the other half', refuse in some such words as these, which should be preceded by a genuinely kindly laugh: 'Another one? No thanks, old laddie . . . *No*, I certainly won't let you buy me one. No – I don't want it.' Then (3) a minute or two later, when his attention is distracted, buy him, and yourself, the second drink. The boy will feel bound to accept it, yet this enforced acceptance should cause him some confusion, and a growing thought, if the gambit has been properly managed and the after-play judicious, that he has been fractionally put in his place and decimally treated as if he was a juvenile, and more than partially forced into the position of being the object of generosity.

Straight drinkmanship, *of a kind*, is known all over the world and, of course, long before Simpson and I incorporated it in gamesplay, the fellow who 'was shy of his round' was the menace of club and pub. But genuine drinkmanship is very different, if only because no true gamesman is, I hope, ever either mean or bad mannered.

In my larger work I have planned twelve chapters for the twelve principal drink plays – and while I was working out the details of dialogue and positional play I often asked myself: 'What is *the true purpose* of the tactic – what is it all about?'

Whatever the details, remember the basic drill. (1) Remember always that (except in the case of the Nice Young Chap) 'ONE DRINK UP IS ONE HOLE (OR IN LAWN TENNIS ONE GAME) UP'. But (2) Remember also that to achieve the best results your opponent should not realize that you have avoided paying for a drink *at once*. Optimum realization time: standing on the first tee, or, better still, when he makes his first bad shot. Therefore the ordinary escape tactics, e.g. (*i*) turning aside to ask 'was that telephone call for me?'; (*ii*) going vague; (*iii*) producing a treasury note too big to be changed, etc. – these are not successful against an opposing drinkman of average recovering power.

NOTE. – After your opponent has lost the game, angered by the thought that he has been outwitted in the bar-room – *then*, after the game, make him still more annoyed by saying: 'By the way, I owe you a drink – and a large one.' You will thereby not only prepare the ground for the next match by obscurely irritating your man with *Winner's Heartiness*: you will at the same time maintain the gamesman's standard of hospitality and good manners.

Guestmanship

Elwyn Courthope – brother of G. L. – made a special study of 'putting your man in the drinkdrums', as we used to say at Prince's (the tie of which I still wear, though I was never a member[1]). But his one-sidedness enforced this penalty on his game: that it was only successful against opponents at his own club or in an hotel or pub. As a guest, where drinks were going to be bought for him anyhow, he was lost.

That is, of course, why G. L. Courthope – known from time immemorial as 'Court' – invented guestmanship, of which, in spite of the later experiments of Thomas and Riezenkühl, he can justly be called the Father.

The object of guestmanship is difficult to achieve. The host is at an advantage. He is playing on his home ground. He knows the ropes. He has armies of friends. There are plenty of opportunities for making his guest feel out of it. But by the time Court had finished with him, an average host would wonder whether he was a host in any valid sense except the unpleasant one of having to pay: indeed, he would begin to wonder whether he was really a member of his own club.

G. L. used to start, very quietly, (A) by some such question as this: (1) 'Have you got a card-room here?' (knowing that, as a matter of fact, they hadn't). Or (2) (In the Wash-place): 'Do you find you manage all right with two showers, in the summer?' He would then (B) find some member whom he knew, but his host didn't, and carry on an animated conversation with this man. Discover 'at the last moment' that his host had never met him. Introduce them, with surprise apologies, and tell the host later that he really must get to know this fellow – his interest and influence, etc. At luncheon, Court would always know some special ale, or even only a special mustard, the existence of which in the club, after fifteen years' use of it, the host

---

[1] At Oxford, though never a blue, I used to wear a blue's tie – particularly when playing games against nicemen who knew I had no right to wear the honour. This simple trick, which is said by psychologists to induce the 'pseudo-schizophrenic syndrome', or doubt, was most effective in moving-ball games.

had rather lamely to explain he knew nothing about. Court then would ask why X was on the Committee, and why Y wasn't, and make use of a host of facts which he had been able to pick up from a lightning study of lists, menus, pictures of former captains, etc., which he had studied during his host's temporary absence paying some bill.

6

LOSEMANSHIP

'. . . For the glory of the gamesman who's a loseman
in the game.'

THE READER WHO has thoroughly absorbed the first four chapters will
know something of the fundamentals. He will be prepared, I believe,
now, to take that little extra step which will put him on the way to
being a gamesman. And he will realize that he cannot comprehend
the thing itself, unless he knows how to turn the tide of defeat, and,
with alertness and courage, with humour and goodwill, learn to play
for the fun and glory of the gamesplay.

Straight now to the underlying principle of winning the losing
game. What is the chief danger from the opponent who is getting the
better of you? Over and above the advantage in score comes the fact
that he is in the *winning vein*. He is playing at his best. Yet this is
but one end of a balance. It is your job to turn the winning vein into a
losing streak.

The Primary Hamper

There is only one rule: BREAK THE FLOW. This act – for it must be
thought of as a positive *action*, dynamic not static – may bear directly
on the game itself (*Primary Hamper*) or the net may be cast wider, in a
direction apparently far removed from the main target, in an attempt
to entangle the character, or even to bring forces to bear from your
knowledge of the private life and intimate circumstances of your opponent's everyday existence (*Secondary Hamper*).

To take the simplest example of a Primary, let us begin with an
illustration from golf (the 'gamesgame of gamesgames').

This is the rule.

Rule I:[1] CONSCIOUS FLOW IS BROKEN FLOW. To break the flow of the
golfer who is three up at the turn, select a moment during the playing

[1] In all previous editions Rule I was Rule II.

of the tenth in the following way. This moment must be prepared for by not less than three suggestions that he is 'playing well', 'hitting the ball grandly', etc., made at, say, the second, fifth and ninth holes. Then as opponent walks up to play his shot from fairway, speak as follows:

> GAMESMAN: I believe I know what it is.
> LAYMAN: What do you mean?
> GAMESMAN: I believe I know what you're doing.
> LAYMAN: What?
> GAMESMAN: Yes. Why you're hitting them. Straight left arm at the moment of impact.
> LAYMAN (*pleased*): I know what you mean. Oh, God, yes! If the left arm isn't coming down straight like a flail—
> GAMESMAN: Rather.
> LAYMAN: Like a whip—
> GAMESMAN: It's centrifugal force.
> LAYMAN: Well, I don't know. Yes, I suppose it is. But if there's the least suggestion of – of—
> GAMESMAN: A crooked elbow – (*L. is framing up to play his shot*). Half a sec. Do you mind if I come round to this side of you? I want to see you play that shot . . . (*L. hits it*) . . . Beauty. (*Pause*).
> LAYMAN: Good Lord, yes! You've got to have a straight left arm.
> GAMESMAN: Yes. And even that one wasn't as clean as some of the shots you've been hitting . . .
> LAYMAN (*pleased*): Wasn't it? (*Doubtful*). Wasn't it? (*He begins to think about it*).

There is nothing rigid about the last few lines of this dialogue, which are capable of some modification. But the shape – Praise-Dissection-Discussion-Doubt – is the same for all shots and for all games. I often think the possibilities of this gambit alone prove the superiority of games to sports, such as, for instance, rowing, where self-conscious analysis of the stroke can be of actual benefit to the stroke maker.

Potter's Improvement on the Primitive Hamper

The superiority of Primary Hamper over Primitive Hamper needs no elaboration. But it is worth remembering that some of the earliest tentative ploys in what Toynbee calls, in an amusing essay, the Palæogamesman period, were directed to this essential *breaking of the flow*. They consisted of such naïve devices as tying up a shoe-lace in a prolonged manner, after the opponent at squash or lawn tennis had served two or three aces running: the extended noseblow, with sub-sequent mopping up not only of the nose and surrounding surfaces, but of imaginary sweat from the forehead and neck as well; leaving your driver on the tee and going back for it, etc., etc.

My own name has been associated – against my will[1] – with an attempt to bring the Primitive Hamper up to date. The essence of the modern approach is the making of the pause *as if for the sake of your opponent's game.* E.g. at lawn tennis, opponent having won six consecutive points:

GAMESMAN (*calling*): Wait a minute.
OPPONENT: What's wrong?
GAMESMAN (*turning to look at a child walking slowly along a path a hundred yards behind the court. Then turning back*): Those damn kids.
OPPONENT: Where?
GAMESMAN: Walking across your line of sight.
OPPONENT: What?
GAMESMAN: I said 'Walking across your line of sight'.
OPPONENT: I can't see anyone.
GAMESMAN: WHAT?
OPPONENT: I say I CAN'T SEE ANYONE.
GAMESMAN (*continues less distinctly*) . . . bang in the line of sight . . . ought to be shot . . ., etc.

Or, in a billiard room, your opponent has made a break of eight and looks as if he may be going to make eight more. If two or more people are present they are likely not to be especially interested in the game, and quietly talking, perhaps. Or moving teacups. Or glasses. Simulate annoyance, *on your opponent's behalf*, with the onlookers. An occasional irritated glance will prepare the way; then stop your opponent and say:

GAMESMAN (*quietly*): Are they worrying you?
LAYMAN: Who?
GAMESMAN: Compton and Peters.
LAYMAN: It's all right.

Or say to the whisperers, half, but only half, jokingly.

Hi, I say. This is a billiard room, you know. Dead silence, please!

This should not only put an end to opponent's break. It may cause him, if young, to be genuinely embarrassed.

[1] I wished it to be called 'Linlithgow', after that great Viceroy and good man.

Further 'Improved Primitives' are (*a*) the removal of an imaginary hair from opponent's ball, when he is in play; (*b*) licking of finger to pick up speck of dust, etc. For squash, badminton, rackets, tennis or indoor lawn-tennis courts or fives-courts in rainy weather, it will usually be possible to find a small patch on to which water is dripping. When opponent is *winning, particularly if he is winning his service*, become suddenly alarmed for his safety.

1. Make futile efforts to remove water with handkerchief or by kicking at it.

2. Talk of danger of slipping, and

3. If necessary call for sawdust, which, of course, will be unobtainable.

The Secondary Hamper

(NOTE. – This section is for *advanced students only*. All others move straight to Chapter 7. Students who have made no progress at all should go back to the beginning.)

The Secondary Hamper is still in an early stage of development: and there are at least three London Clubs where it is not used. As followers of a recent *Daily Telegraph* correspondence will know, the Secondary Hamper is not allowed on the GWR.[1] But my view, for what it is worth, is that Bristol will have to follow where Manchester led.

The *object* of the secondary hamper is to bring to bear on the game *private life* – your own or your opponent's. The whole ploy is based, of course, on the proved fact that in certain circumstances, and at certain times, such a simple remark as 'We're very lucky in our new son-in-law' may have a profound effect on the game. Or take such an apparently innocent sequence as this:

GAMESMAN: I was fortunate enough to meet your daughter on Sunday.
LAYMAN: Yes, indeed – I know. She told me.
GAMESMAN: What wonderful hair – a real Titian.
LAYMAN: Oh – no – that can't have been my daughter – that was Ethel Baird.
GAMESMAN: *Really*. But I thought I was talking to your—
LAYMAN: You were, but that was earlier on.
GAMESMAN: *Was* it – but what was the colour of your daughter's hair?
LAYMAN: Well – a sort of brown—
GAMESMAN: Of course. Of course. Of course. Of course.

[1] Gamesmanship West Regional.

Simple and ordinary as such a conversation seems to be, the master gamesman, in play against the less experienced, can turn it to his advantage. A feather-weight distraction . . . a fleeting annoyance . . . a handicap of a sort if only because the victim is made to feel that he *is being got at* in some way.

These dialogue attacks or 'parlettes' led to many other secondaries, still more intimately personal in approach, including especially, of course, those taught me by Edward Grice just before the recent World War.[1] I now use them more than any other gamesmanship gambit: and Grice himself was good enough to say, in 1939, that the basic 'Second Secondary' which I evolved for my own use was not less useful than one or two of his own. Nothing was printed, and then the war came, and I remember telling my wife with some pride that there was a security stop on my little invention! So now, in 1947, it appears in print for the first time.

The idea grew out of a memory from my pre-gamesman days. My friend J.J. (as I will call him) and I played croquet together in a relentless and unending series of singles. In those days J.J. could beat me. But there was a certain memorable spring, a certain March to June, when the upper hand was just as regularly with me.

What happened? I searched through old letters and diaries, to try to find the cause. The explanation was simple.

During those three months, J.J., for the first and last time in his life, had had a very marked success with a girl I was fond of. J.J., in fact, had, or felt that he had, snatched this girl away from me. I may have been upset. I believe that – in so far as one could be upset in the midst of a croquet series – I did feel it. But whatever the facts, J.J. *found himself constitutionally unable to win his games against me during this period*. With his blue and black both on the last hoop, he would unaccountably allow me to hoop and peg out one of his balls. Or he would fail to get started at all, till I was half-way round with my red, his two clips remaining on the first hoop pathetically, forlornly and lopsidedly perched like a fox-terrier's ears.

And now, in a flash, I realized the cause of J.J.'s lapse. He could not bring himself to strike a man when he was down, *particularly since he himself was the cause of the trouble*, or so he believed.

From the games point of view, it was a fortunate situation for me. J.J. never quite regained his superiority – and, in fact, in our present series I am three up. Years later, in my gamesman days, it struck me

[1] In 1937.

that what was successful before, might be successful again. In the
autumn of 1935 I again found myself engaged in a long series of
singles against my old games friend 'Dr Bill', as I will call him. This
time the game was golf; but again I found myself in the position of
regular loser.

I chose the day and the time. I had suffered my seventh consecutive
defeat. The conversation ran something like this. I spoke of a mutual
friend to whom I had purposely introduced Dr. Bill six weeks before.
Her name was Patricia Forrest.[1]

S.P. (*suddenly, à propos of nothing*): What a grand girl Pat is.
Dr Bill: Yes, isn't she? You see quite a bit of her, don't you?
S.P.: Well . . . we're kind of old friends.
Dr Bill: I thought so.
(Pause).
S.P.: Which exactly describes it. Alas!
Dr Bill: What do you mean?
S.P.: Well – you know.
Dr Bill: What do you mean, sort of—?
S.P. (*gruffly*): I shall always like her – very much.
Dr Bill: I'm sure I would if I knew her.
(Pause).
S.P. (*with glance*): She was talking about you the other day.
Dr Bill (*slight pause*): Me?
S.P. (*giving him warm-hearted, Major Dobbin look*): I think she likes you,

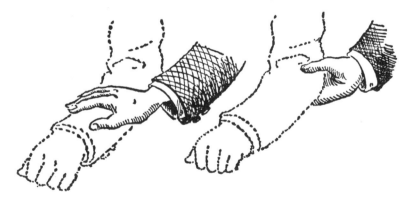

Advanced Secondary Hamper (1). (*a*) Hand laid on forearm (right). (*b*)
Transient grip of the elbow (better).

[1] I have tried, in this book, to avoid pseudonyms. The reader will forgive
me if on this occasion I break my rule.

Advanced Secondary Hamper (2)

   (*a*) Dandelion swing (wrong)

   (*b*) Dandelion swing (right)

bless you. (*At this point a hand may be laid on the forearm. But a transient grip of the elbow is better. See p. 44.*)

Dr Bill: I don't think she even knows I exist—

S.P.: On the contrary, she's very well aware of it indeed . . . damn your eyes!

'Damn your eyes!' is said, of course, in a friendly, nicechap voice. If opponent is still mystified, then gamesman should (1) become despondent and silent or (2) he should knock off head of dandelion with any iron club either by means of (*a*) an ordinary rough golf stroke, or (*b*) better, with a one-armed 'windmill' swing (see above and p. 46).

(*a*) Wrong.

Now what happens? Your Dr Bill will feel pleased and flattered *as a ladies' man*. 'I am a success with Pat' (or whoever she is), he will say to himself. But being a success with Patricia is a very long way from, in fact definitely opposed to, being at great pains to defeat your unfortunate and unsuccessful rival at anything so comparatively trivial[1] as a game. Indeed, arranged properly the gambit will lead him to feel that having pinched your girl it is more or less incumbent on him to allow you to win.

Note. – There is of course an obvious countergame to this gambit, and it is a fascinating 'show' for the spectators to watch two gamesmen trying to prove that it is the other one whom the girl really prefers. Leonards and McDirk used to draw a big crowd when they were fighting out a match on these lines.

[1] I do not apologize for 'comparatively trivial'. Love is more important than games. And I also believe that love is more important than gamesmanship.

(*b*) Right.

I was once dangerously counter-gamed in the teeth of my own gambit. My opponent cut in on the words, 'We're very old friends' with a new line of thought which ran as follows:

COUNTER-GAMESMAN: Well, I ought to play well today.
GAMESMAN: You always do. But what's up? Anything special?
COUNTER-GAMESMAN: I'm a free man.
GAMESMAN: Splendid. What do you mean?
COUNTER-GAMESMAN: I'm one of the idle classes.
GAMESMAN (*genuinely interested*): What – you haven't left the North British and United?
COUNTER-GAMESMAN (*stiffly*): They are very sorry. They are cutting down staff.
GAMESMAN: You mean you've got the sack?

In the face of this disaster to my friend it was hopeless to go on

with the 'You're a lucky fellow' sequence. And I'm bound to admit
that my contra-counter ('Well, we must moan together: the doctor
says this is the last game I shall ever be able to play') seemed lame and
forced. But the small band of us who are interested in this branch of
the game, believe me, will continue to improve and experiment; though
bold man would he be who could boast a defence against every conceivable counter-hamper.

Hampettes

'Hampettes', or minor hampers, exist in plenty. Many of them are
of occasional use to the losing gamesman. Many of them come under
the heading 'Of course, this isn't really my game' (see 'Ruggership',
p. 22). While playing squash, let it be known that rackets is *your
Game*, and that squash is that very different thing, a game which you
find it occasionally amusing to play *at*, for the fun of the thing. R.
Simpson first drew my attention to this gambit when I was playing
lawn tennis with him on a damp grass court on the borders of Lyme
Regis. I happened to be seeing the ball and for once in my life really
was driving it on to that precious square foot in the back-hand
corner of the base line. After one of these shots, Simpson was 'carried
away' enough to tap his racket twice on the ground and cry 'chase
better than half a yard'. I only dimly realized that this was an expression from tennis itself, which had slipped out by accident; that he was
familiar with the great original archetype of lawn tennis, compared
with which lawn tennis itself (he wished to make and succeeded in
making me understand) was a kind of French cricket on the sands at
Southend.

I lost that game. But I learnt my lesson. I walked about the real
tennis-court at Blackfriars (Manchester) two or three times 'in order
to be taught the game'. I took lessons from the pro (I showed no
aptitude). I put by a few shillings in order to buy that most games-
manly shaped, ungainlily twisted racket. I keep it in the office. And
although it has never hit a ball since those Manchester days, I make
admirable use of that racket almost every week of my life.

The Natural Hampette

There is a hampette which I like to use against a certain type of
player. It has no official name: it obeys no code and no rule. Among
my small group of students I used to call it 'After All'.

'After all there are more important things than games.' There are often occasions, when losing against a particularly grim, competent, unemotional and ungamesmanageable opponent, when this motion may be suggested, as a last resort.

I use it in golf. Without warning, I assume the character of a nature rambler. 'Good lord,' I say, bending down suddenly and examining the turf on the side of the bunker, into which, for once, my opponent has strayed. 'Good lord. I didn't know Bristle Agrostis grew in Bucks.'

LAYMAN: What's that?

GAMESMAN: Look. Lovely little grass, with a sharp leaf. It ought to be sandy here.

LAYMAN: Well, it's sandy in the bunker.

GAMESMAN: No, I mean it's supposed only to grow on sandy soil. Ah well!

Then later:

GAMESMAN: What a day! (*Breathing deeply*). And what a sky!

LAYMAN: It's going to rain if we don't look sharp.

GAMESMAN: That's right. It's a real Constable sky. That's the glorious thing about golf, it brings you closer to England.[1]

LAYMAN: How d'you mean?

GAMESMAN (*Breathes deeply*).

Layman's game may not yet have been affected, but a tiny seed of doubt has been planted. Is he missing something? Also, his opponent is showing a suspicious lack of anxiety over being two down. A little later you pick up a loose piece of mud behind your ball, as if to throw it out of the way, and then you suddenly stop, and look at the scrap of muck.

GAMESMAN: Look. Pellet of the tawny owl.

LAYMAN: Pellet?

GAMESMAN: Yes. I wonder if she has rodings round here.

LAYMAN: Rodings?

GAMESMAN: Yes, there has been a great increase of the tawny owl in Wilts., and if we could show that she was something more than an irregular visitor in Kent it would be good.

LAYMAN: But this is Berkshire.

GAMESMAN (*thoughtfully*): Exactly.

---

[1] This phase of the play is sometimes called Sussexmanship. In a book such as this, which deals with First Principles, it has been my aim to use as few technical terms as possible.

LAYMAN: I suppose they're useful. (*Layman now feels he must take a halting part in the conversation.*) I mean – mice—

GAMESMAN: As a matter of fact we *don't know*. The chances at present are fifty-fifty.

LAYMAN: Oh, yes. Chances of what?

GAMESMAN: We're working on her now. All amateur work. The amateurs have done wonderful work. Absolutely splendid.

This conversation, with identical wording, will do of course for any bird. If a faint crack is now apparent in your opponent's game, re-double your references to the 'marvellous work of the amateurs' whenever you are in earshot. That this gambit (the '*natural hampette*', I want it to be called) works, is a matter of fact. Why it works, is one of the mysteries of gamesmanship.

NOTE I. – This technique has no connection with the ploy of the gamesman who says 'Whoosh! I wish I'd got my .22 with me', whenever he sees a bird get up.

See in this same series *Bird Gamesmanship*, especially the chapter on Game Birdmanship. Also the pamphlet published by the Six Squires Press – *Big Gamesmanship and Blood Sportsmanship: Fact and Fancy*, 8*d*, and the graph, prepared by Ernest Tile, on p. 79.

NOTE II. – Grass court tennis and croquet are equally fruitful fields for the natural (or Naturalist's) Hampette.

See *Gardens for Gamesmen*, or *When to be Fond of Flowers* (15*s*.). To give verisimilitude to your natural history asides on the field of golf, or polo, or cricket, any good nature lover's booklet is recommended. O. Agnes Bartlett's *Moth's Way and Bee's Wayfaring* is a prettily illustrated general account.

NOTE III. – Against some players it is more irritating to point out any minute little grub and say, 'Who would think, from its appearance now that that little fellow will one day turn into a Peacock Blue!'

7

GAME BY GAME

'All ob one swallow am too much big swallow.'
Up at Odoreida's

GOLF

IF I HAVE not said more about golf gamesmanship it is because I am afraid of saying too much. The whole subject would make a volume in itself. It is a book which I feel should be the work of a younger man. Yet the fact remains that there are many gamesmen who are not golfers. Indeed, many good steady gamesmen, knowing that golf is to me 'the gamesgame of gamesgames', have started their games-play of rackets or squash or whatever it may be by saying to me 'I'm afraid I don't play golf. Do you know, I've never been able to see the point of it?'

My counter to this simple gambit has always been to say: 'No – it is, of course a game of *pure* skill. It is the best game because no shot one plays can ever be quite the same as any other shot. Luck scarcely enters into it, all one wants is fitness, a good eye, a good nerve and a natural aptitude for games. That's why I like it.'

The truth is, of course, that fitness counts for less in golf than in any other game, luck enters into every minute of the contest, and all play is purely incidental to, and conditioned by, gamesmanship.

To a young man about to undertake the teaching of our science in its special application to golf, I would stress the fact that he must make the student realize the extreme importance of Advicemanship, Bad Luck Play, with special attention to Commiseration, Luncheonship and, of course, the Secondary Hamper.

Then, when the student has properly mastered what I have nick-named (and somehow the nickname has stuck!) 'Four-up Friendliness', and when – but not before – he is *really familiar* with, say, *ten* of the basic ways of walking off the tee after the drive with, or not with, the opponent – *then* go straight, say, to Caddie Play – but *don't* learn caddie management *or try to learn any other* secondary ploy, until the primary ploys have been mastered.

Then, for part two – the secondaries can be approached. I suggest that their importance should be emphasized in this order:

1. *Splitting*

In the foursome of four-ball game, this, quite simply, is the art of fomenting distrust between your two opponents. And do not let the student forget, in the maze of details, that the basis of Split Play is to make friends with your opponent A, and in that same process undermine his carefully assumed friendship – so easily liable to strain – with his partner, your opponent B, in order that, after the first bad shot by B, the thought, 'Poor you!' may be clearly implied by a glance from you, a shrug of the shoulders or the whistling of two notes as recommended by Gale (descending minor third).

NOTE. – Attention to detail is important here, and may lead to results of even wider value. It is possible to weaken your opponent's attack even in a straightforward single, if you can show sufficient parallelism of tastes and interests. Groundwork includes the preliminary hunting out of the pursuits or hobbies most favoured by the opponent to whom you want to reveal the possession of those common interests which may well be, you will wish him to feel, the basis of a lasting friendship. And – one tip – DON'T RUSH. Slow and steady wins this race. Or, as I always tell them: 'Keep off Tintoretto till the tenth!'[1]

In the forefront, then, of secondary ploys, remember: Study the interests and tastes of your opponent. For

THE GOOD GAMESMAN IS THE GOOD FRIEND

2. *Caddie Play*

The old rule still holds, 'Be nice to your caddie and the game will be

---

[1] R. Smart had a passion for Tintoretto so intense, that if an opponent admitted to a similar interest in his paintings, Smart could scarcely ever bring himself to beat him. On one occasion, however, my friend G. Odoreida had an unfortunate experience. His match with Smart was of supreme importance. He had practised for it by an intensive three-weeks' study not only of Tintoretto but also of Trienti, Tintoretto's celebrated pupil. He paid a flying visit to the Mauritshuis, where there was a recent Tintoretto acquisition. At the first hole, Odoreida plunged straight into the subject, not without genuine enthusiasm. But when, in consequence of this, he found himself four up at the ninth hole, he made his first mistake. He corrected Smart on a point of Tintoretto scholarship. Smart, furious, fought back and beat him at the twentieth hole.

nice to you'. Demonstrate, always, that caddies instinctively like you and respect you more than they respect or even notice your opponent. Play to the caddie. Ask his advice. Create a pleasant caddie-liaison, and, when you whisperingly ask your opponent, in the neighbourhood of the sixteenth hole, what he proposes to offer as a tip, let your reply to his suggestion be: 'What – do you mean two shillings as a *total tip*? Oh, I think we ought to give a little more than that.' For remember that

THE GOOD GAMESMAN IS GENEROUS

NOTE. – Though this small ploy may work well against a diffident man playing on a strange course, it is sometimes advisable to say: 'Oh, I don't think we ought to give them as much as that, you know. Members don't like it, you know. Do you remember when that Argentine Film Company was down here, flinging their money about? I'm not sure they weren't asked to leave the club. Of course, I see the Committee's point, in a way . . .' For remember that

THE GOOD GAMESMAN IS THE GOOD CLUBMAN

An Isolated Instance

While these papers were still in the proof stage I was beaten in a certain golf match. I have not time to discuss the matter in full. I do not even know whether it comes in the province of gamesmanship. The incident was absurdly simple – almost comic. At the first hole, my opponent, D. Low, of Golders Green, drove into the edge of the rough. On reaching his ball, before playing it he picked it up and placed it in the fairway, saying, 'I always do that. Do you mind?' Thinking that he intended not to play the hole at all – that his intention was perhaps to accompany me largely as a spectator – I laughed heartily, said, 'Of course not,' and settled down to a practice knockabout. Imagine my amazement when he proceeded thenceforward to play seriously and without further infringement. In my own mind the game was null and void from the beginning, but that did not prevent Low from presuming, indeed from saying, that he had in fact won.

Is this gamesmanship? And if so, what is the counter?

Simpson's Statue

I have been asked to give an exact explanation of a phrase used by many young gamesmen who do not, I fancy, properly know the meaning of the term, much less its origin.

I refer to the phrase 'Simpson's Statue', a simple gambit often used in croquet or snooker, but as it has its origin in golf, I place it here. R. Simpson had the idea of standing in the 'wrong place' while his opponent was playing his shot – beyond the line of the putt in golf (or the pot in billiards). Or in the 'wicket-keeper's position' during a golf shot off the fairway (or, in bowls, simply standing in the way). Having elicited a remonstrance, Simpson then proceeded, before every subsequent shot, not only in that game but in all subsequent matches against the same opponent, to remember that he was in the wrong position more or less at the last moment, leap into the correct position with exaggerated agility, and stand rigidly still with head bowed. (See right and p. 54.) Simpson, the originator of this ploy, used sometimes to increase its irritating effect by resting his club or cue head downwards on his boot, facetiously, in the 'reversed arms' position. A simple but good gambit. And remember, to make it effective, repeat it again and again and again.

Simpson's Statue:
the billiards
position.

BILLIARDS AND SNOOKER

Although the close proximity of the players makes the billiard table almost as important to gamesmen as the golf-course, I have little to add to the much we have learned from this game. If snooker is inextricably bound up with gamesmanship, billiards is no less important. The ardent snooker gamesman plays billiards in order that he can say that 'billiards is his real game'. There are the long periods, at billiards, during which no score is made. Its ancient history, and dignified aroma of cigars and professional markers, adapt the game perfectly to this purpose. It is useful for the snooker gamesman to be in a position constantly to remind his snooker opponent that 'billiards is *the* game', also, that 'billiards is the best practice for snooker', and that he 'will never improve his potting game until he has mastered the half-ball in-off at billiards'.

Snooker-player's Drivel

I strongly recommend Rushington's one-and-sixpenny brochure

on *Snooker-talk Without Tears*. This booklet contains full vocabularies of the drivellingly facetious language which has been found to be equally suitable to billiards and snooker, including a phonetic representation of such sounds as the imitation of the drawing of a cork, for use whenever the opponent's ball goes into the pocket. This

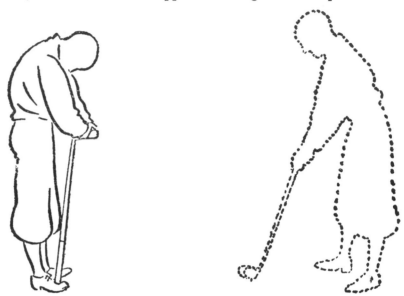

Advanced Simpson's Statue: the golf position, with 'reversed arms' irritant (see p. 53).

is a most useful ploy against good billiard players of the older generation, who believe in correct manners and meticulous etiquette in the billiard room. I often saw Rushington at work in the good old days before the war. His masterpiece, I always thought, was never to say 'five', 'eight', etc., after scoring five, or eight, etc., but always 'five skins', 'eight skins', etc.

Remind students, here, that

THE GAMESMAN IS FAMOUS FOR HIS SENSE OF FUN

SQUASH-RACKETS

Unlike golf and billiards, squash is very far from being a gamesman's paradise. Most of the gamesman's work must be done beforehand, in the dressing-room or at the luncheon table. There is far too much ordinary play in this game, with all its dangers of physical distress, so fatal to the well-timed thrust of the gamesman. To counteract this disadvantage I always bring with me an old and even slightly punctured ball which I refer to as the 'new, specially slow ball, recently authorized'; and I add that it is in general use now because 'otherwise the rallies would never end'. If losing, stress inferiority of squash to rackets, which, in turn, of course, is so inferior to tennis. Thus, the sequence of talk runs as follows: 'I was playing tennis at Lord's yesterday. This game's all right, but you know, after tennis, squash seems – well – you do feel rather like a squirrel running about in a cage, don't you?'

BRIDGE AND POKER

Miss Violet Watkins – name of ill-omen in gamesmanship circles on the Welsh border – has said that 'Gamesmanship can play little part in bridge and poker, which are themselves games of bluff'.

The association of the word 'bluff' with gamesmanship does small service to the art. True, there is a difficulty with poker. There are those who believe that the sole duty of the poker gamesman is to build up his reputation for impenetrability and toughness by suggesting that he last played poker by the light of a moon made more brilliant by the snows of the Yukon, and that his opponents were two white slave traffickers, a ticket-of-leave man and a deserter from the Foreign Legion. To me this is ridiculously far-fetched, but I do believe that a trace of American accent – West Coast – casts a small shadow of apprehension over the minds of English players.

Bridge, up to 1935, was virgin ground for the gamesman, but every month – owing largely I believe to the splendid work of Meynell – new areas of the game are being brought within his field. I will name one or two of the principal *foci of research*, in the new but growing world of bridgemanship.

1. *Intimidation*

We are working now on methods by which the gamesman can best suggest that he usually moves in bridge circles far more advanced than the one in which he is playing at the moment. This is sometimes difficult for the mediocre player, but a primary gamescover of his more obvious mistakes is the frank statement, with apologies, that the rough and ready methods of this ordinary kind of bridge, played as it is for amusingly low stakes, are constantly putting him off. 'Idiotic. I was thinking I was playing duplicate.' Refer to the 'damnably complicated techniques' with which matchplay is hedged around. During the post-mortem period after each hand, give advice *to your opponents* immediately, before anyone else has spoken about the general run of the play. Tell the opponent on your left that 'you saw her signalling with her third discard'. At first she will not realize that you are speaking to her, then she will not know what you are talking about, and will almost certainly agree. Invent 'infringements' committed by your opponents in bidding, tell them that 'it's quite all right – doesn't matter – but in a *match* it would be up to me to ask you to be silent for three rounds. Then if your partner redoubles, my original bid resumes its validity.' Refer frequently to authorities. Mention the Portland Club and say 'I expect you've only got the 1939 edition of the rules. Would you care to see the new thing I've got here? "For members only"?' Never say 'It doesn't matter in the least what you throw away because I am leading this card at random anyhow.' Refer to some formula in the *Silver Book of End-Play Squeezes*.

It is usual, as part of intimidation play, to *invent a convention* (if playing with a fellow-gamesman as partner). Explain the convention to your opponents, of course, e.g.:

GAMESMAN: Forcing two and Blackwood's, partner? Right? And Gardiner's as well? O K.

LAYMAN: What's Gardiner's?

GAMESMAN: Gardiner's – oh, simply this. Sometimes comes in useful. If *you* call seven diamonds *or* seven clubs and then one of us doubles without having previously called no trumps, then the doubler is telling his partner, really, that in his hand are the seven to Queen, *inclusive*, of the next highest suit.

LAYMAN: I think I see . . .

GAMESMAN: The situation doesn't arise very often, as a matter of fact.

The fact that the situation does not arise more often than once in fifty years prevents any possible misunderstanding with your partner.

This phase of Intimidation Play is often called 'Conventionist' or 'Conventionistical'.

2. *Two Simple Bridge Exercises for Beginners*

(a) *The Deal.* Better than ten books on the theory of bridge are the ten minutes a day spent in practising how to deal. A startlingly practised-looking deal has a hypnotic effect on opponents, and many's the time E. Hooper has won the rubber by his 'spiral whirl' type of dealing. A good deal of medical argument has revolved round this subject. 'Hooper's deal' is actually said to have a pulverising effect on the Balakieff layer of the cortex. Myself, I take this *cum grano salis*.

(b) *Meynell's mis-deal*. This is, in essence, the counter-game to intimidation play. Against a pair of opponents who know each other's game very well indeed, who have played together for years, and who pride themselves on the mechanical and unhesitating accuracy of their bidding, it is sometimes a good thing to make a mis-deal deliberately (so that your partner has fourteen and yourself twelve, say; or the disparity may be even greater – see below). Then pick up the cards and begin a wild and irrational bidding sequence. This will end, of course, in a double from E or W. As you begin to play the hand, discover the discrepancy in cards. The hand is then, of course, a washout. Your opponents will (*a*) be made to look foolish, (*b*) be annoyed at missing an easy double, (*c*) be unable to form a working judgment of your bidding form.

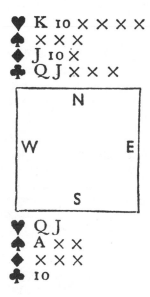

Bridge hand: Distribution after typical Meynell mis-deal.

3. *Split Bridge*

The old splitting game in golf foursomes has already been des-described (see p. 51). Of late years – it is, in fact, the most recent development in bridge – we have seen the adaptation of splitting, and the re-shaping of it, for the junior game.

The art of splitting, in bridge, is, quite simply, the art of sowing discord between your two opponents (East and West).

There is only one rule: BEGIN EARLY.

The first time the gamesman (South) makes his contract, the situation must be developed as follows:

GAMESMAN (South): Yes, just got the three. But I was rather lucky (*lowering voice to a clear whisper as he speaks to East*) . . . as a matter of fact your heart lead suited me rather well. I think . . . perhaps . . . if you'd led . . . well, almost anything else . . .

Ten to one West will seize this first opportunity of criticizing his partner and agree with Gamesman's polite implications of error. The seed of disagreement is sown. (Particularly if East had in fact led a heart correctly, or had not led one at all.) At the same time the gamesman's motto MODESTY AND SPORTSMANSHIP is finely upheld. It is never his skill, but 'an unlucky slip by his opponent', which wins the trick.

The principal lawn tennis ploys have already been discussed. I should like to add here one word more of general advice. If there is one thing I hate to see on the lawn tennis court, it is sloppy gamesmanship. And much more attention should be paid, I think particularly, to the following evolutions:

(1) How to pass opponent when changing ends, particularly the choice of the right moment to stand elaborately aside in order to allow your female opponent, in a mixed doubles, to come through first: and equally when to allow her the minimum room for getting by.

(2) When to make a great show of encouraging your partner, and say 'Good SHOT', whenever she gets the ball back over the net.

(3) How to apologize for lobbing into the sun.

(4) When to get the scoring wrong (always, of course, in your opponent's favour).

NOTE. – I have already referred (p. 10) to Farjeon's use of asymmetrical lengths, slopes and grass surfaces of his lawn tennis court at Forest Hill. It has been said of Farjeon that he raised lawn tennis to the status of a Home Game. It was after association with Farjeon that I began that develop-ment of Home Croquet which has placed it so far ahead of the championship game. Major West, of Gamesman Accessories Ltd., where Gamesman Accessories may be obtained, has constructed an artificial hawthorn tree for asymmetrical insertion into the normal croquet lawn. Illustrated below is Major West's 'Baskerville' lawn tennis lawn-marker for home courts. This reliable machine imparts the standard '3″ wave' to lines even on the most level lawns.

The Baskerville Lawn-Tennis Marker for imparting asymmetry to home courts (see text).

HOME GAMES

There are a variety of odd local games, and games developed in the home – 'roof-game', 'tishy-toshy', etc. Unorthodox games, like billiards fives, or *boule* – the game of bowls played with metal balls.

All these need careful gamesmanship, and are admirably adapted to a wide variety of ploys.

The player on the home court stands at a tremendous advantage, specially if he has invented the rules of the game. He must rub this advantage in by every method at his command.

Terminologics

To counteract any suggestions that the game is 'silly', he should create an atmosphere of historical importance round it. He should suggest its universality, the honour in which it is held abroad. He should enlarge on the ancient pageantry in which the origin of the game is vested, speak of curious old methods of scoring, etc.

Meynell uses the word 'terminologics' to describe the very complete language we have built round the game of *boule* (which in our game consists of rolling old bits of brass into a cracked gutter).

NOTE TO TEACHERS. – It is most important that the student should develop methods of his own. Encourage originality. But perhaps teachers may be helped by seeing this specimen of a 'correspondence' which 'passed' between Meynell and myself. This we incorporated in a privately printed pamphlet *English Boule* which we leave about in the bathrooms, ctc., of the boule court house. The specimen may suggest, at any rate, a general approach.

DEAR MEYNELL,

I forgot, when I was writing to advise you on the financial matter, to say that I had checked up on the point you mentioned, and it is not uninteresting to note that the expression *bowels* (i.e., boules) *of compassion* 'first used in 1374' has no connection with the ancient etiquette, recently revived as we know, according to which the gouttie-etranger (the gutstranger, or guest player new to the boule 'carpet') is supposed to allow his host to win the 'bully-up', or first rubber sequence. The term, of course, acquired its modern use much later in connection with the boule game which the Duke of Rutland played for a wager against Henry, son of Shakespeare's 'old Gaunt, time-honoured Lancaster' at Hove Castle in 1381, beating him on the last throw with a half-pansy, and dubbing his victim 'Bouling-broke', an amusing nickname which, spoken in jest, became as we know the patronymic of the Dukes of Lancaster.

Yours,

'My Man Over the Hill'

There is an excellent alternative to the development of a private game in your own home. That is to do the same thing in a house belonging to someone else. This is not only inconvenient to the real owner of the house; it places you in the fine games-position of 'playing on a strange court'.

J. Strachey has invented a form of indoor hockey which is played with the pointed end of an ordinary walking-stick as the club. As a game it is feebleness itself. But Strachey uses an interesting games-play in its execution.

The game is played in an old shed, five to fourteen a side. Early in the game Strachey says:

'Hi – whoa! – Look everybody. Wait a minute, wait a minute. Wait a minute, everybody. We mustn't lift our sticks above the knee, must we. Or else one of us will get the most awful cut. Right.'

He then proceeds, quite deliberately, to lay about him to right and left so that nobody can come near him. Through this method he has amassed an amazing sequence of wins to his credit.

CHESS

The prime object of gamesmanship in chess must always be, at whatever sacrifice, to build up your reputation. In our small chess community in Marylebone it would be modesty on my part to deny that I have built up for myself a considerable name without ever actually having won a single game.

Even the best players are sometimes beaten, and that is precisely what happens to me. Yet it is always possible to make it appear that you have lost your game *for the game's sake*.

'Regardez la Dame' Play

This is done by affecting anxiety over the wiseness of your opponent's move. An occasional 'Are you sure you meant that?' or 'Your castle won't like that in six moves' time' works wonders.

By arrangement with another gamesman I have made an extraordinary effect on certain of our Marylebone Chess Club Rambles by appearing to engage him in a contest without board. In the middle of a country lane I call out to him 'P to Q3', then a quarter of an hour later he calls back to me 'Q to Q B5'; and so on. 'Moves', of course, can be invented arbitrarily.

JUNIOR MEMBER: I can't think how you do it.
SELF: Do what?
JUNIOR MEMBER: Play chess without the pieces. Do you have a *picture* of the board in your brain . . . or what is it?
SELF: Oh, you mean our little game? I am actually up at the moment. Oh, you mean how do we do it? Oh, I've always been able to 'see' the board in that way, ever since I can remember.

Potter's Opening

This is supposed, now, to be the name of an effective opening, simple to play and easy to remember, which I have invented for use against a more experienced player who is absolutely certain to win. It consists of making three moves at random and then resigning. The dialogue runs as follows:

Potter's opening (1) KP–K4 : KP–K4
(2) B–Q B4 : B–Q B4
(3) Kt–B3 : Kt–B3
(4) White resigns

SELF: Good. Excellent. (*Opponent has just made his third move.* See above.) I must resign, of course.

OPPONENT: Resign?

SELF: Well ... you're bound to take my Bishop after sixteen moves, unless ... unless ... And even then I lose my castle three moves later.

OPPONENT. Oh, yes.

SELF: Unless you sacrifice there, which, of course, you wouldn't.

OPPONENT: No.

SELF: Nice game.

OPPONENT: Yes.

SELF: Pretty situation ... very pretty situation. Do you mind if I take a note of it? The *Chess News* usually publishes any stuff I send them.

It is no exaggeration to say that this gambit, boldly carried out against the expert, heightens the reputation of the gamesman more effectively than the most courageous attempt to fight a losing battle.

Chess and Parentship, or Gamesplay against Children

Many of the regular rules have to be adapted, with a tender hand, I hope and trust, when one exercises gamesmanship against the young. E.g., much use can be made of the fact that *children cannot remember their own infancy* (Grotto's Law). For instance, if beaten by my son at chess, I tell him (*i*) that I have only just taken it up, and (*ii*) that 'my first recollection of him was of a tiny figure sitting astride a wall, swinging his legs and playing chess with his minute friend Avrion. Neither of them can have been more than five at the time. How glad I am that I encouraged him to take it up'.

Basic Chess Play

'Sitzfleisch'. I have the greatest pleasure in assigning priority to F. V. Morley who first described this primary chessmanship gambit (see Morley, F. V., *My One Contribution to Chess*, Faber and Faber, 1947). Morley's wording is as follows:

Sitzfleisch: a term used in chess to indicate winning by use of the glutei muscles – the habit of remaining stolid in one's seat hour by hour, making moves that are sound but uninspired, until one's opponent blunders through boredom.

Johnsonian Capture

The name of Miss C. Johnson will always be associated primarily with certain specialized techniques or styles, recommended, of course, for women only, in the method of capturing pieces. It is, in essence, Differentiated Intimidation play. Playing against men, she has had extraordinary success by soundlessly and delicately removing her opponent's piece before quietly placing her own piece on the square. But against women, particularly nervous women, she bangs down her own piece with great force on the occupied square, so that her opponent's piece is, of course, sent sprawling over the board.

By the way, it is not true to say that Miss C. Johnson, who for some years now has been giving lessons in the 'Johnsonian Capture', is the first PGWA.[1] Readers will remember the unfortunate case of Miss J. Wethered, whose name in golf might now be forgotten were it not for the famous case in which she was deemed to have infringed on her professional gameswoman status by a series of matches, much too long to pass unnoticed, which were later proved, beyond possible doubt, to have been genuinely friendly.

[1] Member of the Professional Gameswomen's Association.

DARTS AND SHOVE-HALFPENNY

Basic play in these games must always be a variation of the Primary Hamper. Question your darts opponents closely on the exact area of the dart where he deems it wisest to exert maximum thumb-and-finger pressure. Continue to ask if he will be so kind as to demonstrate for you the precise position of the hand in relation to the head at the moment when the dart is released. In the case of shove-half-penny, hold up game continually by asking your opponent if he 'will touch with the end of a match the area of the ball of the thumb which should be regarded as the target-of-impact between skin and receiving edge of disc of "halfpenny" '.

In playing these games on home boards, where you might be presumed to have an advantage, keep talking about 'How you prefer old pub boards . . . nothing like genuine pub boards . . .'.

CRICKET

If there is one thing more than another which makes me regret those pressing requests of my friends which forced me to 'rush into print' with this volume, it is the fact that the huge subject of Cricket must remain a blank in this edition of my work. GRC(C) (or, to give it its full, rather ponderous, title, Gamesmanship Research Council, Cricket Division) has been in existence scarcely five years. A devoted band of workers have spent their spare time in its service for no other reward than a nominal expenses account, an entertainment allowance, and the nominal use of the Council's cars and petrol. It will be re-membered that after five researchers had found 8,400 instances of gamesmanship in a match at Hove, reduced by rain to a bare one and a half days' play, between Sussex and Derbyshire, the investiga-tion was completely reorganized, following the resignation of the Chairman, Sir William (now Lord) Tile, the brother of E. Tile, the sportsman. This meant, virtually, the scrapping of two years' work, when the researchers were given their new briefing, and sent out all over again in an effort to discover some game, or some act in some game, of cricket, in which gamesmanship was *not* involved.

But results are beginning to come in now. Four instances have been recorded from Surrey alone. By 1949 there should be something in print, till then, good luck to the GRC(C), and good hunting. The chapter on 'Spectatorship', or the 'art of winning the watching', as it has been called, is to be, I am glad to say, in the able hands of Colonel Debenham.

NOTE. – Historians of gamesmanship often ask the following question: 'It is said that there is some mystery about the connection between cricket and G. Odoreida, the celebrated gamesman. What is it?'

The answer is simple. There is no mystery, for the facts are known. Odoreida did well in his early cricketing days as a spectator, particularly at Old Trafford. He was the first to enclose the Complete Records of Cricket in the cover of Bradshaw's Railway Guide, so that when, in order to win an argument, he was 'recalling', say, Verity's bowling average of 1931, he was able to achieve accuracy up to two places of decimals, while to the admiring onlookers it seemed that he was casually verifying the time of a train.

But this spectatorship of Odoreida's soon had too many imitators: and after he took to the game itself, he was never really successful. When it came to such straightforward irritation gambits as the movements of sightscreens, Odoreida found that the ordinary average cricketer could outgame him every time. Some of the devices he fell back upon were not very happily chosen. He spent an entire season acquiring absolute ambidexterity as a batsman. Coming in eighth wicket down, he was able to irritate an already wearied field by playing alternate balls left- and right-handed, forcing the fielders to change position after each delivery. As a bowler (according to F. Meynell, quoting H. Farjeon), his habit was to shout 'no ball', imitating the accent and voice of the umpire, as the ball left his hand. This gambit got him an occasional wicket, but it was frowned upon by the older generation of gamesmen.

8

LOST GAME PLAY

'... for the game is one of a series,
And a fractional loser thou.'

THE VALUE OF gamesmanship as a training for the British citizen, and for young people in particular, is shown not only in the special qualities it enhances among those who habitually find themselves on the losing side. If it is true that the typical Britisher never knows when he has lost, it is true of the typical gamesman that his opponent never knows when he has won.

The true gamesman knows that the game is never at an end. Game-set-match is not enough. The winner must win the winning. And the good gamesman is never known to lose, even if he has lost.

To take one example. Tony Gillies was no snooker player, and no golfer either. But he had this gift – of turning defeat into something very near complete victory. If the match was 'serious' – Club event or handicap – he would paint himself as the Abe Mitchell of club golf, who had won everything but the cup. He would bring out astonishing details of unpopular members who had won the event, and refer to their dull struggles, their ant-like methods of overcoming difficulties ... characters without temperament, and without interest.

Conversely, of course, if the match he lost had been 'only a friendly', he would say, 'I don't think I've won a *friendly* match this year. There is some devilish twist in my character which condemns me only to win a match if it is really important. Sheer blind desperation, I suppose.'

Bookmanism

This is the place to mention the basic Lost Game Play originated, I believe, by Rupert Duff, of water-polo fame. And I should like to say here that I bear no grudge against the followers of the Oxford Group for their punning use of the term 'Buchmanite' transliterated from my own 'Bookmanite', 'Bookmanism', etc. But let me remind readers that the term BOOKMANISM, in its original sense, bore no reference to gamesmanship in religion, but was used to cover that small, highly specialized, but very valuable ploy in the Lost Game, which includes the possession of books on the game, and the knowledge of the right moment to recommend them, and to lend them.

This is more effective even than the suggestion that your opponent, 'now that he is doing so well', should 'have a couple of lessons from the pro (and mind you stick to what he says)'. In at least three respects it is more likely to undermine his game.

'Take my tip,' you say to him, 'and study this little book by Z. It's worth a dozen practice games. Don't take another practice shot till you've mastered the first twelve chapters. Then make up your mind to put into execution what you've learnt. Even if it means losing a game or two.'

Use of Bookmanism in Opponent's Putt-Ploy

I am supposed to be something of a fanatic in the use of Bookmanism where Golf is concerned. I have collected a small library of books on the different aspects of the game. The book I select for lending is determined when I have decided which aspect of my winning opponent's play it is most advisable to undermine. But, in general, all 'golfgamesers' are agreed that 'the putt is the thing to go for'. 'ANALYSE YOUR OPPONENT'S PUTTING' is the Golden Rule. Ask him what muscles he brings into play, and from what part of the body the 'sequence of muscular response' begins. To deal with opponents who say that they 'aren't aware of using any muscles in particular', O G A are issuing the accompanying diagram-leaflet, with instructions on how to present it. (See next page.)

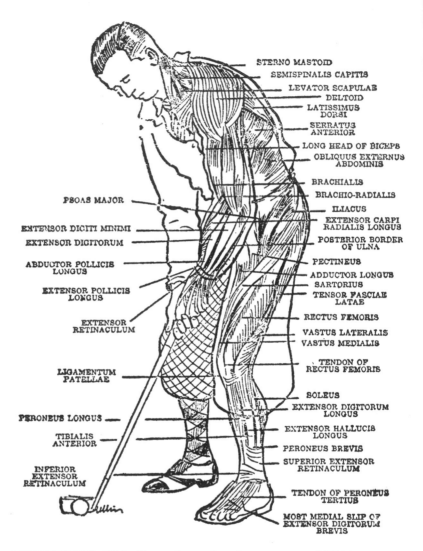

STERNO MASTOID
SEMISPINALIS CAPITIS
LEVATOR SCAPULAE
DELTOID
LATISSIMUS DORSI
SERRATUS ANTERIOR
LONG HEAD OF BICEPS
OBLIQUUS EXTERNUS ABDOMINIS
BRACHIALIS
BRACHIO-RADIALIS
ILIACUS
EXTENSOR CARPI RADIALIS LONGUS
POSTERIOR BORDER OF ULNA
PECTINEUS
ADDUCTOR LONGUS
SARTORIUS
TENSOR FASCIAE LATAE
RECTUS FEMORIS
VASTUS LATERALIS
VASTUS MEDIALIS
TENDON OF RECTUS FEMORIS
SOLEUS
EXTENSOR DIGITORUM LONGUS
EXTENSOR HALLUCIS LONGUS
PERONEUS BREVIS
SUPERIOR EXTENSOR RETINACULUM
TENDON OF PERONEUS TERTIUS
MOST MEDIAL SLIP OF EXTENSOR DIGITORUM BREVIS

PSOAS MAJOR
EXTENSOR DIGITI MINIMI
EXTENSOR DIGITORUM
ABDUCTOR POLLICIS LONGUS
EXTENSOR POLLICIS LONGUS
EXTENSOR RETINACULUM
LIGAMENTUM PATELLAE
PERONEUS LONGUS
TIBIALIS ANTERIOR
INFERIOR EXTENSOR RETINACULUM

IMPORTANT: This illustration, taken from p. 472 of Weil's *Primer of Putting*, should not be shown to opponent until the third week.

RANDOM JOTTINGS OF AN OLD GAMESMAN
by
'Wayfarer'

'. . . And the gamesman's gone from the ghyll.'

When the first crocus breaks cover, and the branches of the still-bare trees are peopled once more with sound as the birds begin to practise their spring song, that is the time when the hearts of gamesmen, young and old, stir at the thoughts of triumphs to come. They stir in another way, too, when the last leaf falls and the branches grow silent – stir with memories, then, of a season past, remembrance echoing with the small victories, the tiny conquests, recalling to their minds some grand old phrases of the games-play – 'Loseman's Hamper', or 'the weak heart of Morteroy', memories of the triumphs and failures of the gamesacre.

Which reminds me – by the way – that the Old Gamesman's Association continues to grow. OGA or 'the Ogres', as they are affectionately called, meet twice a year to deliver judgment on their validity, as a body, and to describe advances in technique. Welcome, also, to the new Ogre tie – and what a sensible notion it was to make the colours and pattern of this special tie precisely the same as that worn by the I. Zingaris! This has the triple advantage of (1) doing away with the need of designing a special tie, (2) allowing the gamesman to be mistaken for one who has the very exclusive honour of belonging to

IZ, and (3) irritating any genuine IZ against whom the gamesman
happens to be playing.

A QUEER MATCH

No, the OGs don't take themselves too seriously. And what a good
thing that is! I had the good fortune to be present at the celebrated
badminton match between G. Odoreida and the Yugo-Slav champion
Bzo in the West Regional Finals – one of the longest games I have
ever watched. Both were poor players. Both were at the height of
their gamesmanship powers. The match started a good hour before
the game began. Odoreida kept Bzo's taxi waiting twelve minutes and
then was short of change when the time came for payment. But the
younger player succeeded in exacting his share and came out of it a
shilling to the good, only to find himself one rum and orange to the
bad on the drink exchange before their sandwich lunch. In the chang-

ing-room Bzo prettily pleaded a cut on the palm of his righthand,
which he had swathed elaborately in a special grip-improving elasto-
plast earlier in the morning. Odoreida Frith-Morteroyed in reply,
displaying his little finger, the top joint of which was missing. 'Jet
plane,' he said. 'The skin has just healed.' This was dangerous, for
many of us knew that the accident happened thirty-five years ago,
when Odoreida caught his finger in the chain of a toy tricycle.

The game itself started with some efficient crowd play. Odoreida
opened by exchanging jokes with the umpire, and Bzo countered by
patting the head of the shuttlecock boy and comically pretending to
be hurt when a return from Odoreida hit him gently in the middle of
the chest. Odoreida drew level by smashing into the net on purpose,
after the umpire had (quite correctly) given a line-cock decision in his
favour. The applause had hardly died down when Bzo jumped into

the lead again. Odoreida had made the mistake of achieving his first hard shot of the game, and Bzo made no attempt to reach it but stood stock still, shaking his head from side to side in whimsical respect, and sporting acknowledgment of his opponent's skill. Odoreida did well soon after this by discovering a 'sprung string' in his racquet and asking with delightful informality whether 'anyone had got another bat' as he had not got a spare. This double thrust shook Bzo for a few points, but he soon pulled himself together by asking a spectator 'not to wave his programme about' as it was 'bang in his opponent's line of sight'. Bzo seemed in full spate. Odoreida, now badly rattled, fought back well with a couple of broken shoe-laces and a request for a lump of sugar. Thus gambit after gambit was tried, and each in turn was effectively countered. After an hour's play they were still on the first game and the score was deuce for the sixtieth time, when suddenly Bzo came up to the net and spoke as follows:

'Let's' (or 'Why not let's') 'drop gamesmanship and just play?'

Odoreida assented and the game was then *played*, to the end. It had, of course, lost all interest to the more understanding spectators, who were puzzled, to say the least, although a small group applauded.

At the same time, I do not feel we should blame them too heavily. For

GAMESMANSHIP CAN BE TAKEN TOO SERIOUSLY

GAMESMANSHIP
AND LIFE

As I was endeavouring to think of a phrase which would express some of our deeper feelings on the subject of this queer Science of ours, the heading was supplied, as if by chance, in a way which was as unexpected as it was kind. When my wife brought me my post I knew, from the superscription, whence the letter came. 'My dear,' I said, 'here is something from the Dean of Southport.' He had written to ask me to come along and chat to his lads up there on the theme of Gamesmanship and Life. It is certainly amazing – and I was favourably astonished – to see the interest expressed by Young People of all denominations in my small theories.

I noticed how readily gamesmanship appealed to the young when I watched my own two lads picking it up with increasing aptitude, and using it, too, in boyhood games of ping-pong and lawn tennis, croquet and chess. And how pleased we were when, sometimes, their little efforts succeeded against us.[1]

I think it is the fact that sportsmanship and chivalry are the so frequently repeated watchwords of gamesmanship, which makes it appeal so strongly to young persons, and to much older people also, like the Dean of Southport, who must have noticed the constant use we make of these phrases in our magazines and pamphlets.

I think my visit was a success. I know it was of benefit to myself. When I went up for my lecture – group-chat would describe it better – I soon had them smiling and asking questions. And I was glad to do even this small office towards the ensuring of that continuance of growth, that ever-widening circle, which will help us to look to the future, while we are remembering the past.

[1] v. 'Counter-Gamesmanship, Parents and', p. 63.

APPENDIX I

THE KÖNINCK PORTRAIT OF DR W. G. GRACE

THERE ARE STILL certain points which need clearing up on the subject of the disputed portrait of the great doctor.

The dust of controversy has settled, by now. Yet it is amusing to recall that fifty years ago the Köninck portrait of Grace was always reproduced as a proof that the famous beard was false. Grace certainly

The Köninck Portrait of W. G. Grace (see text).

used his beard like a good gamesman, and no doubt this fact, and the obvious advantages of a large black beard, gave rise to the rumour. It was said that the join of the beard to the neck (N on the picture) was faked. Mr Samuel Courtauld first came into prominence as an investigator of pictures by stepping forward to point out that at the mouth (M on the picture) the join was obviously natural.

The extraordinary success of Grace as a gamesman has led to an astounding crop of stories associated with his name. Half the cricket theorists in England have vied with each other in the invention of the unlikeliest tales.

The Gladstonian Theory

Ridiculous theories were particularly rife in 1888 as to the 'real identity' of the great doctor. The Köninck portrait usually figures largely in these discussions. If the cap in the portrait is supposed to show the colours of the Wanderers, why the monogram? And if the monogram shown is that of the Gloucester Colts, why the button on the top of the head? Microscopic examination has shown, too, that the shirt, instead of buttoning left over right, folds right over left. Was Grace a woman?

The theory that Grace was really Gladstone became, of course, the sporting sensation of the century. The doctrine is based on the 'concealed meaning' of two words, the most important words spoken by Gladstone in the whole of his career, or at any rate, the words which *he seemed to wish the world to believe* the most important. This was his asseveration, when he first assumed the office of Prime Minister, that PACIFY IRELAND was to be his mission. The theory is, of course, that when Gladstone spoke of Ireland, he was referring not to the famous country but to J. H. Ireland, the Australian fast bowler.

The one man who knew the answer to the secret – R. G. S. ('Flicker') Wilson – kept his mouth – now closed for ever – firmly shut during his lifetime. It is certainly true that Gladstone, if he had in fact been Grace, would have had more reason to fear the Ireland of the cricketing world, and indeed Gladstone's suddenly assumed interest in Ireland is difficult to explain. Gladstonians have gone to fantastic lengths to read double meanings into the wordings of Gladstone's Home Rule Bills. They prove, to their own conviction at any rate, that it was Home Rule for England which was Gladstone's main concern, foreseeing as he undoubtedly did the menace of Australian Test Match cricket.

But the whole theory breaks down, surely, on the question of dates. Is it true that Grace was never seen batting at Lord's during the Midlothian campaign? What is the value of the evidence of D. Bell that his grandfather once 'thought he heard Grace laughing in the Long Room' during this period? Again, J. H. Ireland was only twenty-six when Gladstone assumed office. His play had been reported in *The Times*, but only three members of the MCC had seen him bowl, including Price. And it is I suppose just conceivably possible that Gladstone did frequently refer to 'Price's Message', if by a simple transliteration references to Lord Rosebery can be shown to be references to Price.

But Grace or Gladstone, who cares? As any sportsman will say, here was some magnificent cricket played by a magnificent cricketer, who gave pleasure to the world, be his name what it may.

APPENDIX II
NOTE ON ETIQUETTE

IT IS extraordinary how often, among gamesmen, the etiquette of gamesplay is instinctive, and there is little need, I am glad to say, to reduce etiquette to the formality of print.

There are two points, nevertheless, on which questions are sometimes asked. I append the official answers.

(*a*) When two gamesmen are playing together, it is usual for the senior gamesman to make the first move.

(*b*) When two or more gamesmen are playing against opponents *or with partners* who are not gamesmen, none of the gamesmen should make any reference to gamesmanship either directly or by using such phrases as 'don't take any notice of what he says', 'he's pulling your leg', etc.

APPENDIX III
CHAPTER HEADINGS FROM 'ORIGINS AND EARLY HISTORY OF GAMESMANSHIP'

Play Among Primitive Animals: the Limpet – Significance of 'Fishy' – Cat and Mouse and the Study of *Ur* Gamesmanship – The Neolithic Gap – Some Unexplained Greek Vase Paintings – The Indecipherable 'Prayer Sheets' Found in Londonderry – Persian Origin of the Phrase 'Velvet Glove' – St Augustine's Find – Chinese Emblem for 'Playing a Losing Game' – Gift of 'Tennis Balls' to Henry V – Gamesmanship and the Battle of Agincourt – Symbolism of the Pawns, in Chess – Renaissance – of what? – Boyhood of Francis Drake – Difference Between Machiavelli and Cervantes – Use of Latin Quotations – Rembrandt's first 'Tam-o-Shanter' Self-Portrait Examined – The Nineteenth Century and After – After That – Dawn of

Cricket – Dawn of Not Cricket – W. G. Grace's Beard: False or Genuine? – Use of Linesmen in Wimbledon Lawn Tennis – End of the Era of Actual Play, in Games.

APPENDIX IV

DIET

I DO NOT favour any fads or frills where diet for gamesmanship is concerned. Eat what you please seems to be the Golden Rule. But in moderation. A sufficient breakfast, wholesome lunch – and there is no reason why it should not be palatable as well. 'A little of what you fancy' at tea-time. And a well-balanced, well-cooked evening meal completes the scheme, and should satisfy the wants of the average gamesman. Fats are important and carbo-hydrates should not be neglected, provided that protein content is kept in mind. But always remember that the meal before play should not be too heavy, nor the meal afterwards too light.

APPENDIX V

SOME EXTRACTS FROM THE 'GAMESMAN'S HANDBOOK' FOR 1949

THE *Gamesman's Handbook* (1949) is now in preparation and it is hoped to publish it at the beginning of December 1948 – not in order to take advantage of any adventitious catch-sale at Christmas, but because the birthday of our popular treasurer falls in that month. It is hoped to make the volume a combination of Wisden and Baedeker, with full accounts of the principal clubs, hotels which cater for the OGA, garages which will accept custom, etc, etc.

Here is an extract from the earliest of many interesting tables:

OPEN CHAMPIONSHIP
1929 Miss E. Goodhart
1930   ,,
1931   ,,
1932   ,,
1933   ,,
1934   ,,
1935 G. Odoreida

The professional side of gamesmanship will receive full attention. Extracts from an article by 'V.V.':

The low status of the amateur gamesman, in Great Britain, is a factor which we should never be allowed to forget. In America it is difficult to tell the pro from the amateur. In Britain, the feeble clothes and general appearance of the amateur single him out at once. We amateurs have to fight against the growing menace of young people who insist on playing their various games for the fun of the thing, treating it all as a great lark, and indulging rather too freely, if the truth were known, in pure play.

There is no doubt that a knowledge of the game itself sometimes helps the gamesman. But there is a growing tendency to carry this too far in some professional circles. An interesting point arose when Kinroyd of Hoylake, the local Professional Gamesmen's Association representative, holed the course in seventy-two, the standard scratch score. Had he or had he not lost his professional status? And, if so, what profession?

RECORD GAMES AND QUEER INCIDENTS

A selection from the Handbook List

(8) In March 1929 G. Wert won the Isle of Purbeck Shield Knock-out Competition. In the six rounds played, he never holed out in less than ninety-two net. On presenting the prize, Lady Armory complimented him on his success in the face of wretched play and referred in her speech to the 'literally unadulterated' gamesmanship of the player.

(22) On eight separate occasions, all within a fortnight, playing in the same club, against the same group of opponents, J. Batt won his match, using the same gamesplay on each occasion. ('I'm an awful fool, but I've had no food for twenty-four hours'). After one match, the loser actually sent him a present of butter.

(41) Captain E. Mawdesley Hill, in the autumn of 1938, won three successive matches against –. Johns of Forest Grove, in three successive weeks, by asking him, with great delicacy, *on each occasion*, whether he (–. Johns) was in financial difficulties and would he accept help. It is interesting to note that a fourth game was also lost when –. Johns realized not only that no kind of help was forthcoming, but that on the contrary Mawdesley Hill owed him for two lunches. –. Johns was too angry to control his game.

(182) *Distinguished Visitor Play.* J. Strachey made beautiful use of this gambit in a recent lawn tennis doubles 'friendly' in which 'Wayfarer' was concerned. The game was played at a time when Anglo- * * * *ish relations were cordial, but delicately balanced. 'To my surprise,' writes 'Wayfarer', 'Strachey, asking if he could bring his own partner, astonished us by turning up with the * * * *ish Ambassador. Before the game began Strachey took me aside to "explain the position". He suggested that the game should be played, "for obvious reasons", without gamesmanship. On the whole (he tipped me the wink) it would be no bad thing if the Ambassador (who was, of course, Strachey's partner) ended up on the winning side. "Someone on the highest level" had hinted as much to him.

'Pleased to comply, my partner and I obediently lost the first set. Before the next set began, however, Strachey let it slip out that he had been pulling our leg, that it was not the * * * *-ish Ambassador at all, but – and here it seemed to me that I recognized the vaguely familiar face – one of the Oval Umpires who in his spare time played lawn tennis as a member of the East Kennington LTC. This silly trick angered me, and my play in the second set was not improved in consequence, particularly as we both drove hard at the Oval man's body but, in our annoyance, usually missed it. Two sets to Strachey.

'In the third set Strachey out-manoeuvred us once more. He told us, finally, that in fact his partner really was the * * * *-ish Ambassador, who, indeed, he turned out to be. This, of course, completely upset us, the remembrance of our rude behaviour in Set II rendering us almost incapable of returning the simplest ball. This gave Strachey the third set and the match.

'The whole game, which was played on an asphalt court, lasted exactly fifty-eight minutes.'

NOTE. – J. Strachey writes: 'I note that "Wayfarer" actually left the court under the impression that the player in question *was* the * * * *-ish

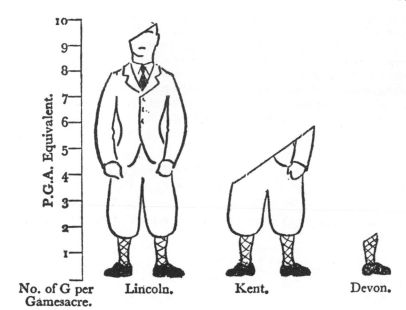

No. of G per   Lincoln.   Kent.   Devon.
Gamesacre.

Diagram showing the distribution of Gamesman's Associations in three typical English counties, to explain the zoning of OGA in relation to PGA.

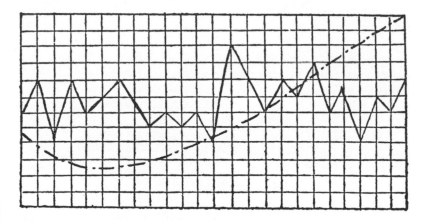

Graph showing the relationship between Mean Bird Gamesmanship and Mean Game Birdmanship.

Ambassador. Be that as it may . . . has not our good "Wayfarer" for once missed the point, or rather perhaps the principle *behind* the point, of this little incident? The real crux was the creation of doubt in the opponent's mind. In this case, for example, our opponents sometimes supposed themselves to be facing the * * * *-ish Ambassador and sometimes one of the Oval Umpires; not unnaturally they failed adequately to adjust their play. But that does not exclude the possibility that the fourth player in the set was the Ambassador of another power, or alternatively, of course, an Umpire, not of the Surrey C.C., but of an *entirely different* County Club.'

We are glad to say that the *Gamesman's Handbook* will be, in its new edition, plentifully pictured with half-tone blocks and illustrations in photogravure. GGP[1] and GO[2] have completed their survey by including the areas of West Riding and Lanarkshire. We reproduce two illustrations (page 79) representing the results of their pooled researches.

[1] Gallup Poll, Gamesman's Division.
[2] Gamesmen's Mass Observation, usually shortened to Gass O. or GO.

Some Notes on

LIFEMANSHIP

With a Summary of Recent Researches in
GAMESMANSHIP

SACERDOS DUX VATES
PARENS ET CONJUX.

OUR FOUNDER
(In the background, Station Road, Yeovil)

1

INTRODUCTION

MILLIONS OF PEOPLE have formulated the wish, often unexpressed, that the lessons learnt from the philosophy of Gamesmanship should be extended to include the simple problems of everyday life.

It has been, indeed, a wonderful surprise to me to find that my little book has sown the seed in so many and, if possible, in such tremendously diverse hearts: that it has been popular both with the extremely young and the extremely old – perhaps more so. And maybe it is true that today we stand in need of precisely that kind of formulation, more actual if only because it is less concrete, which finds its expression in the contrastingly manifested *temporal* problems, themselves reflections of a wider principle, which is yet capable of a not less personal approach.

What does Lifemanship Mean?

Easy question to pose, difficult to answer in a phrase. A way of life, pervading each thought and conditioning our every action? Yes, but something much more, even though it only exists, as a pervasion, intermittently. 'How to live' – yes, but the phrase is too negative. In one of the unpublished notebooks of Rilke[1] there is an unpublished phrase which might be our text: ' . . . if you're not one up (*Bitzleisch*) you're . . . one down (*Rotzleisch*).'

How to be one up – how to make the other man feel that something has gone wrong, however slightly. The Lifeman is never caddish himself, but how simply and certainly, often, he can make the other man feel a cad, and over prolonged periods.

The great principle of Gamesmanship we know. More humbly but not less ardently, if still on the lower rungs of the ladder, comes the

[1] See page 126 under 'O K-names.'

Lifeman, pursuing each petty ploy till he, too, has achieved this 'state of One Upness', this *Bitzleischstüsse*.

Who is the Lifeman?

'You, me, all of us.' That is the answer. But there is another answer, too. It is to be found in the presence and existence of the accredited or practising Lifeman, entitled so to be called. A small band yet a growing one,[1] we work from half a dozen centres co-ordinated, of course, from our 'HQ' at Station Road, Yeovil. Every post brings its new crop of notes, reports, postcards of all kinds, and *ana* out of which, cut to the bone, this conspectus of work in progress has been made.

Day by day our centres send out young men, yes and women too, to assess the lifemanship approach for each district, relatively to the stratum or mode of life incorporated within that district, and suitable to it.

You will find your Lifeman, I hope, genial, encouraging, and, provided you are ready to accept the One Down condition, sometimes apparently genuinely helpful. Yet they are always alert and ready for the slight put-off, the well-timed provocation, which will get the other fellow down.

Opening Remarks of Gattling-Fenn

It is the ordinary, simple everyday things of life, wherein each one of us can, by ploy or gambit, most naturally gain the advantage. When I speak, for instance, of the Opening Remarks of Gattling-Fenn, I am referring to that great Lifeman Harry Gattling-Fenn, and his opening remarks.

With his ready smile and friendly face, his hair artificially tousled, his informal habit of wearing a well-cut old tie round his waist instead of braces, and his general air of geniality, Gattling seemed permanently in the off-guard position. It was only by his opening remarks, power of creating a sense of dis-ease, that one realized, as one used to say of him, that Gattling was *always in play*.

To a young person, for instance, who came to visit him he would say, genially of course, 'Sit you down.' Why was this putting off? Was

[1] According to Hulton Research, the number of lifemen who drink tea but never buy fireworks is 79 (correct for income-group B up to June 1946). The figure for those who are interested in soap substitutes and have not yet been to Portugal is, however, 385.

it the tone? When the young man nervously took out a cigarette he would say, 'Well, if you're smoking, I will.'

He would say, 'You want a wash, I expect,' in a way which suggested that he had spotted two dirty finger-nails. To people on the verge of middle age he would say, 'You're looking very fit and young.' To a definitely older man, of his still older wife he would comment that he was glad she 'was still moving very briskly about'.

In conversation he would lead people to tell stories against their friends and then, when his turn came to speak, he would say (speaking as always from the point of view of the good-natured man) that he 'wished B. was here' because he 'never told stories behind people's backs'.

Thus a 'lifeman's wicket' was prepared – i.e. a sense of distrust, uncertainty and broken flow, and Gattling would be in a position to prepare some more paralysing thrust.

'A little club at Hayward's Heath'

It was four years ago that I first saw Gattling in action. It was at Hayward's Heath, I remember, at a sort of social club we had formed, a get-together of people back from Burma, where I, in fact, had never actually been.

The atmosphere was meant to be one of jolly reminiscence. We were drawn together by a mutual interest in Gamesmanship, and a curiosity about the genuineness of each other's war records. 'Lifemanship', as a word, had not then been invented. The atmosphere was pleasant, easy – apparently invincibly so. How well I shall always remember the quietness, the deftness of touch, with which Gattling dried us all up.

There was one ploy of Gattling's which I found particularly effective, and I believe it must have been about this time that I first murmured to myself the word 'Lifemanship'.[1]

Some of us, though not in fact me, had had some pretty hair-raising experiences on active service; whereas the most dangerous thing that had happened to Gattling, I knew to my certain knowledge, was firewatching outside Sale, two miles beyond the raiding area of Manchester. Without actually lying, Gattling was able to tell the story of this totally uninteresting event, in the presence of three submariners and a man who had been twice captured by and had twice escaped from the Japanese, and to tell it in such a way that these

[1] It was certainly not later than November 1947.

people began apologizing for their relatively comfortable war. 'My God,' said Commander Wright, 'I never realized it was like that.'

'A little club at Hayward's Heath.' The curious may be interested to know that the northern side of the room (right-hand window) was 'committee corner', with table and chairs. The left side, scene of the original 'incident', was kept clear for general talk and friendly argle-bargle.

'I stamped out the flaming stuff with my foot,' said Gattling. Some cinder from a small and distant incendiary had, by a stroke of luck, landed in his garden. 'It wasn't a question of feeling frightened, I just found myself doing it. It was as if somebody else was acting in my person.'

He had eventually buried the cinder with a small trowel.

'It was as if I was in a dream,' said Gattling.

For all my admiration, I really couldn't let Gattling get away with this. 'While Mostyn, here, was raiding St Nazaire,' I said . . .

'Oh, my God, don't I know it,' said Gattling. 'Those chaps were risking their lives not only every day, but every hour of the day and night. That's why one longed to be doing, doing, doing something. To make some contribution. And that is why I was glad, that day at Sale . . .' And so on, for another three or four minutes. I got angrier than ever. But I must say I mentally took off my hat to Gattling, not because he probably did less, during the last war, than anybody I met or could even imagine,[1] but because the mere fact that I was getting angry made me realize that here, in Gattling, was our little science of Gamesmanship bearing new fruit. A new colony had been added to Gamesmanship's Empire.

[1] Gattling had more than one way of suggesting that he had been 'rather in the thick of things' during the war. For wear in the Sale Home Guard he managed to fiddle a tropical bush shirt. When he began to wear this over corduroy trousers while playing croquet in peace-time, it was noted that the shoulder straps seemed to be scored with the markings of the removed insignia of a brigadier, and there was an unfaded portion on the left breast which looked like the tracery of four rows of medals.

It was small justification to reply, when challenged, that the device was in direct imitation of a gambit invented by R. Hart-Davis.

CONVERSATIONSHIP

And now in the next three chapters, we get down to Lifemanship Basic. Read through quickly for the general sense, and then back to the beginning to memorize each individual gambit. It is not easy, but you will enjoy the small discipline.

IN CONVERSATION play, the important thing is to get in early and stay there. There are always some slow or feeble-witted people in any conversation group who will turn their heads towards the *man who gets going first.* Any good average Lifeman should be able to succeed here. A simple method is to ask a question and answer it almost immediately yourself, after one person has said 'Oh' – or 'Well'. E.g.:

LIFEMAN: I wonder what the expectation of life of, say, an advertising agent of thirty really is – at this moment of time, I mean.

Having read up the answer to this question[1] in *Whitaker's Almanack* just before coming into the room, Lifeman, after only a second's pause, can answer his own question.

Another *opening*, more difficult to guard against, is the encouraging personal remark aimed at your chief rival, e.g. 'Good lord, how do you always manage to look so *well?*' There are many variants. 'I'm glad to see you looking so fit' can suggest that at last your friend has cut down to a bottle of whisky a day. More subtle, and more difficult to answer is:

LIFEMAN: You're looking wonderfully relaxed.

I have noted J. Pinson's reply (known as 'Pinson's Reply') to this clever gambit:

LIFEMAN: You're looking wonderfully relaxed . . . I thought something good had happened to you.

---

[1] But remember that each gambit has its answer or *counterlife.* Do not be downed by the difficulty of Lifeman's question, but answer back with a will *before* he has had time to answer himself. Thus:
COUNTERLIFE: (i) 'I should have thought that question has lost validity in our contemporary context' *or* (ii) 'I wondered how long it would be before somebody asked that question.'

PINSON: You're looking tremendously relaxed, too.
LIFEMAN (*counter-riposting*): Ah, but I'm not looking nearly so relaxed as you are.
PINSON: Oh, I don't think I'm very relaxed.
LIFEMAN: Oh, yes, you are.

Two lifemen may go on in this way for twenty minutes, but to a layman the statement that he is relaxed can suggest that normally he is nervy and abstracted, if not on the verge of a breakdown.

Glaciation

This is the name for the set of gambits which are designed to induce an awkward silence, or at any rate a disinclination to talk, on the part of possible opponents. The 'freezing' effects of these gambits is sometimes of immense power, and I list them here in order or strength, placing the weakest first:

(*a*) Tell a funny story (not advised).

(*b*) If someone else tells a funny story, do not, whatever happens, tell your own funny story in reply, but listen intently and not only refrain from laughing or smiling, but make no response, change of expression or movement whatever. The teller of the funny story, whatever the nature of his

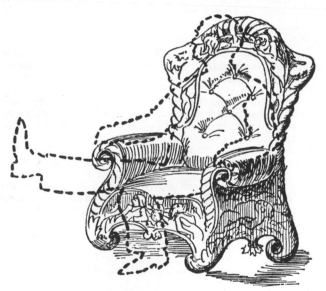

Suggested simulation of false or badly lamed leg, for the Bad Taste gambit in Counter Funny Story play (see text).

joke, will then suddenly feel that what he has said is in bad taste. Press home
your advantage. If he is a stranger, and has told a story about a man with
one leg, it is no bad thing to pretend that one of your own legs is false, or at
any rate that you have a severe limp. This will certainly silence Opponent for
the rest of the evening.

(*c*) 'Spenserian Stunser' – this is the facetious name for Quotationship.
The nickname probably arose because the quotation of two or three lines
of a stanza from Spenser's 'Faery Queen' is probably as good an all-round
silencer as anything.[1]

(*d*) Languaging up. To 'language up' an opponent is, according to
Symes' *Dictionary of Lifemanship and Gameswords*, 'to confuse, irritate
and depress by the use of foreign words, fictitious or otherwise, either
singly or in groups'.

The standard and still the best method is the gradual. If the subject is the
relative methods of various orchestral conductors, for instance, say something early on about the '*tentade*' of Boult. Three minutes later contrast the
'*fuldenbiener*' of Kubelik, and the firm '*austag, austag*' of his beat 'which
Brahms would have delighted in'.

A general uneasiness should now be developing and the Lifeman may
well feel he has done enough. But for Advanced Languaging I recommend
the Macintosh Finisher, invented by H. Macintosh, the tea planter. During
one of the lengthening pauses, he will quote one of seventeen genuine
Ballades in Medieval French which he has learnt by heart. 'Of course,
you know this,' he begins . . .

'Ah, vieille septance du mélange'

[1] It is best for beginners to stick to Spenser. Students who wish to experiment should beware of pitfalls. In general, the older and more classic the
quotations, the more depressing the effect; but they should not be too well
known, or they may be taken for a joke. It's no good just saying 'The play's
the thing,' for instance, whenever the conversation changes to the subject of a
play. And do not, if somebody mentions Italy and Florence, quote Browning:
'Florence lay out on the mountain side,' for this may merely raise an easy
laugh – the last thing you want to do.

No, let your quotation be apt and obviously classic. If someone shows signs
of capturing attention and admiration by travelmanship, for instance, he can
be undermined thus:

TRAVELLER: I'm just back from Florence, too. Where did you stay?

LAYGIRL: An excellent little hotel, recommended by Cook's. Quite cheap.
Near the station. Pensione Inglese. It was quite nice. Do you know it?

TRAVELLER: Well – I never stay *in* Florence . . . too noisy . . . and surprisingly suburban . . . but Cyril Waterford lets me use his rambling old
castle just beyond Fiesole. Very haunted, very beautiful, five ancient
retainers – and fun.

LIFEMAN: Ah—'Give me a castle, precipice encurled, in a gap of the
wind-grieved Appenines.'

Traveller, who has been scoring all along the line against the Laygirl, made
to feel awkward about her wretched English-speaking Pension, finds himself
entombed in the wave of silence which follows this.

and so on, with reverberating accents on the silent 'e'. After two of these, half his audience will be completely silent for fifteen minutes and the rest may actually have gone.

There is a rare counter to this which I have heard once brilliantly used with wonderful effect by B. Meynell, son of F. Meynell the Gamesman, when he was a mere lad of eighteen. This is to tell, *as if to brighten the atmosphere*, a funny story *in French*. If I had to choose an example of brilliance in Lifemanship it would, I think, be this. For a cover to any lack of knowledge of the language or the accent, he told it, or made as if to tell it, 'in a strong dialect'.

'Il a répondu "Favoori", in the Toulouse drawl.'

I have never been able to discover whether this was a genuine Toulouse accent or not, nor, indeed, whether B. Meynell can speak any genuine French at all.

(*e*) If the Lifeman is a late-comer and the conversation is already well-established, a different gambit-sequence altogether must, of course, be used. In order to *stop the flow* he must judge the *source of eloquence* and deflect the current into a *new channel* by *damming the stream*.[1]

If, for instance, someone is being really funny or witty and there is a really pleasant atmosphere of hearty and explosive laughter, then (*a*) join in the laughter at first. Next (*b*) gradually become silent. Finally (*c*) at some pause in the conversation be overheard whispering, 'Oh for some real talk.'

Alternatively, if there is genuinely good conversation and argument, listen silently with exaggerated solemnity and then whisper to your neighbours, 'I'm sorry but I've got a hopeless and idiotic desire to be a little bit silly.'

I strongly recommend this last phrase which indeed might be dignified as a Gambit, though it is usually regarded as a ploy of Lowbrowmanship, which we may discuss under the even more main heading of Writership and Critic Play.

But never forget the uses of Lowbrowmanship in conversation and the phrases 'Oh, I don't know' and 'I'm awfully sorry'. Thus:

LAYMAN: I don't advise the new musical. It's certainly a leg show but the harmonies are trite, the dialogue is unfunny and the *décor* is just a splurge.

[1] There is a *physical* method of making the too eloquent and successful speaker self-conscious and causing him, in the end, to break down. In brief the ploy is:
1. To watch not the man but his gestures – his moving hands.
2. To alter the position of some flower-pot, suggesting by your way of doing it (*a*) That some movement of his hand may be going to knock it over; (*b*) That these gestures are a queer, somewhat Latin business, a little out of place to our English way of thinking.

LOWBROWMAN: Oh, I don't know, I rather like a good bit of old-fashioned vulgarity. And I'm awfully sorry but I like leg shows.

If the Lowbrowman happens to be a Professor of Æsthetics, as he usually is, his remark is all the more irritating.[1]

Countering and cross-countering in the more serious conversations reach extraordinary depths among advanced Lifemen. The ensuing notes are condensed from my Brochure.

How to Make People Feel Awkward about Religion.

The man who lets it be known that he is religious is in a strong life position. There is one basic rule. It is: Go one better. Fenn went too far. This is his method – in his own words:

To take the most ordinary instance – the simple Sunday church-goer. 'Are you coming to church with us?' my host says. It is a little country church, and my host, Moulton, who has some claims to be a local squire, wants me to come, I know, because he is going to read the lesson. He reads it very well. He enjoys reading it. I heard him practising it to himself immediately after breakfast.

'Yes, why don't you come to church for once, you old sinner?' Mrs Moulton will say.

Do *not* mumble in reply to this: 'No, I'm afraid . . . I'm not awfully good at that sort of thing . . . my letters . . . catch post.'

In the contrary, deepen and intensify your voice, lay your hand on her shoulder and say, 'Elsa' (calling her by her Christian name perhaps for the first time):

'Elsa, when the painted glass is scattered from the windows, and the roof is opened to the sky, and the ordinary simple flowers grow in the crevices of pew and transept – then and not till then will your church, as I believe, be fit for our worship.'

Not only does this reply completely silence opponent; but it will be possible to go out and win ten shillings on the golf course, come back very slightly buzzed from Sunday pre-lunch drinks, and suggest, by your direct and untroubled look, before which their glance may actually shift, that by comparison with yourself your host and hostess, however innocently, have been only playing at religion.

That is Religious Basic. A harder character to tackle is the man of big personality with a grave, good-looking, rather biscuit-coloured

---

[1] Make your choice of the three principal ways of saying, 'I'm awfully sorry but I like leg shows,' with careful reference to the character and personality of your opponent.

face who digs himself in, so to speak, by being tremendously under-standing and humorous, and by letting it be known that he belongs to a Group, and you needn't talk to him about it unless you feel like it.

The basic counter is, of course, to ask him about it almost before you have got into the room. Get him to explain, and after a few sentences say:

'Yes. Indeed I agree. I expect we all of us do. The only trouble is, it doesn't go far enough. In other words, it's not a religion. It's an ethic. And a religion is what we want. Now many of us . . .' and then get going.

This works with the layman, but many an expert in Religionship is, in fact, an expert Lifeman of the first water.

If so he will seem to appreciate and indeed admire your answer and reply, 'Good. Good. Good. I'm not sure I don't rather agree.' Leaving you stuck with what we call the 'so what' diathesis.[1]

No. Deeds not words must be the rule in religious play. Take Jack Carraway. Effective enough in his way; but put him up against a real Lifeman like Brood or Offset or Odoreida and what happens?

The Carraway Group believes in cheerfulness and helpfulness.

Freehand drawing of Redhill Station from the North. The cross shows Platform 2, with Carraway's point of entrance.

Every morning Brood meets Carraway on the platform of Redhill station for the eight fifty. Every morning Brood says, 'Still sowing the seed, Carraway?' And the constant repetition of this joke, now for four hundred successive weekdays, is said, by Brood at any rate, to be imparting a one-sided effect to Carraway's smile.

Brutal methods against brutal men. Offset's plan was subtler. He used to catch Carraway's train at East Croydon, and whenever he happened to get into Carraway's carriage, Carraway would appal Offset by taking Offset's hand and helping him up the step, putting

[1] For 'diathesis' see O K-words (p. 94).

his bag on the rack for him, offering to 'swop papers' (which Offset was sometimes embarrassed to do owing to the nature of the paper he usually read), making room for him, and indeed, on two occasions, actually *giving up his seat*, telling Offset that he 'looked tired'.

But Offset soon developed an effective counter. Whenever Carraway showed signs of helping, quick as a knife he went one better. He kept sharpening pencils and giving them to Carraway, 'for the crossword', although in fact Carraway never did crosswords. He would be waiting at East Croydon with a large cup of absolutely boiling tea, an armful of magazines, and a piece of gingerbread, all for Carraway.

Arriving at London Bridge he would insist on helping him from the carriage, and on one occasion I saw Offset actually lift him out. It was on that occasion that we gave Offset the high place of 84 on our list of Leading Lifemen.

Odoreida's method, if you can call it a method, was, of course, quite different and, if I must say so, typical of Odoreida. He not only allowed Carraway to help him in

COUNTER RELIGIOUS
PLAY: Offset lifts down
Carraway.

and to lift his usual small brown paper parcel on to the rack. He actually sent him on errands for cigarettes or matches, got Carraway to give up his corner seat 'because of my train sickness' and usually borrowed five shillings because he had 'no change to tip the porter'.

Note on OK-Words

My use of the word 'diathesis' reminds me that this is now on the OK list for conversationmen. We hope to publish, monthly, a list of words which may be brought in at any point in the conversation and used with effect because no one quite understands what they mean, albeit these words have been in use for a sufficiently long time, at any rate by Highbrowmen, say ten years, for your audience to have seen them once or twice and already felt uneasy about them.[1] We are glad to suggest two words for November:

[1] I have often been asked whether there is an accredited counter for use against OK-words. Mrs Johnstone made a note of the following conversation

Mystique
Classique

between myself and J. Compton, the educationist (Lifeman 364). Compton used to do splendidly with the word 'empathy' when it was O K in the twenties, but we are none of us as young as we were. He was trying a fairly up-to-date O K-word which has been on our list since October 1938: 'Catalyst'.

COMPTON: I think Foxgrove acts as a useful catalyst to the eccentricities of his chairman.
SELF: Catalyst?
COMPTON: Yes.
SELF: Yes. I suppose 'catalyst' isn't *quite* right.
COMPTON (*surprised*): Not quite right?
SELF: Not quite what you mean. A catalyst is an agent of redistribution literally.
COMPTON: Oh, yes.
SELF: is a re-alignment of the molecules rather than an alteration of their potential . . .
COMPTON: In a sense . . .

Compton knows, and I know that he knows, that I am as ignorant of physics or chemistry as he is; yet nothing he can say will alter the general impression that in the feverish pursuit of the O K-word he has misfired with a metaphor, ployed by his own gambit.

2

LIFEMANSHIP PRIMORDIAL I

The first lesson learnt, what better than to put that lesson into practice with a will? You may already have increased your chances of being one up on the layman by fifty per cent. Where is this condition more necessary to achieve than the social gathering or week-end party? Yet, remember, that it is just on such occasions as this that an appearance of geniality is most important.

LET ME, to start with, transcribe here a few notes, I believe not unimportant, on the typical Week-endman – based, I should add, on that grand Lifeman with that fine old week-end name, G. Cogg-Willoughby.

What to record? I remember Cogg-Willoughby's first action, coming down to supper – a late cold meal, on the first night – the Friday night. The F. Meynells of Suffolk live (he is of course the Gamesman) in a charmingly appointed cottage,[1] but suffer, with one excep-

[1] This cottage of the Meynells is in fact a beautifully altered and luxurious Georgian house, but it is an *important general rule* always to refer to your friend's country establishment as a 'cottage'. Why? Because it is an extraordinarily difficult gambit to counter. Impossible to reply 'My *what?*' 'It's not really a cottage' is no better if not worse.

T. Driberg, noted Essex Lifeman, himself possesses a beautifully appointed and luxurious Georgian house, and, in the intervals of concentrating on his great work *M P-manship*, promised for 1953, he has done a good deal of work on Counter Cottaging, a summary of which he has sent us.

T. Driberg suggests that as answer to the generalized question 'Are you going down to your cottage this week-end?' the reply should be a firm 'Yes,' followed after a small pause by one of the following 'phrases of extended qualification'. These should either refer (*a*) to the house, or (*b*) to the grounds.

(*a*) The House. (i) 'We've had to close the south wing altogether, except of course to the half-crown trippers.' (ii) 'I'm afraid Palladio didn't know much about the English climate! There's nothing like a classical colonnade to make the north wind whistle.' (iii) 'We're just having the octagon room done up. I wish I could get the Gainsboroughs back.' (iv) 'The man from the National Gallery has just been down to look at the Angelica Kauffmann mantelpiece.' (v) '*Nothing* takes so much dusting as a dome.'

(*b*) The Grounds. (i) 'The park looks lovely from the belvedere these summer mornings.' (ii) 'We have to keep an extra bailiff just to fill in forms.' (iii) 'I'm hoping to get some advice from Kew on restoring the maze.'

tion, from an almost complete absence of staff. Immediately the meal was over, Cogg-Willoughby would take off his coat, roll up his sleeves, clear the table in a trice, and then, 'Let's get down to it,' he said, and would do all the washing-up, if not part of the drying-up as well, expertly and thoroughly, with a quick swish round even of one or two saucepans, and clean a cup, used at some previous meal with which he had no connection. No need to add that, having planted this good impression in the mind of his hostess, 'Cogg' for the rest of the weekend would lift not one finger in the kitchen or the garden, nor bring in so much as a single log of firewood from the shed.

Cogg-Willoughby and Anti-Game Play

Cogg was in his element, as we all remember, at week-end parties where there were plenty of games to be played and plenty of people to play them. Incapable of any kind of sport, it was here that Cogg established his mastery.

While the rest of the guests were feebly organizing bowls, ping-pong

Cogg-Willoughby at Ashton Broad Elm, graceful home of Lady Tilden, from a water-colour. The meaning of the lettering is uncertain. Note pediment, said to be the twelfth highest in East Anglia.

TCU—D

or cricket, Cogg would look on encouragingly. Soon he would produce an enormous pair of field-glasses.

'Well, I'm going off for *my* game. See you all later.' Sometimes it was bird-watching, sometimes butterflies, occasionally wild flowers. Cogg, of course, was almost entirely ignorant of all these pursuits, but it was 99 to 1 the rest of the guests would know still less. Cogg would suddenly stand stock still. 'Listen,' he would say. Some feeble quack would be heard from the willow beyond the pond. 'That's an easy one to tell. The frog-pippit.' Then he would add, for a safety measure, 'as I believe they call it in these parts'.

By the Sunday most of the women guests would be following him round, standing stock still, in a trance, listening or looking at some bit of rubbish, while Cogg explained.

What I liked about Cogg was the cleanness and openness of his play. Only in one gambit did he seem to me to show a trace of unpleasantness, but I must say I was glad to see him employ it against that confirmed hostess-nobbler, P. de Sint. In his specious, dark-haired way, de Sint was a typical hostess's favourite.

De Sint's first action at a summer week-end was always to strip to the waist and sun-bathe. Unlike Cogg (who remains white and sluglike) and myself (who quickly turn beetroot), de Sint will develop a rich honey bronze straight away.

Cogg was at his best in this situation. I have never more admired the easy coolness with which he dealt with a crisis. Late on the Sunday afternoon, it might be, he would look de Sint up and down. He would speak thoughtfully.

COGG-WILLOUGHBY: By Jove, you brown easily.
DE SINT: Do I?
COGG-WILLOUGHBY: Yes. You're one of the lucky ones.
DE SINT: Oh, I don't know.
COGG-WILLOUGHBY: They always say that the Southern types brown more easily.
DE SINT: Well, I don't know, I'm not particularly . . .
COGG-WILLOUGHBY: Oh, I don't know . . . Mediterranean . . .

Cogg-Willoughby was able to speak this phrase with an intonation which suggested that de Sint was of Italian blood at least, with, quite probably, a touch of the tarbrush in his ancestry as well. On three or four occasions, after this attack, I have noticed that de Sint spent the rest of the week-end trying to cover up every exposed inch of his body.

I do hope the reader will understand that I have only scratched the

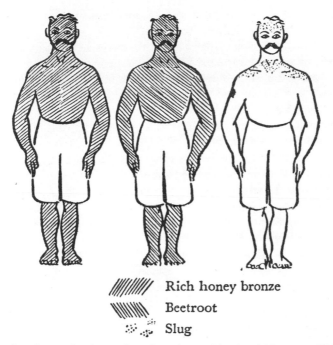

/////// Rich honey bronze

\\\\\\ Beetroot

∴ ⁖ Slug

Types of sunburn. Students of week-endmanship should learn to distinguish these three 'sunburn results' at a glance.

surface, in these notes, of week-endmanship; and that this account of Cogg-Willoughby, even, is far from complete.

The Odoreida Diagnosis

For basic week-end I should perhaps acknowledge, for once, the work of Odoreida.

Odoreida is usually incapable of pioneer work, but one must admire his occasional flashes, such as this, reported to me (Odoreida in play against Redruth's Decline Gambit).

G. F. C. Redruth was basically a poor week-end man. With his tweedy skin, podgy legs, and boringly healthy cheeks, he looked like a fine Game Birdsman. But the fact is, he was an appallingly bad shot, and it was necessary for him to keep this fact concealed. In the old days, at the Blessinghams' when the Saturday morning shoot was being planned, 'Count me out of this,' he would say.

'Why?' (Mrs Blessingham – then Lady Blessingham – asked.)

'Not my cup of tea. Stupid old conscience at work. Don't like birds, but feel I wasn't created to take pot-shots at them. Besides, I think the creatures are rather beautiful.'

Odoreida, who always loathed Redruth, couldn't make much headway by murmuring, 'I suppose you miss them on purpose,' and when, in the evening he said 'I see you don't mind *eating* the beautiful creatures,' he was again put out by Redruth's technique of vaguely quoting the Bible.

'Let he who casts the first stone . . .' said Redruth, and all this went down more than well with the Blessinghams, this being the time when they dropped their title[1] on conscientious grounds, and opened the grounds of their house and the annexe of the servants' quarters to the Basingstoke Liberal Summer School.

But later, with General and Constance Ould, Redruth realized that Conscienceship was out of the question. Here, in order to conceal his feebleness with guns, Redruth used to suggest that, healthy though he looked superficially, it was dangerous for him to stand about even for a minute. The slightest hint of moving air on the skin, he was able to convey, might cause the old T B centres to become active again. It was good by-play on his part to be always wearing a hat, even indoors, if there was the faintest draught.

Odoreida, unable to stand this, countered by a method which none of us could have used, though we can but admire it. He was able to suggest, and indeed actually say, out of Redruth's hearing, of course, that the complaint Redruth actually suffered from was ringworm.

Important Person Play

There is no doubt that basic week-endmanship should contain some reference to Important Person Play. It must appear that it is *you* who in mid-week life are the most important man. I always like to quote here the plucky ploying of poor Geoffrey Field. On the Friday evening he always seemed pretty done in. No question of having to

---

[1] As most of you know, our Glasgow Group has been working for some time on snob and counter-snobship. The results are too unco-ordinated to be included in this manual, but we have published from Yeovil a few promising first-fruits. Here is the list:

No. 8080 *Knights, and How to Reassure them about their Social Position.*
No. 71 *The Renunciation of Titles Bad Form: a Plea and a Counterblast.*
No. 38384 *Christian Names? Never!*
No. 31 *Famous People and When Not to Recognize Them.*
No. 491 *It's All Right Only Having an O B E, or How to Avoid Full Dress; Six Easy Devices for the Undecorated.*

entertain Field, or, indeed, of Field entertaining. He was there for a rest – had to be, got to be, if he was going to get through next week's work. He would lie back, legs out, eyes relaxed, arms hanging straight down on the sides of the chair – content.[1] 'Sh – they won't ring me up because (not a word) nobody knows where I am. Except Bales.'

No one knew who Bales was, and only I knew that he didn't exist, and that in fact Field had been out of a job for nine months. Yet there was a general tendency among the guests actually to wait on Field – tend him. At Liverpool Street on Monday morning Field used to say, 'Taxi? No thanks. The Ministry is sending or is alleged to be sending a car for me.'

When everybody had gone, Field would take a fourpenny tube to Ealing Broadway, and play squash on the public courts, or rather knock up by himself.

[1] It is extremely important to know if and when – and why – a Lifeman may put his feet up at the week-end party.

It suggests that you are important, it suggests that you are relaxed and at home in the house – a favoured guest. It suggests that you are tired. And it suggests another thing, too – that you are young.

Older men who wish to appear younger and have not been trained by us sometimes make the mistake of assuming a smart, energetic step, and generally bustling about. How wrong this is. To appear young, be slow and loose-limbed in your movements and put your feet up if possible over the *back* of the couch on which you are sitting. J. C. Jagger used to continue to do this even when well over fifty-eight and in agonies from neuritis.

It has been often asked: Did Jagger overdo this evolution? We believe, No: but overgambiting, at week-ends, can be a real danger.

CHILD PLAY, for instance (Beinggoodwithchildrenship), is, of course, of the utmost importance at many week-end parties, where your position as Top Man may depend on how you go down with your hostess's offspring. We were never quite satisfied with the work of E. J. Workman, the author, in this field. (For the Workman approach, see under Writership, p. 121.) The Workman gambit is well known enough. 'I talk to the child absolutely ordinarily,' he was constantly repeating, 'absolutely ordinarily, as if he was one of us. Absolutely ordinarily in the morning. Absolutely ordinarily at mealtimes,' said E.J.

It was before mealtimes, unfortunately, that Workman occasionally took one or two too many appetizers. I remember his turning to little Albert Groundhill then aged five, and saying: 'Don't you agree? This endless physical exercise is a fetish?' Of course, Albert made no reply. Nor did small Judy Homer, aged six and a half, when after four rum and oranges E.J. asked her whether she 'didn't think, in some parts of England, people in villages were a good deal more immoral than people in towns. Whoopee.' This last was an unsuitable question for a child of six, or at any rate unsuitably put. Gambits are for use, not for over-use.

4

LIFEMANSHIP PRIMORDIAL II
EXPERT MANAGEMENT

Do not hesitate, now that you have learnt some simple rules, to use them. The thrill of the young Lifeman, when he first puts his precepts into actual practice! How to be one up on the expert – worthy ploy. But this, too, is basic, since superior-knowledge counter-play, the doing down of the specialist, is primary whether life or Lifemanship is involved. Indeed, my Bude audiences will remember that I made this the first, not the third, of my lecture series.

Counter Expert

I ALWAYS BELIEVE that some kind of ABC of counter expert play is the best grounding for the young Lifeman. Without any special knowledge, without indeed any education whatever, it is possible not only to keep going in conversation, but, sometimes, to throw grave doubts on the value of expert knowledge in general.[1] There is no finer spectacle than the sight of a good Lifeman, so ignorant that he can scarcely spell the simplest word, making an expert look like a fool

---

[1] There is no need to stress the failure, here, of the sloppy expertship of the old school. The man who depended on mugging up the subjects of his week-end fellow guests never went very far. The classical example of this was, I always thought, G. Protheroe. On one occasion, for instance, hearing that Dr Lowes, the expert on Coleridge, was to be present during a week-end holiday, he spent the previous month (he was a very slow reader) trying to memorize the facts of a small, mass-produced life of S. T. Coleridge printed in the These Men Have Made Their Mark series.

By the Sunday evening, when the visit was coming to an end, he realized only too well that as yet *no reference to Coleridge had been made*. During a pause in the conversation he decided to speak.

PROTHEROE: I am right in saying, I believe, that there are two versions of the 'Ancient Mariner', and they are not the same.
LOWES: 1798 and 1800?
PROTHEROE: 1798 and 1800 . . .
LOWES: Yes – they are not the same.
PROTHEROE: Not the same.

And here the conversation ended. Easy to find fault with Protheroe. Not so easy to formulate the basic rules which turn failure into success.

in his own subject, or at any rate interrupting him in that stupefying *flow*, breaking the deadly *one upness* of the man who, say, has really been to Russia, has genuinely taken a course in psychiatry, has actually read history at Oxford, or has written a book on something.

A few simple rules, then, for a start.

The Canterbury Block. We always encourage youngsters to *practise as they learn.* Why not an easy exercise to warm up? The expert on international relations is talking. He is in full spate. How can he be jolted? (R. Bennett's variant).

EXPERT: There can be no relationship based on a mutual dependency of neutral markets. Otto Hüsch would not have allowed that. He was in Vienna at the time . . .

LIFEMAN (*As if explaining to the rest of the audience*): It was Hüsch who prevented the Archbishop from taking office in Sofia.

A suggestion only. But no matter how wild Lifeman's quiet insertion may be, it is enough to create a pause, even a tiny sensation.

Nor is the typical Block necessarily complex. The beauty of the best Canterbury is its deadly simplicity, in the hands of an expert. Six words will suffice.

EXPERT (*Who has just come back from a fortnight in Florence*): And I was glad to see with my own eyes that this Left-wing Catholicism is definitely on the increase in Tuscany.

THE CANTERBURY: Yes, but not in the South.[1]

'Yes, but not in the South,' with slight adjustments, will do for any argument about any place, if not about any person. It is an impossible comment to answer. And for maximum irritation remember, the tone of voice must be 'plonking'.

Here, then, we have two forms of what is known as the Canterbury Block.[2] For 'plonking', see next paragraph.

What is Plonking?

If you have nothing to say, or, rather, something extremely stupid and obvious, say it, but in a 'plonking' tone of voice – i.e. roundly, but hollowly and dogmatically. It is possible, for instance, to take up and

[1] I am required to state that World Copyright of this phrase is owned by its brilliant originator, Mr Pound (diagram on next page).

[2] This word has nothing to do with Block; nor has Canterbury with Canterbury. The phrase is good 'White Celtic' and almost certainly derives from Kan-tiubh bribl-loch (literally the 'war-winning man-of-words' in the 'porcelain-expert foray').

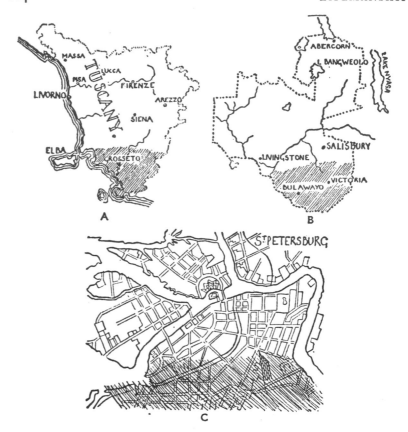

CANTERBURY BLOCK ('Not in the South' gambit). To give added effect to this phrase, some Lifemen carry a small packet of a dozen districts chosen at random with the southern area shaded. Tuscany (*a*), Rhodesia (*b*), and St Petersburg (*c*) are suitable.

repeat with slight variation, in this tone of voice, the last phrase of the speaker. Thus:

TYPOGRAPHY EXPERT: ... and roman lower-case letters of Scotch and Baskerville have two or three thou. more *breadth*, which gives a more generous tone, an easier and more spacious colour, to the full page—

YOURSELF: The letters 'have width'.

T.E.: Exactly, exactly, exactly – and then if—

YOURSELF: It is a widening.

T.E.: What? – Oh yes, yes.

This is the lightest of trips, yet, if properly managed, the tone of voice, will suggest that you can afford to say the obvious thing, because you have approached your conclusion the hard way, through a long apprenticeship of study.

'Plonking' of a kind can be made by the right use of quotation or pretended quotation. (See under Conversationship, p.88.) Here is the rough format:

MILITARY EXPERT (*Beginning to get into his stride, and talking now really well*): There is, of course, no precise common denominator between the type of mind which, in matters of military science, thinks tactically, and the man who is just an ordinary pugnacious devil with a bit of battlefield instinct about him.

YOURSELF (*Quietly plonking*): Yes, . . .[1] 'Where equal mind and contest equal go.'

This is correct quotation plonking (*a*) because it is not a genuine quotation and (*b*) because it is meaningless. The Military Expert must either pass it over, smile vaguely, say 'yes', or in the last resort, 'I don't quite get. . .' In any case, it *stops flow*, and suggests that whatever he is saying, you got there first.

I was never in Vladivostock

These early gambits mastered, the student can begin his study of more advanced expertship. Here is a slightly more complex ploy against the man, always dangerous, who has actually been there.

This expert can only be attacked on his own ground. And the basis of attack is to take if possible *one foreign place* where you have *actually been*. A convenient one for young British Draftees who have spent their army year in Germany is Munster Lager, transit and demobilization camp, well known to them, but entirely unknown to anybody over the age of twenty-one. Munster Lager is good, because it can be pronounced, by variation, as if it was a placename of any country. The conversation goes like this. Subject, say, Fishing Rights on Russia's Eastern Seaboard. The expert coming in to the attack:

TRAVEL EXPERT: Well, I don't know, but when I was in Vladivostock, I knew there was going to be trouble. Nyelinsky was on the warpath even then, and I was fortunate enough to meet his staff with the Korean Councillor.

AUDIENCE: Really?

TRAVEL EXPERT: The local papers were front-paging it day after day. I

[1] For the vocal equivalent of the printed dot, see my early pamphlet, *Whither BBCmanship?*

soon *sensed* a very nasty situation, even if it didn't blow up then. It wasn't a very *comfortable* visit, but I was glad I'd been, afterwards.

SELF: Yes.

TRAVEL EXPERT: You see—

SELF: I was going to say – I'm sorry.

TRAVEL EXPERT: I'm sorry?

SELF: I was only going to say that though I was never in Vladivostock, I *did* spend some months in Munster Lager, not a million miles away. (*The pronunciation can be slurred into something like Man Stalagin.*)

TRAVEL EXPERT: Oh, yes?

SELF: Of course, I was working as a stevedore among the dockers and porters . . . I didn't see much of the high-ups, I'm afraid. But, Lord, I feel I understood the *people* – the cutters and the quay-cleaners, the dossmen and the workers on the factory fringe. The wives waiting on the quayside, waiting with their children. I needn't say where my sympathies lay.

Often the Travel Expert is completely shut up by this kind of talk; but it is *not for beginners*. The clever Lifeman can continue in this vein indefinitely, without ever having to say, or not, that he has been in Asia, or that, in fact, he has not.

Go on Talking

A very small probe, which yet is not ineffective, has been used by Cogg-Willoughby, who has been fairly successful with a series of counterings from the psychiatrist's angle.

The expert holds the floor. His audience is submissive. Cogg waits, attentive. Sooner or later the expert will say, 'But I'm talking too much' – always a prelude to talking still more. Or, 'What do you think,' he may even say, simply.

EXPERT: But you say. What do you think?

COGG-WILLOUGHBY: No, go on.

EXPERT: But I have been going on!

COGG-WILLOUGHBY: I know. But it's good. It's right. I knew as soon as I came in you were happy. You – you look so natural . . .

EXPERT: Natural?

COGG-WILLOUGHBY: Yes, it's all right: don't take any notice of what I say. It's good.

EXPERT: Good?

COGG-WILLOUGHBY: It means that you're what we call happy. Go ahead. we're all listening to you.

Cogg was extraordinarily successful with this sequence for a time, and it led him to explore, curiously enough, the field of counter psychiatry. Cogg's Anti Psyke, as it came to be called, is not well known, and I have been asked to publish a note on it here. He had two principal tactics, and trained himself to make a spontaneous choice of either.

Tactic One, his favourite, was used against direct attack by an accredited psycho-analyst. This would be the shape of the dialogue – or at any rate these were the words I noted down when he was set against Krautz Ebenfeld. Imagine, if you can, the thick Slovene accent of the one and the quiet Cambridge tones of Cogg for contrast:

COGG: I expect you are always observing and analysing, Dr Ebenfeld.
EBENFELD: It is my job.
COGG: You will make me self-conscious.
EBENFELD: Why is that? It is what you do when you are not conscious that interests me. Do you know that you caress the back of your neck with your left hand when you speak to me?
COGG (*who has been doing this on purpose*): No. Really?
EBENFELD: Do you know why that is?
COGG: Well – you mean . . .
EBENFELD: You had a brother or young cousin who was a fine swimmer, yes?
COGG: Rather!
EBENFELD: And you perhaps were not much of a swimmer. Yes?
COGG (*very warmly*): How glad I am to hear you say that.
EBENFELD: Glad?
COGG: The doctrine of '95, supported by you of all people.
EBENFELD: Ninety-five what?
COGG: Back to the founder of all founders – and how rightly. Hardt's doctrine, as my own father taught it to me.
EBENFELD: Yes – Hardt . . .
COGG: How well did Freud say, in his queer English, 'He is my look up to. I stand to him – pupil.'

'That is very interesting,' says Ebenfeld. But he realized he was gambited. Later Cogg even reduced Sophie Harmon, the great lay psychiatrist, to silence.

SOPHIE: You have a limp?
COGG: No.
SOPHIE: You were dragging your feet as you crossed the room.
COGG (*smelling a rat*): Was I?
SOPHIE: You are not satisfied, fulfilled, today?
COGG: Ah.
SOPHIE: You have *two motives* pulling different ways.

COGG: My limp, you mean?

SOPHIE: Perhaps.

COGG (*lowering his voice yet speaking more distinctly*): Perhaps. Or just an old weakness of the paradeltoid?

SOPHIE: Perhaps.

Sophie keeps her head, but she is ployed, and Cogg knows it, knowing that she never took anatomy.

It is easy to bungle Counter Psychiatry, which is of course, a huge subject (see end of this chapter). But it is essential, we now believe, to work at these opening exercises before the more intricate problems are attempted – before dealing, that is to say, with the experts in painting and music, politics and philosophy.

To murmur 'exhibitionist' or 'Œdipus' or just to whisper the one word 'aunt' when any rival is in full flow is a fine ploy, equalling Lifemanship at its best.

NOTE. – For 'incest' read 'aunt' throughout.

THE LIFEMANSHIP PSYCHO-SYNTHESIS CLINIC

Lifemen have not been backward in the counter-attack: and those of us whose job it is to deal with this kind of thing possess, as some readers will know, a certain top floor room not a hundred miles from Wimpole Street where we are setting up our school – openly lay – of psycho-synthesis. LET US RESTORE YOUR INHIBITIONS is our phrase. SUBLIMATE WITH US. WE can put back the Hamlet into YOU.

Our workers in Wimpole Street make it perfectly clear that they are

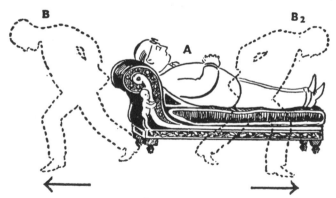

PSYCHO-SYNTHESIS IN WELBECK STREET (diagram) Note the couch, which can be easily adapted from the old psycho-analyst's couch or *tentade*. The 'psycho' himself (A) is, of course, the reclining figure. The patient is, or should be, striding from B to B2 and, of course, back.

not qualified physicians. That they are not recognized by the Medical Council. That they are unattached to any hospital or clinic. We do not prescribe. We do not even advise. All we want you to do is to talk, and talk guardedly. Never mention the first thing that comes into your head. It will seem strange at first to the old-fashioned patient to find the psycho-synthesist lying relaxed on the couch while he the patient will be encouraged to walk up and down feverishly. You are suffering from a suppressed and thwarted conscious. Give intellectual self-criticism free rein.

A charge of a few guineas is made for each visit. The first treatment is bi-weekly for six months. At the end of this period it is normal and natural to hate, and indeed loathe, your synthesist. This is a sign that the thing is working, but that the treatment should continue until the patient gets out of the Dislike Phase.

The natural antagonists of all Lifemen, or shall I call them 'friendly enemies' of the lifeplay, are the psycho-analysts. They have their own organization, their own literature, their own terminology. Lifemen have always recognized the value of their 'psycho-analytic look' for stopping conversation. Now Lifemen have a chance to hit back.

SUPPORT LIFEMANSHIP BY JOINING

A LIFEMANSHIP ORGANIZATION

(All fees and subscriptions are sent direct to Station Road, Yeovil)

THE LIFEMANSHIP PSYCHO-SYNTHESIS CLINIC

5

WI' DOWNCAS' HEID

SOME NOTES ON CONTEMPORARY WOOMANSHIP

We publish these Notes not without some pride, as they are the first fruits of our first Research Gala, as we call it. It is interesting that twelve times as many workers volunteered to send in reports on Woomanship as on any other subject. Looking round at a group of our lads, I think we could say that our features are essentially kind and wholesome-looking, even if we have not got the regular profiles of a haberdasher's advertisement. Still, be we who we may, I am sorry I have space here to include so few of our experiments, most of which, though not uniformly successful, show, I believe it will be agreed, spirit.

History

VOLUMES WILL BE written about the historical aspects of the huge subdepartment of Lifemanship, Woomanship. It was known, certainly, in early China. The Cretans were said to woo and 'enjoy patterns of woo behaviour' before becoming engaged to each other.

May I say here that the question whether or not woomanship should be taught in schools has been answered by me in the affirmative? It is rational, it is perfectly all right, it has great beauty, treated in the proper way; in fact, there is really nothing in it. At any rate, the go-ahead headmaster of the Pennine Grammar School smiled on the class in this subject which I held for his charges.

My task now to collect reports on some of the leading Woomen and Woo-women of today. I have a sheaf of them in my hand now for tabulation and collation. But wooing is, of course, a very human subject and many aspects of it are readily understandable to the general public.

WOO BASIC

'. . . for each approach, the method . . .'

Through the Gears with Gattling-Fenn

Each woman presents a different problem, or, alternatively, each woman presents the same problem. How often that has been said. To that sound old Wooman Gattling-Fenn, the problem, and the approach, was always the same, a fact or situation which may owe its being to Gattling-Fenn's undoubted limitations. He was getting bald in a curious way. Yet he was always falling in love with horrifyingly pretty girls of vacant minds.

To see Gattling-Fenn at work on one such is to see woo basic at its best. There is nothing new about the theory of Gattling's 'gradually-awakened interest' approach. But his practice of it has never been improved upon.

'The rule,' he was always telling us, 'is not so much to seem to be attracted against your will, as to give the impression that you can scarcely bring yourself to speak to her. And this in spite of the fact, you are at the same time able to indicate, that the face you are addressing happens by some racial fluke, some luck of the ethnological draw, of some genetical jackpot, to be as near the perfection of sexual beauty as mortal may be.'

Gattling-Fenn used often to talk in fairly long words. It was part of his method. But he also talked in short words, too; and in the opening stages he was monosyllabic.

Gattling, having succeeded by much pushing and side-stepping in planting himself next some mentally feeble girl, begins as follows:[1]

G.-F. (*Struggling against boredom*): I have, in fact, seen you before. Being important in some film shot. Denham, Stage II.

The girl will be unlikely to deny absolutely that she has ever been in a film studio, but will probably say:

GIRL: Oh – I don't think so.
G.-F.: Sorry, a bad professional blob of mine.
GIRL: Professional?
G.-F.: Yes, I'm sorry. There was one period of my life, I'm sorry to say, when it was my job to stare at Film Faces.

At this moment he suddenly wrenches his glasses out of his pocket, rams them on his nose, stares, and snatches them off again. (See Spectacles, management of.)

[1] The principle of Instantaneous Speech is important. No good, if you get into a railway carriage solely occupied by some wooworthy girl, waiting for half an hour and offering her a cigarette at about Reading, after premonitory mumbles and throat-clearing. Gattling always used to maintain that he would start speaking to the girl while still half in the corridor, saying, for instance (if she is reading *The Times*), 'Good heavens, I thought *The Times* had ceased publication,' naturally and easily, as he entered.

GIRL: Oh?

G.-F.: Selecting the perfect film profile – one of J. Arthur's more surprisingly imaginative ideas. Two hundred and fifty dead straight noses. Two hundred and fifty pairs of brilliant eyes, oh so large and liquid. I'm afraid you're rather the type.

GIRL: Were you really?

G.-F.: How do you mean?

GIRL: I mean, what did you have to do?

G.-F.: Me? Just be the final judge, and take the unfortunate creature to various functions. You don't act at all, do you? I have an office job at the moment, and I'm wondering whether even the theatre isn't better than that. I'm no good at being a ten till five man.

GIRL: Oh, *I* have to be at the office at nine.

First Gear

This, of course, is the moment to slip into Gear One. Gattling leans forward fractionally, and although he has in fact been staring at the girl all the evening he manages to give the impression that he is seeing her, now, for the first time.

G.-F.: What – you have a job?

GIRL: Oh yes.

G.-F.: I mean a real human job, doing things, working, like myself – with all the routine, and sometimes the thrill? How wise of you – to be part of the pattern. You mix with people. Know people.

GIRL: Oh, you see a lot of people. I don't think it'd interest you much.

Gears Two and Three should follow automatically.[1]

NOTE. – Gattling-Fenn's 'Period of Indifference' is not to be confused with the phase, or sub-phase, known as The Impersonal Love-letters of Allchick. This was the ploy, now in frequent use, of T. Allchick, who in the midst of the wildest and most tempestuous love affair would write letters to the girl beginning 'Dear Madeleine', continue for a few lines on the theme 'my cold is very much better', and end up 'Yours cordially'. I remember the original Madeleine well, and these letters certainly added fuel to the flames of her love for T. Allchick. Why it worked is a mystery. Allchick's American imitator, B. Benedict Hume, used to sign himself

[1] According to Gattling. But the truth is he was never very successful. He told me once that he only took up this particular approach because his Dog Gambit had failed so completely. In the old days he used to approach a girl with a dog, and establish affinity by showing his fondness for these pets. 'How's Wog-Wog,' he would say, speaking solely *to the animal*. But latterly, owing to the bizarre appearance of Gattling's hair, all dogs growled with real menace at the first sound of his voice.

'Yours spontaneously'. There are many who believe in the extremely ardent love-letter, twelve pages long: but there is certainly a case against them.

WOOMANSHIP SECONDARY

Being One Thing or the Other, or, alternatively, Being One Thing and Then the Other

Most of the experts agree here. The sound wooman is either fascinatingly rich or amusingly poor. It is bad gambiting to have a normal income.

Similarly, he must either be charmingly weak about women, feckless and extravagant; or he must be slow to move, stolid, and dependably waiting for the 'One Woman'.

Similarly, one must either be the experienced ladies' man, with correct Flower Play; or alternatively, one must be so gauche as to be the kind of man who has never given a bunch of flowers in his life, doesn't know where to buy them, and waits till the taxi has been chugging back to Hammersmith for twenty minutes before he breaks the silence by saying 'Can I kiss you?'

In the same way, the wooman must ask himself: Is he going to be vague so as to get the 'He's so vague, let me look after him without his knowing it' reaction. Or is he going to be quietly definite, precise and well-ordered, so as to make use of the 'I can depend on him' diathesis.[1]

---

[1] It is sometimes necessary to combine both of any two opposed approaches, or rapidly substitute one for another, if the first isn't working. Have you decided that the *dependable* line is not succeeding? Do you wish to seem uncared for and in need of a woman's touch? BILLINGTON'S WOO AIDS LTD supply special Esioff imitation inkstains, a file for fraying cuffs, a pair of 'Break-Phast' shoelaces and their useful 'Odsox' for the man who wants, in a hurry, to look carelessly dressed.* All profits are sent direct to Station Road, Yeovil. HELP LIFEMANSHIP.

* 'Odsox' brand of odd socks, for suggesting that wooman suffers from neglect in his home life. (Billington's Woo Aids Ltd.)

The Wilkes Method

On the physical side it is most important, finally, to decide whether you are (*a*) handsome, or (*b*) ugly. The ugly man, or the half-and-half who decides to be ugly, must learn to suggest, like Wilkes, that though the ugliest man in the country, yet, given half an hour's start of the handsomest man in Britain, he could out-woo him with any girl he liked. Of recent years, P. Wilkes has done well with this. He will get himself introduced to the girl, stare crossly at the floor, and then say suddenly:

WILKES: I'm sorry. I don't seem to have anything to say as usual.

GIRL: Oh, well, it's stupid to talk all the time, isn't it?

WILKES: I was trying to put myself in your place, while I was trying – forgive me – not to stare at your face. You see . . . you have this marvellous *lookability* – this ability, by your face alone, to thaw.

GIRL: Thaw?

WILKES: To melt – melt the *resistance* to making contact which is in all of us. Whereas, in my case, there is this barrier of my pretty fearsome countenance. I think—

GIRL (*looking at him*): But, I don't know—

WILKES: I know what you're going to say. You have got an essential delicious kindness—

GIRL: I think you've got rather a nice face.[1] Sort of.[2]

[1] Wilkes had, in fact, a rather well-shaped and expressive left cheek, with interesting lines and dents in it, deepened by repeated exercises, including the turning on and off of bath taps with his teeth, which he did for five minutes every morning. He would at this point in the above conversation affect an expression of humorous scepticism, lay a special smile (exercise 2) on the left side of his face only, at the same time moving his head underneath a top light, to give a deep-set effect to his eyes. (See opposite page.)

[2] B. Boak, in spite of his unfitting name, decided that it was more suitable to him to be not ugly but the reverse, handsome.

This made little difference to Boak's general manner, except that he would from time to time stand stock-still, saying to himself ten times over 'I am handsome, I am handsome', until he had convinced himself that some girl he was after had been struck by 'the immobility of his features'. The fact that for Boak this gambit was never known to work does nothing to disprove the general soundness of the approach.

It was rather amusing to see Boak at work on the same girl in opposition to Victor Weiss. Weiss preferred the approach from ugliness, and while Boak stood about like a statue saying to himself 'The remorseless precision of my profile', Weiss would pace huntedly up and down in the 'I am an outcast from the world of beauty' stage of his attack.

No progress was ever made, in fact, on either side, because the features of both were only remarkable for their complete ordinariness – indeed it was impossible to remember Weiss's face for two minutes consecutively.

The Staines Method

The necessity of having to be very much one thing or the other oppresses some novice or diffident woomen. They have to decide when making basic plans whether, say, to be a Leonardo (intellectual all-rounder), a Fry (games all-rounder) or just a plain attentive man-in-the-background who 'refuses to do anything unless he can do it perfectly'.

But remember that William Staines elaborated a method which by concentrating on *one part*, he was able to suggest *the whole*.

Staines's particular approach was to establish himself as the 'perfect ladies' man with exquisite manners and real consideration'. Yet anybody who knew anything about Staines when he was off gambit knew that he was slothful, dirty, bad mannered, and had never, off gambit or on, opened a door for a lady in his life. Yet by concentrating on one tiny department of chivalry he somehow captured the whole.

He had a rack of a dozen lighters, which he cleaned and put in order once a week. Before making for his girl, he would select one, fuel it, put in a new flint, taking care to choose a large and manly one for the tiny, frightened girl, or one, for instance, with cigarette case

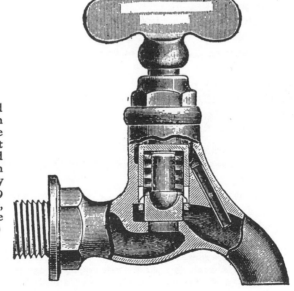

TAP recommended for graded mouth exercises. Its simple shape and wide, flat flanges are adapted for gripping with teeth. Supplied by R. & J. Hart, 69 Cumberland House, Penge. (See footnote [1] on opposite page.)

and pencil attached for the slightly popsy girl. At precisely the right moment in the cigarette manœuvre, fire would dart from his hand. He had trained himself to see a pretty girl feel for a cigarette across three platforms of Waterloo Station, as it were, and to be behind her, flame ready, before the cigarette was at her lips.

The beauty of the Staines method is that once his gentlemanliness with lighters was established, the girl would be so stunned with the perfection of this particular piece of good manners that she would never question his good manners in general, even if she found herself left with the two heaviest bags to carry, and was asked to stand over them while Staines himself went into the refreshment room for a cup of tea.

Boy-play

This sacred and ancient woo basic is too well-known and general to need more than a footnote or two in a modern work. The conception of boy-play arose as a reaction against knightly chivalry and romance an alleviation of the general boredom women were feeling for the knightly gambit, a rebellion first noted at the time of the Third Crusade.[1]

Remember that though the essence of the boymanship gambit is a boy-like gaucherie and enthusiastic barging in, it is not necessary to be an actual boy to practise it, as officially it is part of standard woomanship up to the age of fifty-six: and G. Hollins of Oakwell Park still makes his mark with it at the age of seventy-seven, with no sign of fading success to date (I am writing in September 1950).

Morton's Folly

General rules themselves often go agley in the application. There is the case, for instance, of D. Morton. His method was a variety of the Gattling-Fenn. He would imply to the girl that, frankly, a certain type of woman was inclined to fall for him, suggesting, of course, that a succession of piercingly beautiful girls were for ever hammering at his door.

No man worked harder at this ploy than Morton. If, by a kind of trick, he did succeed in persuading by the promise of some job or other a really thunderously beautiful girl to go out with him, he would

[1] See Trevelyan's *Social History of England*, p. 126, paragraph beginning: 'It was no wonder, after seven years of minstrelsy, foreign travels "in her service," and a red rose bunged into the casement window once a month, that some of the women were beginning to get most frightfully fed up.'

say, 'Look, do you mind if we go into the Six Hundred first, for a drink?' After that, 'I think we might pop across the road to the Avenue Bar. Billy Goatridge might be around.' Morton would then rush the tiring girl round six or seven bars and clubs in the hope of seeing at least one woman he wanted to impress, and demonstrate to them the extra-ordinary beauty of the women who, like the one he was with, he would explain afterwards, 'insisted on his keeping an old birthday date with him'.[1]

'Cigarette Stubs of Jarvis'

Students arc often agley when they are asked to describe the meaning of this phrase. The correct answer to 'What is meant by "the Cigarette Stubs of Jarvis"?' is as follows:

(1) It is a ploy in woomanship.

(2) It was devised, as a variant of Mortonism, by J. Jarvis of Parkstone.

(3) Its object is to impress by suggesting that the wooer enjoys acquaintanceship with several other smart and sophisticated girls.

(4) It needs for its performance (a) a car with (b) a pull-out ash-tray built into the front panel (the 'LUVMATCH' ash-tray, designed by Jarvis himself, is supplied). (All proceeds to Station Road, Yeovil.)

(5) Jarvis's procedure was as follows: He filled the ash-tray with cigarette stubs. He then bought half a dozen lipsticks in striking but contrasted reds (Fatal Apple, Eden End, Oblivion, Cinderella's Pumpkin, Lovers' Lip, etc.) and painted the ends of the stubs with these reds to give an impression not only of the smartness, but of the variety and frequency of his companionship with other girls.

NOTE. – Few, if any, women liked this gambit, but it impressed his fellow-woomen in the Cromer (Norfolk) area.

[1] D. Morton's younger brother, O., used his own variant of the above. He knew three well-known writers whom he had managed to induce to call him by his Christian name. He would bring a handsome girl in to meet these people. A girl like Ethel Baird, for instance, who had read three novels of Dickens and been to the Old Vic. He would introduce her to these literary friends one at a time or together, telling them 'she admires your work'.

Soon Ethel would be getting on with these personalities well enough, but Morton's object, to show this girl his familiarity with the great, was always defeated. His Christian name happened to be the rather curious one of Orlando, and though he really knew J. B. Priestley quite well, and called him 'Jack', Priestley, naturally, could never bring himself to say 'Hallo, Orlando', when other people were present.

The fact may now be admitted, since they have retired from Lifemanship, that the Mortons never had the necessary drive and gusto for this gambit or its derivatives. Both were handicapped by an almost complete absence of chin. A simpler and more radical approach should somehow have been devised for them.

The original ashtray used by Jarvis in his 'cigarette stub' gambit. The side is made transparent, semi-diagrammatically, to show the position of cigarette stubs normally hidden from view. Let the children get to work with crayons or water colours to suggest the contrasted lipstick tints.

Triangulation, or Third Person Play

To prove, if proof were necessary, that approaches must be varied, it is only necessary to consider for a moment the essential Woo Situation.

The very word 'woo' suggests an unwillingness on the part of the object: and that, carried one step further, means a previous attachment.[1] The wooman if he knows his business will, as soon as he knows the identity of this Second Man, leave the girl almost unattended, if necessary for days on end, and make a thorough examination of this person, observe, make discreet enquiries at his place of employment. And then, once he is thoroughly acquainted with the Second Man's character, he can woo with a clear mind and high heart. For he will know what to do. He must be sure that his character, habits, hobbies, tastes and mannerisms are the precise opposite of his rival's.

Supposing Second Man's main interest is geology. Now the wooman may himself be the greatest British authority on this very subject. He may have written the definitive work on the Flora of the Upper

---

[1] From time to time Woomen report painful examples of attachments which are fixed. This is itself the gambit of Darby and Joanmanship, and includes Still-ridiculously-in-love-with-each-othering. Strong gambit as it may be, it is opposed, essentially, to the spirit of Lifemanship.

Cretaceous. But he mustn't reveal it for a second. Keep geology dark, and particularly fossils.

In other words, the wooman must in all respects *be the opposite* of this Second Man, whose preserve, so far from being a hindrance, may in this way be actually turned to advantage.

'I'm not quite sure that I shall *ever* understand how the North Downs and the South Downs are part of a denuded anticline,' says this thoughtful girl, the first time she dines out with wooman. 'I don't even know exactly where the North Downs and South Downs are,' says wooman. She makes no reply, but her eyes grow a shade softer.

Wildworthy's Counter to the Cunningham Indifference

A pretty example of Third Person Play arose originally as a counter to the sound Indifference Play of Cunningham.

E. D. C. Wildworthy, of the Board of Trade, fell in love, from a distance, with Ivy Spring. Cunningham was Second Man, and had been doing well with Ivy through his amazing indifference to everything she did. Whether Ivy appeared in a new hat, an old hat, or an old dress brilliantly renovated and cut in half, Cunningham would never notice the difference, but would always greet her in precisely the same way, 'Well, here we are again.'

Ivy, who had been brought up to 'keep her man on the alert' so as not to let him be too sure of what she was like, doubled and redoubled her efforts to attract his curiosity – I remember on one occasion, for instance, she turned up for a date with Cunningham with a Yale undergraduate in American sporting clothes on each arm, she herself wearing the uniform of a lance bombardier. 'Well,' said Cunningham when he turned up, a little late, 'here we are again.'

This fascinated Ivy at first, of course, as it was bound to do. But actually from the woo point of view, I realized that Cunningham was dangerously liable to be third-personed; and when E. D. C. Wildworthy began to lay plans for Ivy, I watched with interest. He already knew Cunningham. His right procedure was obvious. The danger was, of course, that he might make it obvious to Ivy – as a procedure. He might notice and appreciate every time Ivy remembered to wind up her wrist-watch.

In the end he hit the mark by means of a simple trick. Arriving early one evening at Ivy's flat, while she was shouting at him through the door to make himself a drink, what in fact he did was to take the

Wildworthy's Counter to the Cunningham Indifference. Note that normal relative position of radio set and piano is reversed. The radio is usually *on top* of piano.

radio set, which usually rested on the piano, and reverse the positions, so that the piano rested on the radio set. When Ivy came in he said: 'What a good idea to change those round. It breaks the line of the room *much* better. You really *are* rather a clever girl.' Ivy, of course, couldn't remember having touched them, thought she must have done it in her sleep, but wasn't going to let on that it was luck not cunning. At the same time she said to herself at once, This is the man for me.[1]

[1] Is this the place to point out that there are many woomen who hold that the above gambits are too complicated if not unnecessary and that there are those who believe that it is possible to make love successfully without having read this chapter? A group of Derbyshire Lifemen have done well among woo gambiters by going about with simple straightforward expressions and happy looks suggesting that for them the hectic ploying of the average wooman is unnecessary. 'I am in love,' their silence seems to suggest, 'and the girl is in love with me.'

Odoreida has a counter of sorts to this counter. 'Well,' he will say to some poised-looking wooman in execution of this, 'I have found her' gambit – 'Well, how is your little caper with Julia going?'

This is quite effective.

6

WRITERSHIP

Authorship consists very largely of a succession of enormous gambits. Words-worth is obviously one big ploy. So are Macaulay, Prudence Wheeler, and a hundred others. The boundary between these and our own work in this field is often a very narrow one. However, the Yeovil Trustees have agreed, perhaps artificially, to demarcate the following as genuine ploys of writership.

BASIC WRITERSHIP

WE WILL take Workman as a sound example of the basic writerman.

The novels of E. J. Workman were of the third class in respect-able fiction. He never sold less than 15,000; usually 25,000.

He never trained with us, but it was on our advice that he changed his name. His real name, Cyril Delamere, was much too near the truth to be used in his particular author ploy.

He lived at a sufficiently inconvenient distance from the furthest flung station of Metroland to be regarded as a countryman, in a mod-ernized house one wall of which, after tremendous hacking and scraping, stood revealed as genuine Georgian.

He wore an open-necked flannel shirt in the morning; on country walks usually had a large sheepdog at his heels, though he obviously disliked dogs and knew nothing of sheep; made regular visits to the private bar of his local and played a great deal of darts very badly, got *Picture Post* to photograph him in the ancient bowling alley of the 'Feathers' over the caption 'E. J. ROLLS A PRETTY PUMPKIN WITH THE LANDLORD'. In order to look more like a country author he would screw a camp-stool into uncomfortable but sheltered little corners of his garden, in order to acquire sunburn while writing, well aware that he burnt very slowly and patchily. He would also talk extremely ordinarily to everyone; if possible most ordinarily to some wandering gypsy, noted village crook or village sex maniac – so ordinarily, in fact, that they scarcely knew what he was getting at. He would also talk equally ordinarily to the rector and the local titled woman. He was extremely ordinary about cricket and infected everybody in the team with an unusually ordinary way of hanging about the pavilion.

If anybody asked him some important literary question – the meaning of a word or the place of a preposition – he would say, 'Yes, what the hell is the correct thing there?' as ordinarily as anybody.

Occasionally, with him in the 'Feathers' on Saturday night, I would see him take in a week-end guest, with business-like face, neat town suit and glistening black hair. This unsuitable man would be made to drink pints of beer and play darts till long after closing time. 'Film executive,' I said to myself. For E. J. Workman would in fact so introduce these men with a 'got to be careful of him . . . I'm absolutely hopeless at the money side . . . he understands it all, anyway.'

But I felt sorry for this stranger because I knew that he was probably negotiating for the film rights of one of the Workman novels, and that if so one could be certain that going home after his exhausting time in this Bucks retreat he would find himself £1,200 down on the deal. For though E. J. Workman couldn't write, he was ferociously bright on the finance side, had been his own agent with brilliant success for twenty-five years, and had made the acquisition of almost criminally favourable film contracts his special hobby.

About the middle of August, when the carefully acquired red on Workman's forehead was beginning to turn a colour which might conceivably be called brown, Workman would start complaining of the endless drudge of the farmer's life. Workman had three 1,000-acre farms, each separately run by a first-class bailiff and a large staff, the whole ably co-ordinated by Workman when he met his bailiffs, whom he called by their Christian names, for half an hour on Saturday mornings, and talked to them on comfortably non-technical subjects in the most ordinary language in the world. Workman has never read a line of Milton, as he frequently reminds one. He reads the *Dairy-Farmer's Gazette* every week, from cover to cover.

To cach writer his own play and I am not suggesting that students should imitate Workman in every detail. The *Farmer's Weekly* is just as good to leave lying about as the *Gazette*. But basically, Workman was sound.

Newstatesmanship and Damned-good-journalist Play

Writermen must live in constant awareness of the opposition between these two great gambits. There is a distinct flavour of good writing about the former, fatal to the latter. The morning paper critic has only to remember that he may not be able to write but he is a damned-good-journalist. Being a damned-good-journalist means that you must either praise the film (or book, or play) to the heights, or blame to the depths. Whether praise or blame is chosen depends, if you are a damned-good-journalist, on your last week's article. You must never praise or blame two weeks running.

In Newstatesmanship, on the other hand, definite pros and cons are barred; and they are difficult, anyway, because pro-ing and con-ning is never the best way of going one better.

'Go One Better or You Go One Worse'

In Newstatesmaning the critic must always be on top of, or better than, the person criticized. Sometimes the critic will be of feeble and mean intelligence. The subject of his criticism may be a man of genius. Yet he must get on top. How? the layman asks.

By the old process – of going one better. Hope-Tipping of Buttermere had never really read a book since his schooldays, much less formed an original judgment. But he specialized in his own variations on the formula. He would skim some review dealing with the author involved, find out the quality for which this author was most famous, and then blame him for not having enough of it.

H.-T. first made a name for himself in 1930 by saying that 'the one thing that was lacking, of course, from D. H. Lawrence's novels, was the consciousness of sexual relationship, the male and female element in life'.

Get the Hope-Tipping angle. Talk about the almost open sadism of Charles Lamb, or about Lytton Strachey as a master of baroque. 'The deep superficiality of Catullus' is Hope-Tipping's, too. Never, by any shadow of a chance, was there a hint of a cliché in the judgments of Hope-Tipping.

Another way of going one better is to be surprised. Thus: 'I am surprised that so eminent a scholar as Dr Whitefeet' . . . 'We all owe a great debt to Dr Whitefeet' . . . 'Where should we be without Dr Whitefeet.' Then go for him.

Learn how to smile good-humouredly at Dr Whitefeet's analysis of the early love poems of Sebastian Cromer. Say, 'Surely it doesn't matter whether it was Paulette or Nina to whom Cromer was referring when he wrote "eyes twin pools of onyx". The important point for us who come after, surely, is that here is a man who lived, breathed, moved and had his being. Nay, who loved with warm human passion,

be she Paulette, Nina, or Proserpine herself.' This is the 'for God's
sake' branch of the 'After all' section of writership.

Dr Whitefeet may be rather slow, but he will have a definite feeling
that he is being got at, in some way.

Observe how, in Newstatesmanship, the critic is invariably a
tremendous specialist in the subject under review, and must at all
costs be more so than the author of the book discussed.

It doesn't matter if the subject is as remote as the study of Greek
in Lower California, the reviewer must be there before. An easy
method is to say, 'I am surprised that Mr Sprott does not give more
credit, in the main body of his text, to that fine teacher and impeccable
scholar Dr Kalamesa of Joinstown.' This is considered quite fair,
even if you have never seen the name Kalamesa before, which, of
course, you never will have, except in some footnote or appendix to
Sprott's book.[1]

Remember, too, that it is utterly un-Newstatesmanlike to suggest
that there is any branch of French literature with which you are not
perfectly familiar. K. Digg was rightly banned from Newstatesmanship for stating in a middle page article that he had 'never read a word
of Rimbaud'.

[1] J. Betjeman, in a series of conversations with me, has reminded me that in
Reviewer's Basic, which he has studied for so many years, any attack on the
author under review is essentially friendly. J. Betjeman has kindly turned
aside from his second volume on *Periodship* to summarize for us his findings.
They are as follows:

Friendly attacks should begin with faint praise, but be careful not to use
adjectives or phrases of which the publisher can make use in advertise-
ments. Safe faint praise adjectives are *catholic* – i.e. too wide in treatment to
be anything but superficial; *well-produced* – i.e. badly written. Alternatively
– 'The illustrations, of course, are excellent.' *Painstaking* – i.e. dull.

Useful words for friendly attacks are *awareness, interesting, tasteful,
observant.*

Effective methods of attack are:

(i) To quote from a book no one else has read but you.

(ii) To imply that you are in some college or institution where the subject under review is daily discussed, so, of course, you know better but
think the author quite good for one who has not had your opportunities of
acquiring more knowledge.

(iii) To begin 'Serious students will perhaps be puzzled . . .'

(iv) To say 'In case there should be a Second Edition . . .' Then note
as many trivial misprints as you can find.

It may well be that the author you are reviewing is someone who may be
useful to you in the future. In that event write one signed and favourable
review, and attack the book anonymously in another review in *The Times
Literary Supplement* or the *Listener*. These papers specialize in unsigned
friendly attacks and so do most antiquarian journals.

The absolute OK-ness of French literature, particularly modern French, and indeed of France generally, cannot be too much emphasized. K. Digg made a fool of himself, but everyone must respect the way Digg fought his way back for seven years, publishing in small provincial papers prefaces to catalogues of the exhibitions, in Dundee, of water-colours by children of operatives in jute manufacturing, etc. He would refer to France, somehow, every 250th word and end up with something boldly nostalgic. 'It is at this month of the year,' he would say, in his gramophone notes for the *Cumberland Farmer*, 'that one is dreaming once again of the brilliant colours of the *Cotelons*, whisking and flirting their way between the rotting stanchions of the bridge at Perpignan, while the cool wind, the Dordogne wind, lifts miraculously from the lake, and the garden, and its unkept shrubberies, still tangled with corpiscula as it was when Baudelaire's Remus swam in it.' The part about 'swam in it' may sound weak, but everybody realized that Digg was making a fight of it, and now, of course, all is forgiven and forgotten and Digg is back in Newstatesmanship we hope for good.

Daily Mirrorship

It should not be, but alas is, necessary to remind critics that for Newstatesmanship it is essential to mix in with the knowledge of French an unaffected love of tremendously ordinary and homely things like Danny Kaye, mild and bitter, the *Daily Mirror*, the Bertram Mills circus and Rita Hayworth. This will show that, like all really great authors, you write for, live among, and primarily appeal to, the ordinary common people.

NOTES

Dedicationship. A. C. Y. Davis invented a means of wording his dedications, so that criticism of his book was practically impossible, e.g. 'To PHYLLIS, in the hope that one day God's glorious gift of sight may be restored to her.' Critics and reviewers naturally felt it would be bad taste to be rude about Davis's book (*Spring on the Arun*) with such a dedication. Only I knew that Phyllis was, in fact, Davis's great-grandmother, extremely short-sighted, it is true. And not surprising, at the age of 96.

I'm Afraidmanship. 'I'm afraid' is a splendid life phrase and admirable for showing that you are a nice man and that the reader is a nice man and that your book is a nice book.

I'm afraid I don't like politics . . . mysticism . . .

Rilking

Just as there are O K-words in conversationship, so there are O K-*people to mention* in Newstatesmanship. Easily the most O K for 1945–50 are Rilke and Kafka.[1] It is believed that they will still be absolutely O K for another five years, in fact it is doubtful if there have been any more O K-names in recent times. This gambit is called 'Rilking'.[2]

A NOTE ON RECOMMENDED LIMELIGHT PLAY

Lifemen must always remember that whatever the facts, indeed, whatever the facts the more so, they must always be one degree busier than anyone else.

Our model for this must, of course, be Gattling-Fcnn, Number One Limelight for ever in our hearts.

I first noticed Gattling's methods the first time I met him. One had the impression, even then, that he was a pretty famous man, yet he called me by my Christian name at once. In fact I heard his voice saying, 'Hello, Stephen', before I got into the room. He asked me how I was, and I said as a matter of fact I had just been in bed with a cold.

He said: 'How lucky you are to be able to go to bed with a cold.'

Another thing I noticed about Gattling, that wherever he was, whether he was sitting on the steps of the Members' Enclosure at Cheltenham, or pausing for a sandwich lunch half-way up the Cairngorms, he would always, at one point, pull out a roll of galley proofs and start correcting them.

Though obviously always extremely busy, he was obviously always most frightfully calm.[3]

---

[1] In 1937 Lorca was O K, too.

[2] *Anti-Rilking.* There are types of authors who are not O K names whom it is O K to pitch into. It is all right to pitch into:

Any author who has written a book about dogs.

Any author who has written a book on natural history, illustrated with woodcuts.

Any author who has written a life of Napoleon, Byron, or Dr Johnson, without footnotes or bibliography.

Any author of a life of anybody not yet dead.

Any author of a book on Sussex.

Any author of a a book of unrhymed and irregular verse in the style of 1923.

Any author of a book of thoughtful open-air poems in the style of 1916.

[3] Needless to say, Gattling had been in films, and, in fact, there was a general impression that he had made a tremendous name for himself as a director, when, brilliantly, I am told, he was not calm at all, but feverish,

This calmness of Gattling was emphasized by his habit of arriving two minutes early for an appointment, dictating answers to his letters as he read them through, and showing special knowledge of telephone management.

Telephone Management

He would never, under any circumstances, speak to any man until his secretary had got not only his secretary but the actual man himself speaking on the phone. It was, in fact, rather amusing to see him ring up Tipping, who was equally keen on the same procedure. They devised a means by which, after a count of five, they both started talking simultaneously.

But his general gestures with the telephone, when without his secretary, were always worth watching. He would never express irritation when the bell rang; he would rise slowly, talking all the time, pick up the telephone and continue talking with the mouthpiece buried in some portion of his body, then remove his hand and without a pause and in the same tone of voice say mildly, 'Gattling-Fenn here.'

---

enhancing this effect by crunching up a benzedrine tablet every five minutes. These tables were, in fact, dummies, being made of sugar and water in solidified form.

False benzedrine tablet, magnified 7½ times (Lifemanship Accessories). A genuine benzedrine tablet (below) is drawn to same scale for comparison.

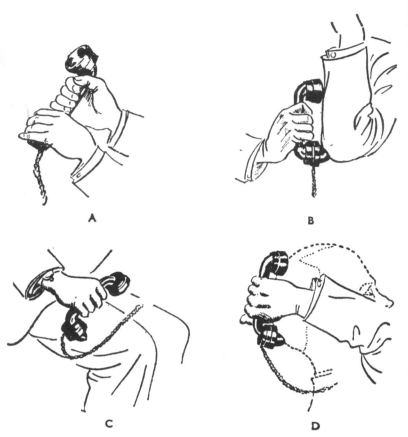

MOUTHPIECE BLOCKING for Important Person Play. While caller is talking, take little notice but continue your conversation with friends in the room, covering mouthpiece 'with the natural ease of long custom' (Pettigrew). *Not* (*a*) by placing hand on mouthpiece but by placing mouthpiece either against elbow (*b*), thigh (rectus femoris) (*c*), or back of head (*d*).

The Modesty of Gattling-Fenn

The main point about Gattling's Limelight Play was, of course, its essential modesty. He was one of the most ignorant and ill-educated men I have ever met, and it was therefore always a particular pleasure to hear him say, to a perfectly ordinary question, 'I don't know', slowly, kindly and distinctly. He was able to indicate, by his tone of voice, that although he knew practically everything about practically everything, and almost everything about this really, yet the mere fact

LIMELIGHT PLAY : HOW TO BE PHOTOGRAPHED IN PUBLIC. A. *Right*. B. *Wrong*.
Note: These sketches were drawn from life by Colonel Wilson, who made a
special tour of fashionable restaurants, etc. Genuine press photographers
were present and we note that the male figure in sketch A was in the habit
of paying £50 for the publication of these and similar photographs of himself
and partner.

TCU—E

that he knew such a tremendous lot about it made him realize, as we couldn't possibly, that the question was so inextricably two-sided that only a smart-Alec would ever dream of trying to pass judgment either way.

Another characteristic of Fenn, was his absolutely unspeakable kindness to underlings, on those rare occasions when for five or six weeks he did manage to hold down some kind of directorship. He would enter into discussions with his inferiors exactly as if he was one of them. His favourite phrase, was 'I am going to stick my neck out, but—' (to show, as it were, how unsycophantic he was to himself).

But Fenn certainly deserved the success he achieved by his really splendid management of public appearances, speeches after dinner, etc.

He knew exactly the expression to put on when being photographed. Having previously bribed the photographer to take his photograph, he would, of course, when the photographer approached him, demur. He would certainly not look pleased, but a little down and a little pained. If in a restaurant, he would see that there were no glasses on his table, except one obviously containing water. He would even bewilder neighbours at the next table by suddenly putting six of his used glasses and a bottle of brandy on their table.

If he was being photographed in a group, he would try and make out, by an encouraging glance, that it was somebody else who ought to be in the foreground, and he would lean forward to speak to the least important person present.

At a public dinner, he would be a tremendously good listener to the least important person near him, taking no notice whatever of the chairman. If Gattling's name was mentioned in a speech and there was applause, he would drag to his feet some confused stranger who had nothing to do with it.

'We all know to whom we owe the "Fenn Wing" as it has been called,' the chairman would say. And once it had been clearly established that the applause was directed at Fenn, who had fiddled the cement rights in the transaction, he pulled to his feet, I remember, a harmless Old Marlburian who happened, through confusing the Pinafore Room at the Savoy with the Princess Ida, to be attending the wrong dinner.

7

LIFEMANSHIP RESEARCH

*Lifemanship is in its early stages still: but our young
workers have not been idle.*

Music

THE GENERAL aim in music is to make other people feel outside it – or
outsiders, compared to yourself. Don't look too solemn when music is
played; on the contrary, be rather jolly about your musical appreciation. Say, 'Yes, it's a grand tune, isn't it?' and bawl it out in a *cracked,
unmusical* voice. Say, 'Ludwig suggests that this theme represents the
galloping hooves of the Four Horsemen of the Apocalypse. But to me
it's just a grand tune.'

Suggestions for conductorship continue to pour in. W. Goehr,
coming North to preside over the Pennine Northern Orchestra, who
for twelve years had taken their lead from the first violin and paid no
attention to the baton of any visiting conductor, got the better of these
men, many of whom came from Bradford, by a piece of what I can
only call brilliant conductorship.

It was a new work by Mahler. The night before the rehearsal, he
altered a B flat to a B natural in a fortissimo passage of the score of the
7th double bass. When the passage was played in rehearsal, he stopped
instantly. 'Someone is playing B natural instead of B flat,' he said. In
the long, brawling argument which ensued, Goehr, of course, came
out on top, and the Pennine Northern, although they did not change
their fixed expressions, did express, or so it seemed to me at the time,
some sort of silent approval.

Talking over a concert afterwards, with someone who has been
there in another part of the hall, it is not a bad thing to say, in a tone
of faint interest: 'What, you stayed for the Debussy?'

Actorship.

R. Simpson (the originator of Simpson's Statue (see
Gamesmanship, p. 52)) is, of course, also an actor. Not only that, he is
the genial secretary and leading light of the Actorship Society, busy

now collecting ploys and amusing gambits. His own 'Simpson Specials' as he calls them can be briefly described:

(1) If a young actor who shows signs of becoming a rival is slightly 'pressing' in rehearsal, tell him afterwards that 'he's never played the scene better'. The chances are that, next time, he will over-act badly, and even lose his touch with the part for good.

(2) The *V-shaped smile*, for fellow-actors who are doing rather well. Stand in the wings and be seen by them clapping soundlessly, as if to encourage.

(3) If an actor has, to your disappointment, been given a part larger than your own, and one which you secretly coveted, take an opportunity of saying to him, quietly and sympathetically, at the beginning of the *second* week of rehearsal: 'My God, you've got a pill!'

Work in Progress (with names of directing Lifemen)

FIELD GLASSES PROCEDURE. When to have field-glasses which are so big that they are actually too heavy to hold; and when to have them so small and inconspicuous that they do not, in fact, magnify at all. (A 'Friend of Lifemanship,' Luton.)

ROYALTYSHIP. The playing of, or threat to play, still ball games especially golf, in a crown. (A. King.[1])

FOREIGN TRAVEL PLAY. (We'll Go Roamin' Branch.) Having booked up hotels all along your route three months in advance, say, 'We're just going to bung the car over the Channel and let it follow its own nose.' (G. Barry.)

CARSHIP. How to deliver over the map to your passenger to read, saying you'll 'leave the route to her', and then not leave the route to her but on the contrary, question every turning so that in the end she confuses North with South, and third-class roads with the signs for windmills. (G. Tsu, Bulawayo.)

GENIUSSHIP. Our Bermondsey group is working on this large and complex ploy. This includes limpmanship, being the son of a tinker, importance of mother, unimportance of father, being different from other boys and wandering off alone in fields with a book, being like other boys only more so, leaving weaker work till later, showing kindliness, goodwill and understanding of others, being absolutely impossible.

DANCINGSHIP. If everyone else is dancing violently, separating from their partners, twirling round on separate axes, etc., how to

[1] Pseudonym of well-known King.

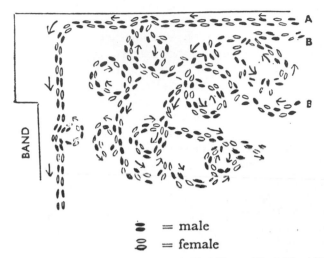

= male

= female

DANCINGSHIP (see opposite). (i) Counter Bad Form Play. Note Lifeman's Path of Disassociation on the perimeter.

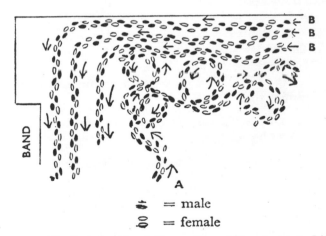

= male

= female

DANCINGSHIP. (ii) Counter Good Form Play. 'A' represents Lifeman's movements throughout.

move slowly and statuesquely, and indicate reproof and superiority by such movement.

How, alternatively, if the dancing is fairly prim, to suggest that this good form is bad form, or at any rate faintly Park Crescent, by being the only pair in the room to dance bebop.

HOUSE WARMINGSHIP. How to comment on a friend's new house. How to say you like it . . . that you think they've got round the awkwardnesses admirably . . . that, of course, they had to have a window there you supposed . . . and would have to make another one there . . . that it's from next door, of course, that you get the really wonderful view . . . that it's much better to have the original coverings if you can't get new ones made . . . that aren't they wise to leave the walls in their original colour – God knows you have to stand over them nowadays to get the colour you really want.

PERIODSHIP. How to specialize in periods which have not yet been specialized. Note on the Coca-Cola period. How to be writing a book on the revival of the Gothic Revival. Lifemanship's *Twopenny List of Unbooked Dates*, for period hunters.

UNDERGRADUATESHIP. Our older Universities are rightly conservative in their introduction of new subjects to their list of studies. There is, as yet, no School of Gameslifemanship. But at Oxford, if not Cambridge, a Research Fellowship is under discussion, and accredited Students already exist. Their researches, in process of co-ordination at Yeovil, rightly seem to concentrate on the essential Undergraduate Situation – the Student-Don syndrome, exemplified in its greatest purity in the weekly visit when Undergraduate reads to Tutor his essay on the theme set the week before.

P. Lewis, expert in Oxford Undergraduateship, has set it down as basic to this ploy that

where the Layman would concentrate on his subject, the Gamesman[1] *concentrates on his tutor.*

Clothesmanship can be used as a distraction in mid-tutorial.

That accomplished Old Hand, G. Cartwright, reduced a shy, shabby Arts don to near-speechlessness for a term by consistently turning up in breeches, boots and spurs, and disappearing at intervals during the interview with the remark, 'Mind if I slip out and see if my horse is all right? You know how restless they get after a hard day.'

[1] For 'Gamesman' now (September) read 'Lifeman' throughout.

There may be good pre-game work to be done the day before. Thus:

GAMESMAN: Oh, excuse me. I just wanted to check a point with you. Was this week's subject, 'The League Machinery AND the Settlement of Disputes' or 'The League Machinery IN the Settlement of Disputes?'

DON: I'm not quite sure. I think it was 'and', but . . .

GAMESMAN: Ah yes, 'And'. Good. Fortunately all my reading has been on that supposition.

It used to be said of that illustrious poineer, E. von Th., that he had so perfected the tone of annihilating contempt with which he used to read out the titles he had been given to write about (he was reading History) that he was ultimately asked to *choose the subjects himself*.

A. Thornton writes brilliantly[1] of Donmanship, suggesting Counters.

Donmanship he defines as the 'art of Criticizing without Actually Listening'.

The experienced Donsman has a store of telling match-points. He challenges all comers by letting it be known that he has a Special Subject, the emphasis falling on the adjective. It may be Turkish Personnel at the Battle of Lepanto, or, Some Unformulated Ideas current in the Eighteenth Century. Timid Donsmen sometimes overstep the mark and confine themselves too rigidly to marginal topics, e.g. Assyrian Woodwind Instruments. But it is the sign of the skilled and formidable Donsman to pick a topic on which there are not only No Books, but No Formed View At All (e.g. the Fourth French Republic), thus scoring an immense lead, or reputation.

In one of his passages A. Thornton ends on a note of what I can only call nostalgic rhetoric which moved me as I hope it will move you. I propose to quote it in full. And let me say now that when the lead passes into younger hands, I shall be the first to step back.

If the Gamesman feels at a disadvantage, playing as he does all matches away, he can inveigle Donsman on to his home ground, and employ Hostmanship on him. He may ask Donsman's opinion on a South African sherry. He may surround him with young Gamesmen and Gamesgirls all talking about 'The Third Man', which either Donsman has not seen, or, if he has, thought it merely a thriller. If young, he can leave feeling old; if old, doubtful. Gamesgirls are a convenience here. Rules of play are of course more sharply defined in this more enclosed space than elsewhere,

---

[1] The full text of all these passages is to be found in the Research Sections of February 1950 numbers of the *Isis*.

but a well-matched pair will welcome the more exacting demands of the Great Game.

There are, indeed, no limits to the ramifications and interpretations of this constant struggle. Let Donsmen always delight to baffle Gamesmen, Gamesmen ever seek new means of outwitting Donsmen. Character is tempered, and the world gains.

K.C.–manship (A. Hawke's gambit)

A. Hawke's work on *K.C.–manship* is still unpublished but he has allowed me to include here this example of his work.

Hawke's gambit may be summarized as follows:

If he, Hawke, is opposed by Y, K.C. (someone else), and if, during the final stages of the case, Y, K.C., speaking of some prosecution ploy of Hawke's, says 'My learned friend has made a point which is of the utmost importance. It is indeed an issue which stands at the root of the British penal system. Legal history is being made in the court today. But . . .', then, at the word 'But', Hawke gets up, and walks, obtrusively and indifferently, out of the building.

8

GAMESMANSHIP RESEARCH

I

It is our purpose here to summarize some of the recent findings of the Gamesmanship Research Committee. Thousands of people, or certainly scores, have sent in their recommendations for new gamesploys and gambits. Our task is to sift, and to co-ordinate.

A SUMMARY OF RECENT WORK ON GOLFMANSHIP

ALWAYS REMEMBER that it is in golf that the skilful gamesman can bring his powers to bear most effectively. The constant companionship of golf, the cheery contact, means that *you are practically on top* of your opponent, at his elbow. The novice, therefore, will be particularly susceptible to your gambits.

Remember the basic rules. Remember the possibilities of defeat by tension. Recorded elsewhere is the 'Flurry', as it is called, in relation to lawn tennis. *It is an essential part of Winning Golf.* The atmosphere, of course, is worked up long before the game begins. Here is the golf variant of Flurry.

Your opponent is providing the car. You are a little late. You have forgotten something. Started at last, suggest that, 'Actually we ought to get rather a move on – otherwise we may miss our place.'

'What place?' says the opponent.

'Oh, well, it's not a bad thing to be on the first tee on time.' Though no time has been fixed, Opponent will soon be driving a little fast, a little tensely, and after you have provided one minor mis-direction he arrives at the clubhouse taut.

In the locker room one may call directions to an invisible steward or non-existent timekeeper. 'We ought to be off at 10.38.' 'Keep it going for us', and so forth.

OPPONENT: Who's that you're shouting to?
GAMESMAN: Oh, it's only the Committee man for starting times.

Your opponent will be rattled, and be mystified, too, if he comes out to find the course practically empty.

If for some reason it happens to be full, you can put into practice Crowded Coursemanship, and suggest, before every other shot Opponent plays, that 'We mustn't take too long – otherwise we shall have to signal that lunatic Masterman, behind us, to come through. Then we're sunk.'

Here are some notes on certain general gamesmanship plays, in their relation to golf.

Mixed Foursomes

In a mixed foursome it is important in the basic foursome play (i.e. winning the admiration of your opponent's female partner) that your own drive should be longer than that of the opposing man who will, of course, be playing off the same tee as yourself.

Should he possess definite superiority in length, you must either (a) be 'dead off my drive, for some reason' all day – a difficult position to maintain throughout eighteen holes; (b) 'I'm going to stick to my spoon off the tee', and drive with a Fortescue's Special Number 3 – an ordinary driver disguised to look like a spoon, and named 'spoon' in large letters on the surface of the head; (c) use the Frith-Morteroy counter.

The general play in mixed foursomes, however, differs widely from the Primary Gambits of a men's four. But beginners often feel the lack of a cut-and-dried guide.

In the all-male game, of course, when A and B are playing against C and D, the usual thing, if all is going well, is for A and B to be on delightfully good terms with each other, a model of easy friendship and understanding. Split Play is only brought into play by the A-B partnership if C-D look like becoming 2 up. A then makes great friends with C, and is quietly sympathetic when D, C's partner, makes the suspicion of an error, until C is not very unwillingly brought to believe that he is carrying the whole burden. His dislike for D begins to show plainly. D should soon begin to play really badly.

In the mixed game, all is different. *Woo the opposing girl* is the rule. To an experienced mixed-man like Du Carte, the match is a microcosm of the whole panorama of lovers' advances.

He will start by a series of tiny services, microscopic considerations. The wooden tee picked up, her club admired, the 'Is that chatter bothering you?' The whole thing done with suggestions, just

discernible, that her own partner is a little insensitive to these court-
linesses, and that if only *he* were her partner, what a match they'd
make of it.

Du Carte, meanwhile, would be annoying the opposing man, by
saying that 'Golf is only an excuse for getting out into the country.
The average male is shy of talking about his love for birds and flowers.
But isn't that . . . after all—'

Du Carte was so loathsome to his male friends at such moments that
they became over-anxious to win the match. Whereas the female
opponent, on the contrary, was beginning to feel that golf was not
perhaps so important as sympathetic understanding.

By the twelfth hole Du Carte was able to suggest, across the
distance of the putting green, that he was fast falling in love. And by
the crucial sixteenth, Female Opponent would have been made to feel
not only that Du Carte had offered a proposal of marriage, but that
she, shyly and regretfully, had refused him.

Du Carte invariably won these matches two and one. For he knew
the First Law of Mixed Gamesmanship: that *No woman can refuse
a man's offer of marriage and beat him in match play at the same time.*

Advanced Caddie Play

Remember the basic rule: *Make friends with your caddie and the
game will make friends with you.* How true this is. It is easy to arrange
that your guest opponent shall be deceived into under-tipping his
caddie at the end of the morning round, so that the news gets round,
among the club employees, that he is a no good, and the boys will
gang up against him.

I, myself, have made a special study of Caddie Play, and would like
to put forward this small suggestion for a technique of booking a
caddie for your guest.

There is usually one club caddie who is an obvious half-wit, with
mentally deficient stare and a complete ignorance of golf clubs and
golf play. *Do not choose this caddie for your opponent. Take him for
yourself.* There is such a caddie in my own Club. He is known as
Mouldy Phillips. It is obvious from a hundred yards that this poor
fellow is a congenital. While preparing for the first tee say:

SELF: I'm afraid my caddie isn't much to look at.
OPPONENT: Oh, well.
SELF: He's a bit – you know.
OPPONENT: Is he?

SELF: I was anxious you shouldn't get him.

OPPONENT: But—

SELF: It's all right, I know the course. (*Then, later, in a grave tone.*) It gives him such a joy to be asked.

OPPONENT: Why?

SELF: Oh – I don't think they'd ever have taken him on here if I hadn't been a bit tactful about it.

It is possible to suggest that in the case of Mouldy you have saved a soul from destitution. Impossible in such circumstances for your friend to refer to, much less complain of, Mouldy's tremor of the right arm, which swings like the pendulum of a grandfather clock, to the hiccoughs or the queer throat noise he will make in the presence of strangers – habits to which you are accustomed.

Meanwhile you have succeeded in your promise to get for Opponent the best caddie on the course. A man like Formby. 'He's just back from caddieing in the Northern Professional,' you say. So he is, and your friend soon knows it. During the first hole:

SELF: I suppose Formby knows this course better than anyone in the world.

FORMBY: Ought to, sir.

Your opponent will feel bound, now, to ask advice on every shot, every club. Formby is certain to give it to him, in any case. After he has done a decent drive and a clean iron shot, Formby will probably say: 'Playing here last week, Stranahan reached this point, with his brassie, *from the tee*. Yes, he can hit, that man.' Here one hopes that Mouldy Phillips will say something.

MOULDY: AA – ooo – rer – oh.

SELF: Jolly good, Mouldy. Yes, he's got us there, old boy.

Here Opponent should be not only distracted but mystified. Formby will redouble his advice, while in contrast Mouldy looks on with delighted admiration at everything I do.

Left-Hand-Right-Hand-Play

I believe it was O. Sitwell who devised this simple rule for play against left-handers. If (as so often happens) your opponent, though left-handed in games generally, yet plays golf with ordinary right-hand clubs, it is a good thing, during the first hole *after the fifth* which he plays badly, to say:

SELF: Do you mind if I say something?

L.H.: No. What?

SELF: Have you ever had the feeling that you are *playing against the grain?*

L.H.: No – how do you mean?

SELF: Well, you're really left-handed, aren't you?

L.H.: I certainly am – except for golf.

SELF: Have you ever been tempted to make the big change?

L.H.: How do you mean?

SELF: Play golf left-handed as well. Chuck those clubs away. Fling them into the bonfire. Damn the expense – and get a brand-new set of left-handed clubs.

L.H.: Yes, but—

SELF: *You know* that is your natural game. Be extravagant.

L.H.: It isn't the expense—

SELF: Money doesn't mean anything nowadays, anyhow.

L.H.: I mean—

SELF: Everybody's income's the same, really.

The fact that your opponent has been advised to play right-handedly by the best professional in the country will make him specially anxious to prove by his play that you are in the wrong. The usual results follow. If he is not only a left-hander but plays with left-handed clubs as well, the same conversation will do, substituting the word *right* for *left* where necessary.

Bemerondsay Trophy Play

C. Bemerondsay was an awkward, tricksy, inventive gamesman, full of devices, many of them too complicated for the older generation. I remember he tried to upset me once by 'letting it be known' that his name 'of course' was pronounced 'Boundsy', or some such nonsense. Players uncertain of their position were, it is believed, actually made to feel awkward by this small gambit, and I have heard G. Carter – always conscious that his own name was a wretchedly unsuitable one for a games player – apologize profusely for his 'stupid mispronunciation'.

On the other hand, Bemerondsay's Cup Trick is well worth following. I will briefly summarize it.

In play against a man like Julius Wickens, who goes in for suggesting he was once much better than he is, the dialogue runs as follows:

BEMERONDSAY: I have a feeling you know more about the game than you let on.

WICKENS: Oh, I don't know.

BEMERONDSAY: What *is* your golf history?
WICKENS: Well, just before the war I was winning things a bit.
BEMERONDSAY: I bet you were.
WICKENS: Spoons – and things.
BEMERONDSAY: Oh, you did, did you?
WICKENS: Then in 1931 I won a half share in the July tea-tray – rather nice.
BEMERONDSAY: Very nice, indeed.

After the match, Bemerondsay asked Wickens round for a drink after the game. 'I keep the stuff in my snuggery,' he says, and in they go.

'Somebody must have put the drink in the cupboard,' says Bemerondsay. 'Why?'

He opens the cupboard door and to his 'amazed surprise' out falls a small avalanche of golf cups, trophies, silver golf balls, engraved pewter mugs, symbolical groups in electroplate. 'Oh, hell,' says Bemerondsay, slowly.

WICKENS (really impressed): These all yours?
BEMERONDSAY: Yes. This is my tin.
WICKENS: When did you win all these?
BEMERONDSAY: I never know where to put it.

It is of no importance in the gambit, but it is believed by most gamesmen that these 'trophies' of Bemerondsay really are made of tin or silver-painted wood, or that at any rate they were bought by Bemerondsay as a job lot. It is doubtful whether he had ever entered for a Club competition, as he was a shocking match player.

Failure of Tile's Intimidation Play

Americans visiting this country for a championship have sometimes created a tremendous effect by letting it be known that, on the voyage over, in order to keep in practice, they drove new golf balls from the deck of the *Queen Mary* into the Atlantic.

I believe that W. Hagen brilliantly extended this gambit by driving balls from the roof of the Savoy Hotel.

When they came to our own seaside course, to play in the Beaverbrook International Tournament, two Americans created a tremendous effect by driving new balls into the sea before the start, to limber up.

E. Tile, pleased with this, determined to create a similar impression before his match against Miss Bertha Watson, in our June handicap.

He cleverly got hold of six old or nearly worthless balls, value not more than twopence each, painted them white, and teed them up twenty yards from the cliff edge to drive them into Winspit Bay. By bad luck, however, not one of his shots reached the edge of the cliff, much less the sea. So his stratagem was discovered.

G. Odoreida

G. Odoreida, I am glad to say, did not often play golf. By his sheer ruthlessness, of course, Odoreida could shock the most hardened gamesman. Woe to the man who asked him as a guest to his golf club.

He would start with some appalling and unexpected thrust. He

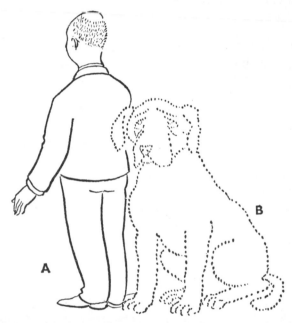

ONLY KNOWN PORTRAIT OF ODOREIDA (A), with ordinary Pyrenean short-haired mastiff drawn to same scale (B).

would arrive perhaps in a motor-propelled invalid chair. Why? Or his hair would be cropped so close to the head that he seemed almost bald.

Worse still, he would approach some average player of dignified and gentlemanly aspect and, for no reason, *ask for his autograph*. Again, why? One was on tenterhooks, always.

I remember one occasion on which his behaviour was suspiciously orthodox. The club was Sunningdale. 'Thank heaven,' I thought, 'such ancient dignity pervades these precints that even Odoreida is subdued.'

I introduced him to the secretary. It was a bold move, but it seemed to work. I was anxious when I saw, however, that on that particular afternoon the secretary was inspecting the course. As he came near us Odoreida was near the hole. Without any reason, he took an iron club from his bag and took a wild practice swing on the very edge, if not the actual surface, of the green. A huge piece of turf shot up. 'Odoreida!' I said, and put the turf back with an anxious care that was perfectly genuine.

Two holes later the secretary was edging near us again. Odoreida was about to putt. He took the peg from the hole and *plunged it into the green.* 'Odoreida!' I cried once more. Surely, this time, the secretary must have seen. But I remember very little of the rest of the afternoon's play. I know that Odoreida won by 7 and 5. I am glad to say that I refused to play the remaining holes.

In other words, gamesmanship can go too far. And the gamesman must never forget that his watchwords, frequently repeated to his friends, must be sportsmanship and consideration for others.

R. and A.-manship

I am delighted that the R. and A., after the usual delays of conservatism and the Old Guard at St Andrew's, have come into line with the spirit, if not with the individual rulings, of the findings of the Gamesmanship Council, 681 Station Road, Yeovil.

It is now the function of Station Road, we conceive, to interpret the new rules in the gamesmanlike spirit of their conception, adding a tip here, a suggestion there.

What a good idea it is, for instance, to place greater emphasis on Etiquette, if possible, than Rules. If Opponent retries his putt he has not broken a rule, and you may feel disposed to point this out to him. But it is against the etiquette of golf. This you will not point out to him, but your expression will become fixed, and distant, for a suitable period.

This will put off many novice gamesmen, but beware of the counter from the old hand. Odoreida, in play against Wickham, after deliberately re-trying short putts, all of which he had missed, on the first four greens, 'suddenly noticed' Wickham's fixed expression on the fifth tee.

ODOREIDA: You look a bit cheap. What's the matter? Hangover or something?

WICKHAM: Really!

Wickham's retort was weak, inevitably, and equally inevitably he lost the match.

New Rules, as a fact in themselves, are an aid to gamesmen. Your opponent will never be quite clear which rules have been altered, and an atmosphere of doubt can be lightly intensified. If putts are equidistant from the hole you can say, 'Who putts first? I believe, now, it must be decided by lot.' This rule has been unchanged, of course, for 250 years. Gamesman can then add, 'But have we got any lots?' You see? Opponent will get fidgety.

Deemcraft

Of classic gamesworthiness is the ruling that the 'player is the sole judge as to whether his ball is playable or unplayable'. Deemcraft Basic should follow this line. During some early hole which the gamesman by bad play has almost certainly lost already, let him deem *playable* a ball which is, say, half-way down a rabbit hole covered with brushwood. After four attempts to hack it out he picks up, but a good impression has been made, and not only will his opponent be scrupulously fair in his own interpretation but fail to see anything wrong till you have taken back your ball from a perfectly open lie in the heather in front of the tee at three holes in the second half of the match.

Trolleyship

No open reference is made in the new rules to the trolley caddie – that 'great new factor in golf gamesmanship', as Lord Morden has called it. But covert references to 'movable objects' are everywhere in the Rules, and it is obvious that trolleys have R. and A. approval.

We have developed trolleys for gamesmen on lines now familiar. Our 'KARRICLUB DUNSTABLE' has the squeaking wheel, our 'HAUNTED HEATH' two holes drilled in the ironwork, which, if there is the faintest breeze, make, according to its inventor, J. L. Hodson, sounds beautifully suggestive of a mouth organ.

Counter trolley play is divided into two parts. Part One is for the gamesman who, in play against opponent with trolley, always has his clubs carried by the best available caddie in the club. His concern is for the physical well-being of his opponent. 'Easy up the slope with

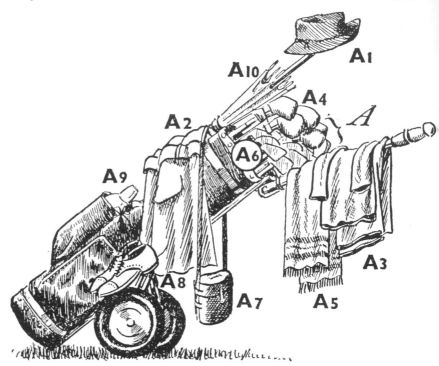

COUNTER TROLLEY PLAY. Optimal normal loading of mean maximum impedimenta. KEY: *A*, Owner's original load (7 clubs). A, Opponent's load, numbered in order of fixment: A1, hat. A2, raincoat. A3, pullover. A4, spare wooden clubs. A5, towel. A6, spare irons, A7, birdwatching binoculars. A8, light shoes. A9, thermos containing lukewarm tea. A10, ordinary umbrella.

that thing,' he will say. 'Let me give you a hand.' Or 'Don't your fingers get frightfully hot/cold/wet/sticky' (according to the weather).

I, however, strongly advocate carrying your own clubs in play against a trolleyman, particularly if the weather is hot. The ploy then is, first, to emphasize the fact that your superior youth and vitality make such things as the use of a trolley absurdly fiddling. Then act as follows. At near or about the seventh hole, *take off tie*, and saying 'May I hang it on your trolley thing?' insert it on opponent's trolley. Two holes later remove sweater and do the same thing. At the 12th, put all spare golf balls in pocket of opponent's bag, saying, 'This won't make any difference to you, will it?' Develop on these lines till 18th. Carry 'by accident' and old copy of an A B C or other heavy book in order to add to opponent's load.

T. Rattigan, who has long specialized in this gambit, uses a specially weighted tie, to add to the burden on his opponent's trolley; and has had made for him spare golf balls which look genuine enough, but which are in fact made of lead throughout.[1]

[1] These notes on Trolley Play originally appeared in the *Sunday Times*. They produced a strange 'reply' from T. Rattigan himself, calling my accuracy in question (*Sunday Times*, 25.vi.50). Both this 'reply' and my answer reprint below, leaving the reader to form his own judgment.

To the EDITOR OF THE 'SUNDAY TIMES'.

SIR – Mr S. Potter, in his recent article on R. and A.-manship, most flatteringly made reference to my foolish trifling device of the weighted tie, for use in encumbering one's golf opponent's trolley caddy ('The Troll King, Mk. III'), but incorrectly, I fear, ascribed to myself the invention of the lead golf balls (or 'Trolley-boggers') for which the credit must surely go to Mrs Bassett. That great gameswoman is, of course, already responsible for the hooting clubhead, adopted by the Gamesmanship Council as long ago as 1936, and for a more recent brilliancy, the reversible umbrella (obverse blue and yellow, reverse violet and rust) not yet submitted for official sanction, but the prototype of which she has already used with remarkable effect in wet after-luncheon play at her home course, Tossem Down.

Having thus corrected our august President on a minor matter, may I now have the great temerity to suggest that he is also at fault on a major one – to wit, the whole question of New Rulesmanship? The heavy burden of his arduous administrative duties has, I fear, blinded the President to the fact that the various ploys which he advocates and which formed the subject of a Council circular letter last January, have, in the rough hurly-burly of practical gamesmanship, long since been superseded by one all-embracing but very simple gambit. It is as follows.

At a given moment, preferably when the opponent has chipped to within a few feet of the pin, give a start of surprise, pull out from the hip pocket a copy of the new rules and, quickly flipping over the pages, study a passage at random with a grave and concentrated frown; after ten seconds raise the eyebrows; after a further ten, shake the head slowly from side to side; then replace book in hip pocket with, if necessary, a short, sharp laugh; finally, gaze thoughtfully at the horizon with the eyebrows in the elevated position, while the opponent addresses himself to his putt – or more correctly, to his putts.

Sunningdale.   T. RATTIGAN

To the EDITOR OF THE 'SUNDAY TIMES'.

SIR – Mr Rattigan must have been joking when he suggested that 'Mrs Bassett' of 'Tossem (*sic*) Down invented the use of lead golf balls for adding weight to opponent's trolley caddy.' Winifred Bassett of Tossem was certainly the first gameswoman to use them, as long ago as 1946, just as, three years later, Mr Rattigan adopted this 'new' device for Sunningdale, a course beautifully adapted by nature for counter-trolley play. But the use of lead, or some alloy of this substance, is as old as gamesmanship itself, dating as it does from the covert substitution of a pure leaden ball when handing a 'wood' to your opponent for some vital shot at bowls.

Mr Rattigan suggests that I am 'too busy with administrative duties' to have heard of a certain New Rulesmanship ploy which consists in taking out a book of the new rules after opponent has chipped to the green, scanning a passage at random, shrugging the shoulders, shaking the head, etc., as opponent is about to putt. Let me say at once that so far from being ignorant of this not ineffective gambit, we have discarded it (B32688 Aug. 1950). The counter, of which Mr Rattigan seems to be unaware, consists in opponent snatching out *his* copy of the rules, showing an equally random passage to his caddy, and nodding in silent unison with the caddy till the gambiter has sheepishly had to put his own copy of the rules back in his pocket. This whole tedious evolution, was, of course, the chief if not the only cause of the insufferable delays in the recent Amateur at St Andrews: and our Council is pleased to fall in with the wishes of the R. &. A. by banning it.

Mr Rattigan is a keen young gamesman of distinct promise, Number Sixteen out of the forty seeded men in the forthcoming Gamesmanship Open. It would be a thousand pities if other entrants followed his example and engaged in long controversial arguments in the public press on the eve of the Championship. Good luck, Mr Rattigan; but let us leave 'the administrative work', and the codifications as well, to older and perhaps wiser heads.

S. POTTER

9

NOTE ON CHRISTMAS
GAMESMANSHIP

IT SO happens that very little has been written about the art of winning Christmas games; yet there is no side of sport in which sloppy technique is more dismally common.

Yet what a field is Christmas for the Gamesman. The reader will understand that there is only room here for a note on basic principles.

The general atmosphere of Christmas family gatherings, with all their jolliness, noise, and sketchy goodwill, is a perfect *climate of operation* for the man who keeps his head. If during any game there is doubt about the score (to give the classical example of Christmas Basic) it is perfectly safe for the man who knows as a fact that the score is one or two points against him, to try a 'let's call it all square'. spoken in the friendly, what-does-it-matter-anyhow tone suitable to the friendly Christmas gathering.

Remember, first, that the essence of Christmas games is their local quality, with local rules, e.g. the rolling of pennies down a groove in the banisters. Sloppy gamesmanship is sometimes seen when one who wished to be regarded as a noted boxer or rugger player suggests that such games are not serious. The correct technique is to *know more about them than anybody else*. And, moreover, to suggest new versions and local variations on the family games, *which can be practised privately for a fortnight before the Christmas holiday*. Instead of the usual Blow Pong Ball (blowing a ping-pong ball into a goal across a table) it is 'much more fun' to use a hazel nut. With his previous practice in the special kind of spitting puff required, he will win easily.

The winning of such games may seem trivial, but it is of great help in the establishment, so essential, of what we call Christmas Control. *You* must be the jolly uncle who 'makes everything go'. It is *your* voice, first heard roaring with laughter in the hall, which cheers everybody up, and makes somebody say 'Hooray for Arthur!' or whatever the name may be. This ploy, known as Life and Soulmanship, is not always easy, and it may be necessary to get some fellow gamesman to shout 'Come on, Arthur, you organize it.' It is even possible, sometimes, to shout 'Hooray for Uncle Arthur!' yourself, in a disguised voice, from behind a screen.

If a straightforward game – e.g. ordinary ping-pong – is suggested, you can then know a 'frightfully good home-made kind' which is played on a small *circular* table, with a net made of volumes, balanced back upwards, of the Home University Library. I have proved that *one day's* previous practice makes success certain.

Life and Soulmanship is even more essential in the great question of Child Play. Children are the special problem of Christmas games. It is, of course, their season – as it should be, I am glad to say – and the Gamesman can at once make use of this fact. For if he wants to suggest a particularly complex card game which he alone can understand, he can whisper to some Mother:

'Do you know who will adore this? Little John.'

Christmas is always the season when we want children, above all, to have a good time. But it is also true that children in certain games needing quick movement have a tremendous advantage over us. It is rightly held, in Gamesmanship circles, that they should be handicapped, and the way to do it is this. In a game like Racing Demon (Pounce Patience or Prawn-eye), children of ten often win because their small hands are defter. Little asides can be given, starting with 'steady on'. Work on the suggestion that they are being too rough. 'No, don't do that, old man.' Then work up a 'fear' that the cards will be bent, and continue perhaps, with 'mind the table'. I have even seen a meaningless but peremptory 'mind the carpet' work as well as anything.[1]

---

[1] *Remember Mrs Wilson.* Failing this, there is always what we call 'Remember Mrs Wilson'. Mrs Wilson is some guest to whom *just because* it is Christmas, we have (you indicate) to be especially considerate. Remember to be polite to Mrs Wilson. Remember not to shout in Mrs Wilson's ear. And remind the child who is at the crest of a winning streak, remind even the child who though winning is sitting quiet and comparatively silent that she 'mustn't be rough in front of Mrs Wilson'. And remember, if all else fails it is always possible to *remove* a child from a game saying 'It's time you had your little rest now.'

G. Odoreida did extremely well with older children and the mid-teens by telling them that the contest he was planning for them was a 'jolly game for Young People'. This had the effect of taking away from them any desire to win.

10

GAMESMANSHIP AND WOMEN

THE WHOLE question of Women and Gamesmanship thrusts into the very roots of the science. There is scarcely a gambit which cannot be used, provided the *basic adaptation* is made, by women against men, and vice-versa.

Let us begin these brief notes with an example of one such gambit. For some readers the names 'Charles and Christabel' may strike a chord. These two remarkably tall, handsome lawn-tennis players frankly disliked each other in private life (there was some affair between them which went wrong). But for years they worked together most effectively as co-gamesters.

Procedure: Charles begins his singles match at the local club. A man's stiff singles. To start with, he plays purposely below his form. Then, with the score 4–1 against him, say, in the first set, by a pre-arranged signal Christabel would appear, to watch.[1] Her appearance blindingly smart, she makes a big entry, in the character of 'Charles's girl, come to back him up'. Charles would immediately begin to drive and serve with more Zonk – would really get going, and if he could manage to win an ace service, Christabel would give him a smile of dazzling encouragement.

Charles's opponent turns gloomy. 'Oh God,' he thinks. 'He's going to play up to this girl.' Christabel, of course, takes not the slightest notice of this opponent.[2]

The effect of this attack is redoubled, of course, if Charles's opponent has as his spectator some plain and dowdy niece or aunt, who

---

[1] In golf, this play is everywhere known as the 'Striking Stranger Gambit.' The girl should first appear on the tenth fairway.
[2] For Christabel's matches against women Charles would turn up late, in the same way: intent and ardent.

looks stuffily indifferent to what is going on. O. Bousfield, however, had a brilliant counter to this. Bousfield's spectator-friend, Miss Grace Perry, was a girl of stupefying plainness: but when Charles's Christabel came on the scene, with smiles of ravished and ravishing admiration, Bousfield pretended suddenly to feel himself under no obligation to conceal his own idiotic 'devotion' to the frightful-looking girl, Miss Perry. He sent her a thousand glances, even blew her a few surreptitious kisses, and played *at* her all the time. Poor Charles, as we all remember, completely lost his game in a daze of bewildered and futile curiosity.

For women, it is now accepted that knowledge of Clothesmanship is all-important: and a good deal of useful putting-off can be achieved by a clever use of better clothes.[1]

Finally, what is the essential strategy of sex war in games? For the man who finds himself playing against a woman, in singles or mixed, a good working knowledge of the Chivalry Gambit is essential.

In lawn-tennis singles, he will begin perhaps by saying, 'The male is allowed this one prerogative, I hope. Do please take choice of side and service.' If this does not have the desired effect of flustering the girl into making the man a present of the first game as she attempts to serve against the sun, it will yet start the average woman off on the wrong foot.

At golf, little attentions, such as picking up the woman's golf-bag for her, will have the same effect, especially if on the one occasion when the woman really wants help with her clubs (scrambling up a steep hill) this little attention is forgotten.

In lawn-tennis mixed, the basic chivalry move is to pretend to serve

[1] But beware of Counters if Miss P. turns up in elegant and correct if dashing shorts. A celebrated woman violinist was able to cast a decided shadow over this visitor and her team by slipping on a skirt and saying, 'I'm sorry about this skirt – but we're under the shadow of our dear old president here, you know – the Countess of Hale. And she says the most awesome things if she sees a girl playing in shorts.'

Mrs Wilder, the golfer, three times a runner-up of York women, would prettily counter-clothe her opponent thus. It was, as it so often is, a question of inflexion. Mrs Wilder herself would spend well over an hour preparing face and costume if anything like a 'gallery' was to be expected for her match. Yet she had a superb way, on the first tee, of saying to her (probably much more humbly dressed) opponent: '*What* an attractive little skirt.' She was able to suggest, by her intonation, that the wearing of such a skirt constituted an obvious and painstaking challenge to the male element among the spectators, an effort to intrigue the course stewards, if not to influence the judgment of the umpire.

less fiercely to the woman than the man. This is particularly useful
if your first service tends to be out in any case.[1]

And what is the woman's counter to the chivalry gambit? Remember, in general don't react *against* the chivalry move. Appear to be
hoodwinked by it – and if your male opponent shows the least signs of
trying the 'I have long adored you from afar' move, treat it immediately
as a formal proposal of marriage *which you shyly accept*. This is one of
the most devasting, the most match-winning, counters in the whole
realm of gamesmanship.

[1] There is, to me, an element of hatefulness about Odoreida's gambit in
Counter Women Play. He carried about with him a two-page privately-
printed pamphlet called, I believe, *Why Women Cannot Play Squash Rackets*.
On page 3 of this there was a large diagram of the female skeleton with the
thigh-bones coloured ultramarine.

11

HOME AND AWAYMANSHIP

LOCAL GAMESMEN continue to do fine work for the Technique and in the provinces they can often be seen in groups comparing the results of their small researches, notebook in hand, dipping into the local, perhaps, for a 'quick one', and sending results to our Yeovil headquarters, where there is an unpaid organization which places their findings in some file.

From these tiny beginnings – the chance finding of a Local Report in a waste-paper basket, perhaps – has sprung a flourishing band of enthusiasts for Playing Fields Play, or, as it is now more usually called, Home and Awaymanship.

There is certainly far too much genuine good spirit displayed in the treatment of visiting teams; and it is my object in this article to suggest some easy correctives.

Do not make your side of the preliminary exchange of notes fixing the date of the match too friendly. On the contrary, start the letter 'Dear Sir' and after signing it, type 'PP Signed in absence' at the end. Say: 'We usually make up our fixture list eighteen months in advance, but we do happen to have one date in the month you suggest.'

This long-range work eventually produces a certain nervousness or stiffness in your opponents without actually increasing their pugnacity.

Against teams visiting you for the first time a friendlier tone can be used to create what we call a 'ploy situation'.

Say: 'You might care to catch an earlier train than the 10.15 if it would amuse you to "do" our little town and see round it for yourselves in the morning.' This will tire the team not only by making them take a much earlier train than necessary (a good ploy in any case), but also they will be wearied of dispirited tramping, particularly if there are no sights more worth seeing than an exhibition of shawls in the annexe to the Town Hall, and a statue of William IV in the public recreation ground.

A still matier tone can be used in this way.

'We shan't turn out to meet you with the red carpet,' you say, 'because in fact the Playing Fields are dead opposite the Station. Turn right and the entrance is diagonally opposite, by the next street.'

The meaninglessness of this direction is not realized till the team find after twenty minutes' search (carrying heavy sports bags) that the playing field they have at last found is the wrong one.

Of course experienced teams will know how to counter this sort of thing by taking no notice whatever of any directions sent by post, and by coming with a small compass, or even better, large-scale map.

There are, of course, many Counters to these effective Gambits and often the real battle is fought in the sports pavilion and changing room, and we get all the pretty by-play of Homeship *versus* Awaymanship.

The offering of extremely feeble lunches to the visitors, for instance, can be countered. if the visiting team is forewarned, by the sudden and unexpected production by them of luncheon hampers, *no part of which, however much is left over, they offer to their hosts.*

The great master of Awaymanship was J. Scott-Dickens. A poor footballer, he was yet for twenty-three years chosen as captain when his side was playing away. He built up his attack by a multiplication of very small ploys. He would make a point, for instance, of mistaking the 12th man for the captain of the opposing side and continue so to do, in spite of repeated corrections, right up to the toss.

If his opponents possessed a star man, a celebrated player, he would elaborately never have heard of him. So far from taking any notice of trains or routes suggested by opposing club secretaries, he would demand to be met with his team at the station, at, say, 9.15, and then not arrive by train at all, but appear at the sportsground two hours later, with all his team in a charabanc.

Good work has been done lately in changing rooms by such clubs as the Basingstoke Tusslers. The china of their washbasins is seamed and cracked. The taps are marked 'hot' and 'cold', but all that comes out of the hot tap is a long sucking noise, and unless the feet are placed at least a yard from the basin, they are resting on what seems to be mud. Instead of mirrors over the basins, there are notices saying, PLEASE LEAVE THE WASH BASINS AS YOU WOULD LIKE TO FIND THEM.

Corner of Visitors' Changing-room at Basingstoke (Reproduced by permission of *Catalogue for Gamesmen*, 1945).

The secretary of this same Basingstoke club, the go-ahead W. Brood, later developed another device for preventing geniality in dressing-rooms. He would dress a junior groundsman in a dark suit and cause him to walk quietly through the dressing-room about twice when the Away team were in it. Later he would come up, full of apologies, to the visiting captain:

'I'm most terribly sorry – I didn't mean him to come in when you were here, but we've lost so many things from the lockers lately – nothing to do with you people, I need hardly say – that we've got this man more or less permanently on duty, watching.'

This sort of thing presented no kind of difficulty, of course, to Scott-Dickens. He knew all about Brood, and he never visited Brood or any of his Club Secretary imitators without bringing an extra 12th man whom he would introduce as 'Our detective. We've had to, you know.'

I consider Brood should have first credit for the development of Playfieldsmanship in its broader aspects. He has made a little name for Basingstoke by his keenness and dash. May I add, as a footnote to this section, that the Brood flair is very much 'in the family'. Charming Molly Brood, his daughter, is gamesmistress at Basingstoke College for Daughters of Gentlewomen. It is pretty to see how, under Molly's training, the College lacrosse team treats a visiting side. The girls stand aside in little groups, never speaking to their opponents when they arrive or when they are looking unsuccessfully for the changing room. With their backs half-turned towards the embarrassed visitors, they will suddenly break into little screams of giggling laughter. Before Molly's advent, things were very different.

An Unusual Instance

Occasionally matches are played *away by both sides*. This curious feature needs a special ploy, seen in its simplest form with Lord's Schools, who play, of course, at Lord's. The match is really fought out in the pavilion, often called the 'sacred shrine' of cricket. The side which seems to be most at ease and to know its way about best is said to have won. It is not generally known that Odoreida is an old Wykhamist.[1] He once managed to get into the pavilion himself for a few minutes. It was during a Lord's Schools match. Everybody heard him ask 'why the picture of Nyren has been moved from the right to the left of the glass case containing C. B. Fry's walking stick'. Later, Odoreida was seen wearing First Eleven colours. It is easy to prove he was never awarded them.

A NOTE ON GAMESMANSHIP AND THE CLASSICS

It is a great pleasure to me to be able to introduce at this early date (July 1950) a reference to the work of the Birnam Society, now centered at Wellington, Berks. In the last of my Bude lectures I spoke of Gamesmanship and Shakespeare, and though most of my remarks referred to Footnote Play I had something to say, as well, of Shakespeare himself as a gamesman. I pointed out that C. Jones had shown that the fight in the last Act of *Hamlet* was swarming with ploys (how exquisite Hamlet's 'These Foyles have all a length?'[2] just before the fight begins). I showed that Coriolanus was the victim of massive ploys on the part of that great gameswoman, Volumnia. I drew attention, in *Macbeth*, not only to the expensive ploy of the 'moving' of Birnam Wood to Dunsinane, but to the splendid Superstition Play of Macduff and the timing of his casual reference to the fact that he was

from his Mother's womb[3]

Untimely Ript.

[1] May 2nd – June 6th, 1922.
[2] I absolutely prefer the First Folio spelling (F1).
[3] Again, see how much more zing in F1 (the First Folio spelling).

On these small beginnings the Birnam (& Dunsinane) Society was founded, with its Homership Fellowship, under the supervision of H. Wright, with whom I was up.

H. Wright (also known as 'H. H. S. Wright' or 'Root') has based his life as supervisor on the theory that Odysseus was the perfect gamesman and that the epithet most often used of Odysseus – πολύμητις – should in future be translated 'gamesmanlike' instead of the feeble 'of many wiles'.

At Wellington, under 'Root's' skilful direction, results are beginning to come in. Let me reprint almost in full this note (by ———) on the funeral games of Iliad XXIII.

The whole art of Homeric gamesmanship as typified in the chariot race is contained in the maxim: 'He, who has the best gods, wins.' It is here, surely, that we see the best and most classical examples of godmanship. It is true that the Gamesman always sticks to his rules, but rules become unnecessary if (a) the gods or (b), more important, the goddesses, are on your side. Eumelus, who had a mere male god on his side, never had a chance: Apollo may have taken Diomedes' whip and left him completely shiftless, but Athene went one better.

Not only did she give Dionysus back his whip, but she heartened his horses, and at the same time she broke Eumelus' chariot pole and ran his horses out of the race. Pallas Athene was obviously interested in the result of the race. Perhaps a little investigation of Odysseus' movements at the time would not be unprofitable!

The secondary gambit, for those not professionally acquainted with the gods and thus unable to command their interest, financial or otherwise, seems to have been plain downright dangerous driving. But we must not deprive the drivers of all credit for their gamesmanship. There is surely some significance in the fact that Antilochus rode level with Menelaus for such a distance and *only* that distance *that a discus might carry when cast for a practice throw*. Evidently there is some subtle measurement here of psychological strain. One feels that Antilochus had practised this manœuvre time and again until he had perfected it. Students of gamesmanship will recognize in his manœuvre a rudimentary but nevertheless definite form of the 'flurry'.

'The first muscle stiffened, is the first point gained.' With a little thought we can diagnose in Diomedes' tactics before the dramatic intervention of Athene and Phoebus Apollo a cruder application of this effective psychological gambit. We are told that Diomedes' horses were breathing 'down Eumelus' back', so close were they; here again there is an application of the flurry. To be quite accurate the word, 'μετάφρενον', means less 'back' than 'the part behind the kidneys' – a section of the body unusually susceptible to this form of irritation. It would have been interesting to see the results of this gambit. But it was not to be. Godmanship decided the issue.

THINGS YOU MAY LIKE TO KNOW

List of Leading Gamesmen: The Ladder

Yes, Gamesmenites, it is true that in our Yeovil office, over the Founder's desk, there is the 'Gamesman's Ladder' – the list of leading
gamesmen in order of merit. There are 600 spaces but some of them
are blank. Any gamesman can challenge any other gamesman *one* or
two places above him, and if in the opinion of the Committee the
lower outgames the higher, the order on the ladder is changed.

Outposts

Besides the ladder for Britain, there is a ladder for the United
States of America, an international Gameswoman's Ladder, a leading
Gameswoman, and a leading Gamesman for individual districts. You
may be surprised to hear that there is a Paris One, a Huntercombe
One, a Boston One, an Aldeburgh One. The Gamesman need never
feel he is alone, and Empire bonds are strong. Wonderful links are
being formed, and techniques exchanged, with all the cut and thrust
of monthly correspondence. The other day, for instance, the First
Gamesman for Ulster prepared a ploy in Clothesmanship which was
turned down by Number One Holy Land.[1]

[1] Author of one of our first Near East publications: 'Dead Seamanship, its
Practice and Exercise' (Pam: 31014).

HORSE EXERCISE
AT HOME

Horse=Action Saddle

HIGHLY APPROVED OF BY
H.I.H. THE EMPEROR OF AUSTRIA.

PERSONALLY ORDERED BY
H.R.H. the PRINCESS of WALES.

ADOPTED BY
SIR HENRY THOMPSON,
AND PRONOUNCED BY
DR. GEORGE FLEMING, C.B.,
Late President of the Royal College of Veterinary Surgeons, and Principal Veterinary Surgeon to the British Army,
to be a most efficient substitute for the live horse.

EXERCISE ON THIS SADDLE
QUICKENS THE CIRCULATION,
STIMULATES THE LIVER,
AIDS DIGESTION,
CURES GOUT & RHEUMATISM,
AND
SAFELY REDUCES OBESITY.

---

*Special Side Saddles
for LADIES.*

THE LANCET says: "The expense and difficulty of riding on a live horse are avoided."

The *Sporting Times* says: "Ten minutes' gallop before breakfast will give the rider a Wiltshire labourer's appetite."

WEEK-ENDMANSHIP: COUNTER GUEST PLAY. An early device for trapping guests into 'entering into the spirit' of home games, not being spoil-sports, and 'joining in the fun'. See Chapter II, page 96. *(Advertisement)*

ONE-UPMANSHIP

*Being some account of the Activities
and Teaching of the*

*LIFEMANSIIIP CORRESPONDENCE
COLLEGE OF ONE-UPNESS AND
GAMESLIFEMASTERY*

OUR COLLEGE

I AM speaking to you now[1] as newly elected President of the Lifemanship Correspondence College. When I look at the list of distinguished names among our helpers and founders here I am astonished and even bewildered at the honour. Ours is a small community, housed quite modestly in a converted section of a converted mansion, yet from the files and the classrooms, the laboratories and the libraries, Lifemanship throws its lifeline from Alaska in the West to Colchester in the East.[2] Linked by vast sea routes,[3] it has been said of Lifemanship that we have been called into being in the role of the Old World redressing the balance of the New World redressing the balance of the Old.[4]

But let me tell you something of our small self-contained University, not a thousand miles from Yeovil. Students from Wyoming, it is true, cannot reach us here. With them we deal, inevitably, by letter. For such, Correspondence College it must be; yet we prefer and welcome the personal touch, the human problem in the flesh; we are proud of the young lads and lasses who come to 'LCC' to study at first hand.

We boast no domes or pediments. In spite of Gamesmanship

---

[1] These opening words form part of a lecture first delivered to a very small group in the waiting-room of Marks Tey Railway Station in January 1952. I am indebted to Sir Ford Boulder, chairman of the catering division of the Great Eastern, as it once was, for not withholding permission to print them here.

[2] There is as yet no Games-Life Association at Frinton, for instance, where one would expect it. Although a happy and natural result of the Aldeburgh Festival has been the founding of a small Lifemanship Club in that resort, it may be said that the Games-Life median line coincides unexpectedly with a Longitude which involves the tip of Cape Cod, famed in Melville.

[3] It is estimated that eleven-twelfths of Lifemanship's vast 'Empire' is covered by water.

[4] But see pp. 264 ff (Hands-across-the-seamanship).

Rallies and GIVE FREELY TO LIFEMANSHIP weeks, our dream of a worthy
Senate House, built in Re-inforced Functional Revival, waits
fulfilment.[1] Every penny of our endowment is spent on equipment,
and it is spent on staff.

I should like to describe to you our workrooms – yes and our play-
rooms as well, not unlike those of one of the older universities, with
whom we co-exist in mutual evaluation and respect.

Here a room which belongs to the Arts Faculty, at first like any
other such; but look again and see how, in a detail, Lifemanship's
doctrine of One-Upness is always followed or imbued. Note the
piano with cigarette stains on the upper notes. But these are dummy
surfaces removable at will, because it is not in all company that such
signs of Bohemian inconsequence impress.

There is the conductor's baton – but where is the orchestra? In the
gramophone cabinet, for it is the conduction of gramophone records
which we teach, splendid way to corner attention and cause confused
irritation when music is being played.

THINKING IN FRENCH
(a Language Life-
gambit)

During a ramble by
the canal after one of
our language tutor-
ials, Cogg-Willough-
by set us all laughing
with this sketch of
himself. 'Some day
you will see yourself
in print,' I said to
Cogg. And here he
is!

---

[1] We are still without the government grant due to our foundation.

Look, too, at the wall devoted to pictures. But how are they arranged? 'O K' in gold letters denotes 'O K to praise this year'. On the right, in black, 'Ex-O K' – pictures which were O K ten years ago and which students must learn therefore to discard, for one-upness in pictureship.

See, too, our modern languages department. See our list of French phrases O K to bring into conversation. See, on the left of the blackboard, correct French; on the right, French translated into English, French, phonetically transcribed, a dialect which our students are taught to cultivate with aristocratic downrightness and amusingly insular don't-care-a-damnmanship.

Here, on this white tablecloth made of india-rubber, coffee-spilling is taught in our Mannership cadre, with demonstrations of how to apologize, or not to, and how, alternatively, to engineer, as host, the awkward pause and the 'Don't-give-it-another-thought' sequence. (Lydall's[1] Reproach.)

In the Gamesmanship section, take a glimpse, now. That strangely shaped racket is a tennis racket, for use in study or office where Royal tennis strokes may be demonstrated to players who are merely lawn.

And why the two lawn-tennis courts? Note that A (left) is humpy, wobbly, the net sagging and stringy, tied to unsuitable sticks. On the right (B) all is taut and accurate, a Wimbledonship atmosphere, with all-steel umpire's chair and chromium seats for linesmen. It is here that lawn-tennis gambits *interchangeably suited to the contrasted gamesacre and lifeclimate of the two different courts* are worked out in detail. On this adjoining putting-green, the now famous intimidation plays and distraction gambits for putters were first taught to men who have since won success in this field on courses as far removed as Studland or Little Canaan. Nearby, in that asphalt corner, see stacked the rubber rapiers of our fencers with the special 'BRUZELESS' boxing-gloves for students who need to say of this sport, too, in later life, 'I once did a bit of it.' That sheer four foot of plaster rock is for the rockman (see p. 242) – the mattress underneath is pneumatic and shockproof.

The seeming shed beyond is in fact the Museum of Clothesmanship, with 'Right' and the equally Lifemanlike and gambitous 'Wrong' clothes standing adjacent for amusement and instruction. Right and Wrong for grouse-shooting, for visiting a coal mine, for the Tate Gallery, for New Year's Eve, for landing in Nairobi.[2] And then,

[1] E. (not J.B.C.W.).
[2] Oh, and countless others.

'681 STATION ROAD'

Note in this recent drawing (A) dummy television aerial. (B) Founder's bed-room, (C) dining-hall with separate tables, (D) eucalyptus tree planted by former member of staff, Miss C. Johnson, (E) eucalyptus tree planted by

Founder, (F) sheer rock for Rockmanship, (G) ordinary putting-green, (H) lawn-tennis court (Vicarage type), (J) museum of Clothesmanship (presented by the Harvard Foundation and Mellon Trust), (K) dummy conservatory.

of course I would show you the College Dining-hall, the Anti-social room and the Library, with its dummy books.

I want the pages which follow to be regarded as an introduction to Correspondence College techniques. It may be asked – why am I revealing all this? But we are not a money-making concern – primarily. If students are attracted by this glimpse of our methods, we shall welcome them. If not, let them admit that Lifemanship is not for them. I have seen some parents ruin many a natural Lifeboy by trying to force our philosophy on him when, at six or seven, he was too young or too obstinate, to receive it.

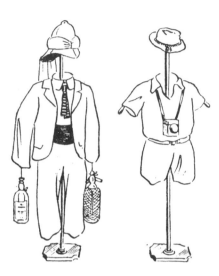

MUSEUM OF CLOTHESMANSHIP
For landing in Nairobi. Wrong (left) and right (right).

Nor will I have it said that there is any mystery about ordinary Lifemanship, even if for obvious reasons its more advanced methods are known to initiates only. There are of course, certain Super-gambits known only to Yeovil, and though we are in full and free consultation with Washington and the Pentagon on the possibilities of their exploitation, the technique of these is still our secret. Therefore it is, I suppose, not surprising that at the time of going to press the newspapers are full of an incident for which some will revile us, though others have shown sympathy A well-known and even liked member of our staff has disappeared. His name – G. Wert. Never high in our confidence, he was yet a leading instructor in our Department of Foreign Enthusiasm, and an expert in Round Tableship and the Exchange of Unpleasantries. Last certainly seen at Ghent (office of our *L'Institution Vie-malheureuse*), glimpsed at Algiers, he probably passed, as a shadow, over the Peloponnesian border and disappeared behind the Iron Curtain. Wherever he is, he has taken his secrets with him, and we now suffer the chagrin of listening, at Round Table

A CORNER IN THE LIBRARY

Note here the new student (H) breaking finger-nails on dummy books. *How will he deal with this situation?* Note desk with signatures of former students. Note empty bust-case. *One day it might be You.* On the left, genuine books. (D) *Gamesmanship* and *Lifemanship*. (F) The complete works of all nineteenth-century novelists in six volumes (shortened). (G) Classic French literature (abbreviated and epitomized for easy reading).

conferences, to elementary Lifegambits from – why not name them? – the Russians. Thus has been inaugurated the era of Marxmanship in the conferences between East and West. Small wonder that the study of Lifemanship and Counter-lifemanship is regarded now as the still more urgent need of all of us.

Universityship

LCC (Lifemanship Correspondence College) is no substitute for three years' academic study at one of the older universities, and we have never made this claim. What we do intend, in our six-weeks' course, is that the student should learn how to be top student, and, when he is launched on the world, how to become the post-graduate top post.

To help us in our work here, university groups form spontaneously, send us their suggestions, or just write saying 'How to help?'

When I get these letters from young Lifestudents, many of them little more than Lifeboys, from Professors, too, of all denominations, my answer to the question is always 'Write about *yourself*, how *you* got away with it, how *you* think it is possible to get by the examiner without actually cheating, Express *yourself*.'

Why the Silence of Yale?

The response, entirely unsolicited, has been extra-ordinary. Oxford and Cambridge have helped with their maturer views; Edinburgh, Bangor and Leeds, in that order, have been perhaps more brilliantly experimental. Stanford, California, is at work, and Harvard has been especially forward with advice and publication. From Yale – I just want to record this as a simple statement – there has been no communication whatever.

The Harvard-Edinburgh

It has been our function to sift and co-ordinate these contributions. To make it clearer to new readers, it can be said that we include in our studies the study of study, and fulfil our function as university University. It is the science of Scientific Attitudeship which we teach; the art of Arts.

I head this section 'The Harvard-Edinburgh' because it will serve to introduce a specifically *Universityship* study theme on which we like to prove our mettle – the basic approach, really, to the examination-room. How to be one up on the lay student before the examinations have started; or how (passmanship) to excel after it is all over. Edinburgh specializes in the former; Harvard in the latter.

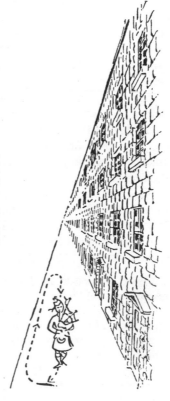

EDINBURGH, 1851
While his friends are working late on the night before the examination, fellow-student distracts them by playing bagpipes outside their windows. Amazing that this example of primitive gamesmanship took place *in the year of the Great Exhibition.*

The phrase 'To edinburgh' implies a spreading, a dissemination of despondency among other students working for Lifeman's examination by an appearance of solid knowledge, of calmness in the face of approaching crisis, and of a desire to help. In his inaugural address, as Senior President to the Edinburgh University Lifemanship Research Group,[1] J. Weatherhead was particularly careful to stress the fact

[1] January 29th, 1951.

(to use his own words) that the Undergraduateman must give one of two impressions, either that (1) he does nothing but work, or (2) that he does not work. Concentrating on (1), he describes the work of J. Reid, who specializes in striding into the reading-room with his hat on, going 'straight to the shelves of a subject he is not necessarily studying',[1] taking a book out as if he knew where to look for it, running down a reference and walking out again *quietly but plonkingly*.

Over the faces of student watchers nervousness runs like a whisper; though in fact Reid has just picked up a book of quotations to verify a clue in a crossword puzzle. By an accumulation of such featherweight ploys as these,[2] Reid was able to oppress his fellow-students with a sense of the hopelessness of any effort of theirs in the face of such competition, and many a promising degree man is virtually failed before he has set foot in the examination-room.

'To harvard' is, conversely, to seem, even when the examination is only two days off, to be totally indifferent to the impending crisis, and be seen walking calmly and naturally about, out of doors, enjoying the scenery and taking deep breaths of air.[3]

Naturally, many Edinburgh men also harvard, and vice versa. But to maintain the truly contemporary nature of their native gambit, Harvard has its own special team – most of them on the teaching staff – with whom I am kept in touch.[4] A recent formulation is that of J. Smail's. This is Smail's wording ('FitzJames' is a fictitious name):

Famed Harvardman (as distinct from Harvard man) J. FitzJames disappeared suddenly from College midway through January Reading Period, just about the time his friends began studying in earnest. Then, on the day of his first exam, he would return, strolling into the examination-room five minutes late, dressed in a light Palm Beach suit and heavily tanned. Sitting down next to a friend he would inspect his papers casually, and begin to write slowly.

Later it becomes known that FitzJames has received an A in the course. What is the explanation? FitzJames has been holing himself up in a miserable rented room in Boston surrounded by the total reading assignment,

[1] Wider Interests Play.
[2] I believe that after putting the book back Reid sometimes speaks quietly to a shy-looking girl student *seeming to impart information to her*, as if to help her.
[3] '*Don't harvard*,' I once, when a visitor to Worcester, Oxford, heard, during a pleasant outing with the Chameleon Club, shouted after an undergraduate who, walking to the bathroom on or about June 18th, was humming.
[4] See *Harvard Alumni Bulletin*, February 9, 1952.

including the optional books, and has been working like a dog for three weeks, stripped to the waist between two sun lamps.

A certain sum of money has been allocated at Harvard for the preparation of a counter to this gambit. Even if the results arrive too late to be printed in this volume, I believe that by concentrating on an aspect of *one* of our activities, Universityship, I have given readers some insight into the *whole*.

2

DOCTORSHIP

MD-MANSHIP, PATIENTSHIP AND THE HEALTH PLOY

I BELIEVE that our College treatment of Medicine illustrates our aims and methods as well as any. Basic medical studentship, doctorship and patientship provide us with the three 'Threes' of Lifemanship teaching. Medical studentship is perhaps too advanced for the lay reader, and we have reserved for a privately-printed edition a technical note on the work of Canada in this sphere.

Our ten-days' course for young doctors – how different, in its brevity, compression and point, from the seven *years* of grinding work in the more orthodox schools of medical education. Not that this latter must be neglected, but we do claim that in our Demonstrator in Harleyship and our Sir J. Boot Reader we have two extraordinarily fine men who can give a helping hand both during and after the period of academic study, not only in the simple Health ploys but also in the establishment of one-up relations between doctor and doctor and doctor and patient and vice versa.

Health and the Normal Lifeplay

Ordinary *health*, remember, is highly gambit-prone. Novice Lifemen are often seen sparring with each other in the friendly cut-and-thrust of the Health move.

'It's only a scratch' is often the first Life-remark of the prattling Lifechild, and the reply made by the infant only slightly less young ('Well, that is a good fing, anyhow') is often the first counter.

In later life it is soon discovered that a slight disability, properly used, can be advantageous, particularly where a desire to live up to a reputation for genius is required. We demonstrate the imperious stammer, the attention-inviting tremor and the romantic limp.[1]

[1] In the lecture-room, where we teach limpmanship and the use of the

Köhler was our first lecturer in this subject, and opposite our portrait of Byron you will see a diagram of the human figure crossed by a wavy line, known as 'Köhler's Line'. Köhler, originally a systematic botanist, attempted to standardize what he called 'O K complaints' for various walks of life, above the line being in general more O K than below the line, though this varied interestingly, as can be imagined, in the case of such contrasted pursuits as those of poet, plasterer, racing driver and diplomat, to name a few.

Odoreida-ism was rife in the early days of healthmanship – with Odoreida's irritating 'You're looking remarkably fit' to Gattling just after he'd been thrown over by Claudia; or his 'You're looking a bit cheap' to Cogg just after Cogg had been attempting to brown himself for ten dangerous days in the Engadine. In general, I believe we have inculcated in our young Lifemen the rule that one must be able clearly to suggest either that one is absolutely healthy or, alternatively, never really free from pain. The two styles MUST NOT BE MUDDLED. On this basis all good health work must be grounded.[1]

Natural One-upness of Doctors

But the first real hurdle to be tackled by the novice Healthman, when he comes of age, is the Doctor. We Lifemen have always been well-disposed towards doctors. Above all professions, except perhaps that of the expert in commercial law, the Box Office Manager, and the man whose special job it is to advise people about having their cars decarbonized, doctors have shown themselves to be apt and natural Lifemen, and their careers are built on a well-sprung framework of ploys and gambiting.

As some readers will not know, there is a *Lancet*[2] Research Group, denominating and codifying procedures. They have defined 'Doctorship', with a rough directness, as 'the art of getting one up on the

---

silver-headed cane, there is a large oil-painting of Byron to remind us that the present decay of Sir Walter Scott's reputation is in no small measure due to the fact that although Scott's limp was just as bad and just as genuine as Byron's, nobody ever heard about it. The Walter Scott picture was removed from the walls.

[1] An effective statement in the right context can sometimes be: 'I have had 140 days' illness in my life.' Listeners are unable, without a lame pause for calculation, to know whether to commiserate or admire.

[2] The official organ of British Medicine, and recognized by us.

DOCTORSHIP: CROFT'S LAW OF INVERSE SUPERFICIAL DIFFERENTIATION IN
TERMS OF MEAN EVOLUTIONARY ADDRESS
Correct clothes for (1) 6A Verlaine Road, Portsea, Hants; (2) 'Fording-
bridge,' Dunting Road, Basingstoke; (3) 16 Redcliffe Gardens, Kensington;
(4) 14 Wimpole Street, W.1; (5) President of the Royal College of Physicians.

patient without actually killing him'.[1] Yes, but doctors, it must be
remembered, are subjected to the healthy rivalry of Lifemanship
from the very beginning of their training; and almost as soon as they
are qualified they must decide (see *Lancet* Research) on whether to
become one of four basic Doctor types.

Type One is the Damn-good-doctor, on the spot, enthusiastic,
breathing common sense, fond of simple remedies, and opposed to
Type Two, the Damn-good-scientist. Damn-good-scientist prides
himself on having 'forgotten the starting symptoms of chicken-pox'.
He 'hasn't listened to a chest since his Finals year'. His clothes are
stained with chemicals. The bulge in his pocket is graph-paper, not a
stethoscope.[2]

A rarer but effective type is (*Three*) the man, continuously being
caught out of reach of normal hospital equipment,[3] who learnt his
Infectious Diseases in the stagnant marshes of the Naquipl foothills,
where he was the only doctor in 15,000 square miles, if that. Finally
there is (*Four*) the doctor who achieves eminence by always replying

[1] 'Nursemanship', the art of getting one up on the doctor and/or the patient
without actually marrying either, is also described, with subsidiary anti-
Sister ploys and contra-Matron gambits.
[2] Additional *Lancet*-sponsored properties include a corked test-tube of
soapy water in the waistcoat pocket, a tuft of guinea-pig fur on the lapel, and
the use of odd bits of cardiac catheter, instead of string, to tie things up with.
[3] 'St Kildaship.' The nineteenth-century term is no longer in use.

to the simplest possible question (after the smallest conceivable pause) 'Alas, we don't know.'

These types, potentially one up as each of them is, can be perpetually at war in the age-old struggle for the Survival of the Lifest. It is always the doctor who knows best how to appear to possess a better car than his nearest rival. The doctor who knows how to be one up in consulting-room equipment and clothes. (For our suggested diagonalizing of clothes in relation to mean fashionable address, the top hat in the outer suburbs and the old fishing jacket for Harley Street, with gradations between, *see* Illustration on page 176.)

Natural One-downness of Patient

What chance, it may well be asked, has even the lay lifeman against the doctor? The doctor holds all the cards, and can choose his own way of playing them. Right at the start, when answering Patient's original telephone call, for instance, he can, and generally does, say 'Dr Meadows speaking' in a frightfully hollow and echoing voice, as if he was expecting a summons to sign a death certificate. Alternatively, a paralysingly brisk voice can be used suggesting that Doctor is busier than Patient in normal life, and in a more important way.

DOCTOR: Hallo, yes. Finchingfield here ... Well, it will have to be rather late this morning, I'll see what I can do.

In the bedroom, this brisk type of M D-man is tidier, better or at any rate more crisply dressed than the Patient, and is able to suggest by his manner not only that Patient's room is surprisingly disordered, but that he, the Doctor, goes in for a more up-to-date type of pyjamas than the ones he observes Patient to be wearing.

The patient starts perkily enough ...

LAYMAN: Thank you, Doctor. I was coming home rather late last night from the House of Commons—

M D-MAN: Thank you ... now if you'll just let me put these ... hair brushes and things off the bed for you ... that's right ...

LAYMAN: I was coming home rather late. Army Act, really—

M D-MAN: Now just undo the top button of your shirt or whatever it is you're wearing ...

LAYMAN: I say I was coming—

M D-MAN: Now if you've got some hot water – really hot – and a clean towel.

LAYMAN: Yes, just outside. The Postmaster-General ...

M D-MAN: Open your mouth, please.

To increase the one-downness, bring in the washing-the-hands gambit immediately after touching hands with Patient. Unpleasant infestant possibilities can be suggested.

The old, now discarded, bedside mannership is still used when Doctor wishes to subdue the sensitive Patient suffering from an eclipsing headache. Doctor used to begin a constant fire of hollowly exploding clubroom stories, so involved in their climax that only the keenest attention revealed the point of expected laughter. We now teach that MD-man should show an *inaccurate familiarity with the Patient's own tastes or profession.* He can suggest, for instance, that some prized first edition 'might be worth something some day', or, if his patient is a horseman, tell him that the first syllable in 'Pytchley' is long. For actor-patients Doctor can tell the story of how as a young student he dressed up as Principal Boy in the Middlesex Hospital Pantomime when a member of the Middlesex Mauve Merriments.

After this opening treatment, Doctor may *under certain circumstances* ask Patient his symptoms. But he will let it be seen that he is not listening to what Patient is saying, and may place his hand on Patient's wrist, or, better, stomach, as if to suggest that he as Doctor can tell more through the sensitive tip of one finger than from listening to the layman's self-deceiving, ill-observed and hysterically redundant *impressions* of what is wrong with him.

Many good MD-men make a point of shepherding their patients in to the consulting-room where, by his way of averting his head as Patient is undressing, Doctor can suggest criticism of his choice of underclothes, socks, &c. The doctor is well; patient is ill: and (if only because he is longing for a cigarette) in more ways than in mere physical health.

Nevertheless the following *Friendly* Consulting-room Approach[1] is basically better. Suppose your patient comes in with, say, a chronic outbreak of warts on the back of the neck. He will be disposed to make light of this. ALLOW HIM TO, BUT FRIGHTEN HIM AT THE SAME TIME, by little asides to invisible nurses. Thus.

MD-MAN: Well, you are a pretty sight. Now, just lower your shirt.

[1] This gambit was invented by a well-known actor, with medical tastes. Shunning publicity, he yet allows me to say that it was evolved in Rome during the filming of *Quo Vadis*. He was in charge of the St John's Ambulance Tent, Block L, during the scenes when the lions were eating the Christians – largely faked. He himself was playing the part of the Emperor Ustinian.

LAYMAN (*enjoying himself*): Not very pretty for sun-bathing at Annecy next summer. I thought—

MD-MAN: Better take it right off. Ah, you lucky man. You know the lake, do you? (*Lowering voice*) Nurse, get me a Watson-Dunn, will you?

LAYMAN: Yes, I love it, we go every year . . .

MD-MAN (*pressing buzzer*): The food of course is marvellous. (*Speaking calmly into some machine*) Oh, Barker, get me the light syringe from the sterilizer – yes, the dual. Yes, we must get you right for that.

LAYMAN: But it's not anything—

MD-MAN: Nothing serious, I'm sure. Now bend down. Yes, Annecy – and you know Talloires? . . . Now nurse, if you'll just stand by while we have a look. Quadriceps, please . . . and – oh, thank you, Barker. Better get the hydrogenizer going (*compressed air sound can be imitated by some assistant in the background going 'zzzz' through his teeth*). Yes, there's a little restaurant – right down, please – the Georges Bise . . . Now.

At the end, with a charming 'au revoir', MD-man, instead of telling him what is wrong, can stare, last thing, at frightened Patient's left eye through a specially contrived speculum which startles Patient with a view of Doctor's own eye, enlarged, inverted and bloodshot (*see* Illustration on page 180).

Some Slight Discomfortship

Doctorship Basic is, of course, to suggest that Patient is worrying either (*a*) too little, but (*b*) far more generally, too much. If (*a*), a good general suggestion is that he is playing games too violent for his time of life. 'No ping-pong after 26,' he will say. Or: 'After 55, more than 18 holes is . . . well . . .'

But for the more common 'Don't make such a fuss' approach, procedure usually recommended for MD-men is as follows:

1. If Patient has a rash, describe some really serious skin disease seen in hospital that morning, as if this mentioning of a few silly spots was futile.

2. For stiff neck, put on an obviously assumed interest, say: 'I'm sorry to hear of that,' and if Patient says he has been woken up six times during the night by really sharp twinges, be overheard saying to some assistant that: 'Patient appears to have had some slight discomfort. I shall not be in to lunch today.'

3. When treating a cold, Doctor can go rather mechanically through a list of prescriptions, remedies and a routine which the patient 'must' follow and then say: 'I've got just the same sort of cold myself, they're about everywhere. What do *I* do about it? Well, personally I do

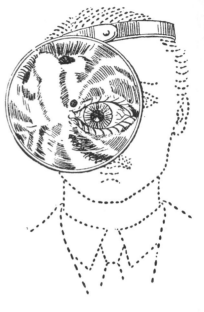

DR J. HOLLIS CARTER'S
EEZISLIPON

This 'speculum' is fitted with coated
lenses which flash in the eye of the
perturbed patient a magnified portion
of doctor's face upside down.
'Sign manual of the well-run
clinic.' – *Scotsman*
'Induces Cheyne-Stokes respira-
tion and a Watts-Dunton anxiety.'
                              – *Lancet*

nothing whatever. Absolutely nothing, I'm sorry to say. Just go on as
if nothing has happened. What? Bed, that is my orders to you.'
All the time, Doctor is suggesting that his constitution, character,
inherited resistance, courage and will-power are in every way stronger
than Patient's.

Gambit Four is for Patient who wants to be made a fuss of. His
warts are painful. His neck is swollen. Make him feel a fool by
writing down everything he says. Thus:

MD-MAN: When did you first notice all this?
LAYMAN: My neck began to get a bit red . . . end of last month.
MD-MAN (*writing*): End of month . . . neck becomes red . . .
LAYMAN: They didn't really hurt till last week.
MD-MAN: After eighteen days . . . some discomfort. Yes. This is the
eighth case of false warts I've seen this week.
LAYMAN: What do you mean, false?
MD-MAN: Only the root is involved.

Modern Methodship

Many Doctors, of course, use Modern Methodship, which consists
in irritating or upsetting the patient by the totally irrelevant diagnostic

approach. E.g. In comes the man with warts. MD-man takes one glance at the warts and then asks him to lie down.

MD-MAN: Right. Relax. Now when did you first notice the warts?

LAYMAN: Oh, about . . . months ago.

MD-MAN: Right. Now try lifting the right leg slowly . . . down . . . now turn the foot sharply to the left – no, *left*. Now sit up. Up. Do you ever relax?

LAYMAN: Oh – *yes*.

MD-MAN: No – I mean every muscle, cheeks, nose, gums . . .

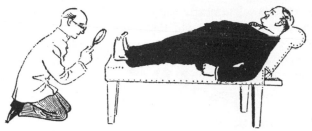

MD-MANSHIP

A simple method of making patient feel a fool. If he complains of ear-ache after bathing, examine his plantar surfaces.

The Totally Irrelevant Question can be brought in here. This is sometimes known as Allergyship.

MD-MAN: Tell me, what sort of nail varnish does your wife use?

LAYMAN (*beginning to get sour*): Not married.

MD-MAN: Not? Do you keep chickens under your bedroom window?

LAYMAN: Sloane Avenue Mansions doesn't encourage chickens.

MD-MAN: Of course not. Look, now, do you mind if I have a look at your fountain-pen? Yes, Thanks. (*Pause*). Yes.

Opposed to this is

Traditional Methodship

Traditional Methodship consists in blurting out every now and then something about 'what she wants isn't psycho-howsit or even deep-ray thingummy but a good slap on the whatsisname'. If Patient turns out to be really ill after all, it is always possible to look grave and proud at the same time, and say, 'You realize, I suppose, that twenty-five years ago you'd have been dead?'[1]

[1] We are working at the moment on a new and somewhat contrasted technique of alarming patients, which we call the Factor of Uncertain Trust.

The Need for Organized Patientship

It will be seen that the whole doctor-patient situation bristles with difficulties for the layman. But is it not precisely this kind of problem – this apparently fixed one-upness of doctors – which we of LCC like best to tackle?

In homely language, how can the Patient get back?

Divers approaches to the problem were attempted in the early days, only to be discarded. It used to be thought that it would curb the Doctor's high spirits to be asked if, after diagnosing mumps, he 'would mind bringing in another opinion'. But it was soon discovered that the doctor's solemn expression concealed a delight in being able to get an extra fee for poor old Pettinglass.

Some success is reported from married couples who have trained their youngest child to say in a clear voice, 'Mummy, I don't like that man' whenever a doctor comes into the room. This is now not much used.

Marvellous Little Manship

This is a proved doctor-irritant, especially if the ploy is executed by a well-dressed woman patient visiting Harley Street address of physician holding dignified position at London Hospital – one who prides himself particularly on never being guilty of Harleyship *per se*.

Recommended dialogue runs as follows:

LIFEWOMAN: I was wondering whether that marvellous little man in Curzon Street would be able to help me, Doctor?

In its present rough state we keep it to a footnote. The doctor adopts a man-to-man attitude, and admits right away that he is not quite sure. To give the wording advised by our visiting Welbeck Demonstrator, C. Hobbs:

MD-MAN: Let's have a look at these warts. (*Begins to whistle a slow tune*) They *are* warts, are they? But isn't there something that looks rather like a wart which you have to take out, or something? Wait a minute – where's my book? Where's Price – big red – here it is. Funny, they haven't got anything about warts in the index. Some long-winded medical word, I suppose . . . here's something. Oh, yes, it says: 'Inject with novo-phosthene.' Do you mind if I just look that up? Little grey book somewhere. No, I haven't got novo-phosthene, but I've got something damned like it. Damned like it. Now, we're supposed to use a squeegee. Oh Lord, I haven't used one of those things for years. Supposed to put it under the tap. All these 'do's' and 'don'ts'. Now then . . . . Now look, you're going to help me. If you'd just mind pushing . . . (*begins a jolly laugh*) Go on, push against it! Push!

A refinement of this gambit has just been received from Ireland. If Price is missing from the Doctor's shelf, as it probably will be, let him take down a book titled in large letters *Veterinary Surgery*. Or, better still, (S. Casey suggests) *A Simple Manual for Dog Lovers*.

HARLEYMAN: Oh yes? What little man?
LIFEWOMAN: Olaf Pepacanek. *How* do you pronounce it?
HARLEYMAN: I'm afraid I've never heard of him.
LIFEWOMAN: Oh, but he's a most marvellous man – he *weighs* everything. He says that English doctors don't realize that what he calls the square foods and the round foods can cancel each other out. He's written a book.
HARLEYMAN: Oh yes.
LIFEWOMAN: It's called *Bricks Without Straw*.
HARLEYMAN: Oh yes.

This is often quite irritating. Our Wimpole Reader, Gattling-Fenn, is working on what he calls rather long-windedly the Patient's Deskside Manner Counter to the Doctor's Bedside Approach. In the consulting-room, the doctor is tapping Gattling's chest. Gattling exudes a confident cheerfulness.

DOCTOR: (*Taps*).
GATTLING: Tap away.
DOCTOR: Now the back.
GATTLING: Thorough is as thorough does. You chaps certainly put us through the hoop nowadays.
DOCTOR: Say ninety-nine.
GATTLING: Dial 999, yes? (*Sings*) I'm ninety-nine today, I'm ninety-nine today.
DOCTOR: Keep still, please.
GATTLING: Still as a mouse.
DOCTOR: Quiet.
GATTLING (*Pause, begins to laugh*): I suppose it's all necessary, but my great-uncle was a bit of a sawbones. Doctors were doctors in those days. Anyhow, I know *he* was able to take his old wooden stethoscope and diagnose lobar pneumonia through two woollen vests and a horse-hair overcoat in thirty seconds dead.[1]

Under examination, Gattling would counter the danger of nudeship ('the natural one-downness of the unclothed'[2]) by arranging telephone calls direct to the consulting-room carefully timed to coincide with the maximum unclothed condition. He had himself rung by an aristocratically confident female voice and would then become involved in a long conversation, obviously with some wealthy and attractive girl, and burst out twice into long telephone laughter,

[1] *Lancet*-sponsored phrasing.
[2] Many will recognize this as the phrase inscribed under the dome of the Hunterian amphitheatre at St George's Hospital.

slapping his bare thigh and shouting: 'This is colossal! Tell me more!' (Bell.)

Further minor counter-doctor ploys are:

GMC-manship, defined as the 'playing on the doctor's fears of seeming to seek either publicity or kudos for medical qualifications which in fact he does not possess'.

It is possible to throw doubt on the very term doctor – 'I am, I suppose, right in calling you "Doctor"?' Again, if the doctor asks, 'Don't you think your symptoms have a psychological basis?' (always a weak ploy), reply at once, 'I had no idea that was one of your subjects. I have always wanted a good psycho-therapist.' Refuse to take in his worried assurance that he is not a trained psychiatrist. You 'will tell your friends' about him.

Under this same heading, if Doctor tells Patient that he has been spending the week-end in deepest Bucks where he saw, say, Bob Hope and his niece, Patient can reply: 'Hope told me, and – surprise for you! – that snap Babette took of you and Bob joking together with a stethoscope in the bathing-pool is being published in the *Tatler*.'

In contrast with this there is:

Title Play, which consists in annoying your personal consultant by pretending to think that all doctors like titled patients. Talk in what is called the Titles Voice about your friend Max Bodenheim who has just been flown over to Dublin to have a look at the Connemaras' little girl and her tiresome attack of thrush. Even if this does not irritate your doctor it will certainly get him off beat. Some Lifemen add: 'I must see if I can get you one or two little plums like that.'

Certain patients, expecially at Christmas-time or on other festive occasions, go to extraordinary lengths to make the doctor feel awkward after a consulting-room examination. When re-dressing, for instance, they will roll their collar-stud under the doctor's couch, grope for it, and appear to 'find' either a small medicine bottle half-full of creme de menthe, or a set of false teeth embedded in a meringue.[1] It only remains to ask. 'Are these yours?' in a plonking tone of voice, and the usual results follow.

Specialist Counter-Lifepatient Play

An intensely effective ply often used by M D-men but overlooked in their published researches is for Doctor to treat Patient not only

[1] Both supplied by Lifemanship Accessories, Ltd.

as if he knew nothing about medicine but as if Patient were as ignorant of all anatomical knowledge as a child of four. Often MD-men will give totally unnecessary technical names and then explain them – e.g. 'that mild rhinitis of yours: sniffles to you'. However determined the Lifepatient may be to show his knowledge, the trained MD-man will get him down in the end. Using the Warts background again, the dialogue might go like this:

LIFEPATIENT (*knowledging*): I came to you because trivial as the condition looks there was this distinct œdematous area under the warts.

MD-MAN: Yes, it is a bit puffy. Tell me, does it go *Pong*-pong, *Pong*-pong?

LIFEPATIENT: You mean does it throb? Are the growths vascular?

MD-MAN: Now don't you worry about that. You see, the heart is a sort of pump—

LIFEPATIENT: Yes-please-but . . .

MD-MAN: It goes squeez-o, squeez-o – no, look at my hand.

LIFEPATIENT: I am, but—

MD-MAN: And the blood isn't just blood, it's full of little soldiers, all fighting against each other.

LIFEPATIENT: Yes.

MD-MAN: Have you ever been in the army?

LIFEPATIENT: Well, no, but—

MD-MAN: You've heard the word 'corpuscles'. Those are the white fellows and the red chaps. Now this is how the battle begins. At the source of the infection – where Something's Wrong—

Even experienced Lifepatients can be silenced in the end by this treatment. Easier to deal with is the Harleyman who tries to put you in your place when you go to him for a stiff neck by suggesting that you are being rather trivial and he is feeling rather tired, 'up all night transfusing a couple of touch-and-go cases of thrombocytopenic purpura'.

It is always possible for Lifepatient to reply: 'I'm sorry to have bothered you with this apparently trivial thing, but my friend Eddie Webb-Johnson[1] persuaded me to go to a really competent general physician if I could find one. He prodded me about for twenty minutes or so and told me to let him know the results of a more careful examination; and who was doing it, what were his qualifications, and so on.

'By the way – just to stop him bothering – what are your qualifications?'

[1] Or some equally absolutely OK medical name.

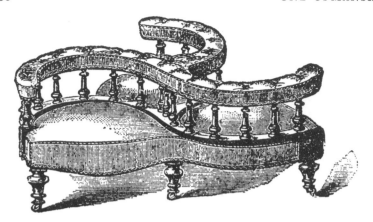

HUNTER-DAWSON'S 'TRI-TRY'
(For taking second opinion)

Custy's Ploy of Poise

There is no doubt that the best of all counter-doctor techniques is some application of the vast Poise Gambit which we are elaborating now for inclusion in Volume IV. Perfected by Miss Antigone Cust, it consists in the overcoming of any crisis by the fixing of the profile in one of six recommended positions and the maintaining, however urgent the cue for a reply, of almost complete silence.[1] The sole word which Miss Cust allows herself to utter is some admonition, spoken in a slightly American intonation, to 'relax'.

The only answer to this gambit so far evolved by our countership department and recommended for doctors is to say either (*a*) 'I haven't relaxed for sixteen years' or (*b*) 'What are you poised *for*?'

[1] Beginners in 'profiling', as it is called, are reminded that Miss Cust owes her success to the possession of perfect classical features. The gambit should not be attempted by others whose noses are (*a*) button- or (*b*) blob-shaped.

3

BUSINESSMANSHIP

YEOVIL'S SCHOOL of Businessmanship is not yet fully formed. It is a strange fact, which we here state in all frankness and without criticism, that vast as are its resources, the business world has made small contribution to our funds. 'We invented Lifemanship before you were born,' said a bulk-buyer of synthetic soup by-products to me the other day, and this conveys the attitude of the whole business community. 'Certainly,' said his friend, who disposed of the residue of the soup by-products, which he patented as compressed fuel. 'And didn't we invent the word Salesmanship?'

'Yes, and Chairmanship too,' said a heavy-jowled older man, who bought up the remains of the residue of this soup by-product for his firm 'Natural Broths, Ltd'.

And of course one must sympathize with this view. 'Businessmanship = Salesmanship = Lifemanship' ... and yet. At any rate, when the concrete request came for guidance, a request from the business quarter of New York City, we were glad to add this youngest of all our student courses to our schedule.

Lifemanship Principle of Negative Selling

What is our approach? On the wall of Commercial Corner, in the East Wing of our College, there hangs a picture. It is taken from the wrapper of a popular American Salesmanship Manual.[1]

[1] This is the only picture in our Business lecture-room, because it can be used to illustrate the right and wrong methods of Salesmanship and anything else as well. E.g. I am sometimes asked, Is there a Lifeman's put-off for insurance salesman? Yes, there is, and this picture demonstrates it. In Method One, the 'prospect' (left) is countering the insurance salesman (right) by a sudden stream of praise for insurance policies in general and a suggestion, since the salesman earns his living by talking, that *he* should insure either (a) his hard palate or (b) his right fist, essential in forceful speech and especially liable to accident. In Method Two, Prospect (right) is asking

Look at the picture. On the left is a figure full of the confidence of the man who knows his job and knows it is well done. The Salesman.

THE 'ALL-PURPOSE PICTUREGRAM'
(*See text*)

('It's men like you we want.'
Alternatively
'It's men like me you want.')

On the right is the prospective client, the 'Prospect', his eagerness to buy only matched by his astonished admiration of this fine and courageous personality who is hypnotizing him into a deal which his reason abhors. That is the implied interpretation.

There you have the business of Business. But in Businessmanship the roles must be reversed. The sitting figure on the *right* is the salesman, trained by us in that bungling diffidence which alone can infuse confidence into the buyer and fill him with certainty that this feeble sap before him couldn't get the better of a milk pudding.

The No-Pen Approach

For our first simple lesson we demonstrate the basic gambit of the No-Pen Approach – easy phrase to remember. Childishly primary, it yet embodies Lifemanship's Principle of Negative Selling.

Lay businessmen when they are anxious – typical business incident – to persuade a client to sign some document containing a clause which on closer inspection will be seen to be to the client's disadvantage, sometimes do it like this. With the document on the desk, the dialogue follows some such Wrong Course as this:

Lay BUSINESSMAN: I think you'll find everything quite in order, Mr Fortinbras.

FORTINBRAS: Oh yes, but what about the—

LB (*oiling in*): You did want us to keep mutually independent? Now, you sit here.

---

salesman (left) if he would mind continuing the conversation at home, take pot-luck with his aunts, and give a comic recitation to help entertain the displaced children of the Papercutters' Orphanage – 'they're quite all right if you know how to handle them, and we ought to be back before 1 a.m.'

FORTINBRAS (*puzzled*): Something about 'giving you right of transference'?

LB: That's right.

FORTINBRAS (*suspicious*): Yes, but—

LB: Now, if you just put your name where I pencilled it in. I think you'll find my pen in working order . . .

What is wrong? The untrained businessman is standing ready with a gleaming fountain-pen full of rich ink. He is hovering. He is amiable. Client is put on the defensive, and ten to one he will begin to ask questions.

Contrast now the *Lifemanship-trained* Businessman in the same position. Once more the document is on the table, all ready for Mr Fortinbras.

BUSINESS LIFEMAN: I think this is the thing you're supposed to sign.

MR FORTINBRAS: I beg your pardon?

BL: Only for goodness' sake let's make sure. Must get my secretary to tidy my desk.

F. (*amused*): Well, here's my name, anyhow.

BL: Let's try and take it in. (*Reading very slowly*) 'Whereas the party hereinafter called the copyholders shall within the discretion of both signatories' – can't understand a word.

F. (*almost paternal already*): Let me. I'm used to this sort of jargon. 'The parties assigned . . .'

BL: Look. Wonderful, isn't it? (*They laugh*).

F. (*taking charge*): That's right, and I'm supposed to sign these – paragraphs individually, aren't I?

BL: Oh? I mean *yes*. Awfully sorry, don't seem to have a pen (*rustles through papers*). I'm most awfully sorry, I've got a new secretary. Josephine! Probably at Coffee. Typical.

F.: It's all right, I've got a pen.

BL (*keen for the first time*:): Oh, isn't that the new sort that writes on ice, or something? Marvellous little thing. Can I look at it? Sorry, after you.

'Sorry', because client is already in the act of signing the document. The client is helping. To make assurance doubly sure in this technique, it is no bad thing if businessman actually puts client's borrowed pen into his own pocket, after admiring it, as if by mistake. Client now leaves, not only having signed the paper but full of a queer sort of confidence. This signature technique was first perfected by Lumer Farr, and it is known as Lumer's Bumbling Approach.[1]

---

[1] In Missouri a fine parallel ploy is in use, invented by St Louis's First Lifeman, G. Palen – 'St Louis One', to give him his proper title. To execute the ploy, used in first business contacts, the Lifesalesman 'should be meticu-

This negative fountainpenmanship sets the note of our course. We teach the students to remember that it is only men *below* the highest quality in any firm who take exact measurements of the carpet in their office room to make sure it is not narrower than Y's or less thick than Z's. But in Supreme Boss-ship we always teach plainness, simplicity and downright ordinariness. No Yeovil-trained managing director ever dreams of being seen behind a desk clanking with telephones, loudspeakers, soft speakers, buzzers, little flashing lights, and silver boxes overflowing with splendid cigarettes and engraved with the signatures of supposedly affectionate colleagues. No. Take Lumer Farr, Yeovil-trained Vice-president (lifeword for Complete Boss) of International Packing Cases. 'You'd never think,' I have heard people say, 'that Lumer Farr controlled three-quarters of the crude teak export trade of Canada.' Actually he didn't, *but why should anyone think he did?*

Lumer likes to be called 'The Guv'nor', but likes it to be thought that he likes to be called 'Bert'.[1] He creeps about in a little black coat. His desk is a plain deal table with nothing on it whatever. The only telephone in the room is an old-fashioned candlestick one in the corner with a winder. He gets up and answers it himself about twice during the morning. Guarding his room, of course, there are ranks and ranks of fashionable men and women and women dressed as secretaries, whose function it is to be extremely busy and to keep anybody except some n'er-do-well nephew[2] from ringing up or speak-

lously dressed, perhaps in a Homburg'. And then present not a shiny clean business card but *one which has been torn, stained with coffee, apparently dipped in beer, sticky on the back, and almost torn in half*. After giving card, Missouri asks for it back *'as it is my only one'*. This lulling tactic is said to soften the hardest business heart, and when he was younger G. Palen, then first using his broken card, is said to have received many offers of *free financial help* from real-estate executives and leading industrialists, including many in chemical research.

[1] In the science of Christian-naming, Lumer is associated with Farr's Law of Mean Familiarity. This can be expressed by a curve, but is much clearer set down as follows:

The Guv'nor addresses
Co-director Michael Yates as	MIKE
Assistant director Michael Yates as	MICHAEL
Sectional manager Michael Yates as	MR YATES
Sectional assistant Michael Yates as	YATES
Indispensable secretary Michael Yates as ..	MR YATES
Apprentice Michael Yates as	MICHAEL
Night-watchman Michael Yates as	MIKE

[2] Lumer's 'Ploy of the Ridiculously Soft Heart'. He always says, 'Suppose I'd better speak to the young scallywag.' But he has never actually given him either help or money.

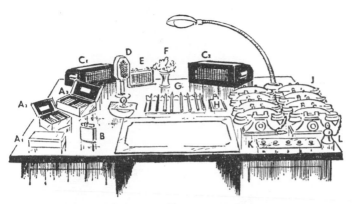

MANAGING DIRECTOR'S DESK
(a) Wrong.

ing to Lumer. These rebuffs in which he has trained this group are delightfully contrasted with Lumer's occasional bemused and affable appearances at the doorway of his office, when he may ask you himself to come in, and apologizes for the lack of courtesy with which you have been treated. Then he will fumble out a broken packet and offer you a twisted cigarette.

Lumer is always slipping out of the room and slipping into the room in a way which is supposed to be unnoticed, but which in fact everybody is supposed to notice. Whe he gets out of a car or a plane, or even coming out of the theatre, he will slip quietly away, head down, as if he were avoiding a reporter. And quite late at night he will be seen, by arrangement, alone at this empty desk, on the plain deal chair.

2. COMMITTEESHIP

I have enunciated a general principle: let me now outline the work of one of our study circles, Committeeship.

It is axiomatic that Committeeship is the art of coming into a discussion without actually understanding a word of what anybody is talking about. But this entry can only be made effective if the speaker *decides what sort of person he, the speaker, is, and sticks to it.* The sort doesn't much matter, consistency is what counts; but the following committeeship types are especially recommended:

Type One, MULSIPRAT. The man who, pretty high and perhaps

MANAGING DIRECTOR'S DESK
(b) Right.

chairman, is yet rather muddled. At the same time he is never in a
flap about his mistakes, but says, 'There I go again' or 'There's another of my beauts.'[1] This is endearing and in fact the point of
Mulsiprat is being adored by everybody. He may employ two special
secretaries, one male and one female, whose exclusive difficult duty
is to[2] obviously adore him.

Type Two, GALEAD, is also rather mad. But this rather-madmanship
is of a totally different sort. Galead is manic, never cuts nails, has one
shoe-lace undone, wears new jackets *with one button missing*, reveals
faint tremor of the left hand, chain-smokes (dummy nicotine stains
may be varnished on to the backs of the fingers). He sometimes adds
to this a speech-disability-sign – e.g. starting every remark with a
long downward-cadence whistle – it (*whistle*) 'cures my stammer'.

In committee he is the permanently 'difficult' one: '(*Whistle*) Yes,
but *how*?' Early in the meeting he finds himself in definite disagree-

[1] May I gratefully acknowledge that the wording here, and certain other
ploys in this section, were hacked out in committee with a dissatisfied group
of low-ranking members of the editorial staff of *Fortune*.

[2] For our lifesponsored split infinitive, see our next publication, *Womanship*,
1954.

ment with the Chairman and Managing Director on some minor issue, which makes it all the easier for him to be overwhelmingly on their side round about lunch-time.

Type Three, LUDLOW, is the tremendously ordinary chap, valuable because he is in close touch with tremendously ordinary people and can, himself, talk tremendously ordinarily.[1] We can't do without Ludlow, because he is the man in the street.

Type Four, MAIDENHAIR, we draw especial attention to because he represents a totally new type, of high value, as we believe, and something we are perhaps rather specially proud of, because he has been developed entirely through Lifemanship-sponsored organizations. He is the man not in the street. Sometimes he has taken a First or possibly read a biography of Verdi.

DIAGRAM OF MAN IN THE STREET

Type Five, TEMPESTRIAN, is not brilliant at all but sensible. He counters suggestions of brilliant-type Maidenhair by saying 'Yes, but don't let's forget the picture. What, after all, are we trying to sell?'

DIAGRAM OF
MAN NOT IN
THE STREET
(Reduced
scale)

Type Six, CO-AX, is in a way wicked, or at any rate puts business first and says so. In the world of journalism he is so hard-boiled about tender feelings that rival committeemen are thought to feel awe. His voice is thin and waxy. 'What we want on this page here,' he says, 'is a picture of a displaced crippled sick orphan of exiled alien parents and plug it for all we're worth.' One day, we were discussing the insertion of a rather daring portrait of fairly pretty Paulette O. in our little mag. 'Page Three,' Co-ax said,

[1] Not to be confused with the man who talks tremendously ordinarily to children. See *Lifemanship* ('Week-endmanship').

TCU—G

hard-boiling. 'We want sex on page three, nine inches by eight. Always assuming that we have a story about cruelty to animals on page seven.' This always goes down particularly well with the shyer shareholders, who may be strong family men and churchwardens. 'Co-ax knows his job,' they say afterwards, downing their small gin-and-limes in one.

Type Seven, HOSPITER, can be any of the foregoing, and yet none. He is the natural counter-committeeman, the underminer. It is not what he is, but what he says, that matters.

Hospiter Parlettes, many of them silent, are as follows:

(*a*) When rival committeeman is speaking:

i. Look sadly at boots (it is best to have actual boots).

ii. Doodle and continue to doodle with the faintest possible deepening of the corners of the mouth. Try to suggest that you see something irresistibly inappropriate or comic in what your rival is saying, but wild horses wouldn't make you spoil his little speech by mentioning it now. This delicate and highly expert ploy was first described to me independently by H. Whyte and F. Anderson, and named by the latter the 'Mona Lisa Ploy'.

(*b*) When rival committeeman has finished speaking, say:

i. 'Well, we sort of came to a decision about that, didn't we, after a fairly full discussion last week, a rather good discussion, I thought. I mean we agree.' Or alternatively say:

ii. 'Well' (*pause and look hard at chairman, as if only you and he knows this*), 'there are definite reasons why that is going to become impracticable fairly shortly, aren't there?'

Or say:

iii. 'Yes, but we have got to think of the effect on the ordinary nice people we meet in the street. They are not terribly brainy, but they are quite nice people really.'

If rival makes obviously good bold and original point, counter it

(i) by saying: 'Yes, I think that's a good idea – I wonder if we were right to discard it five years ago when there was all that row.' Or

(ii) if you can only think of something conventional and commonplace as alternative, *make* your flat suggestion in an 'of course I'm completely mad' voice (*Flairship*) and add: 'I know you'll think I'm making a fool of myself, but I think some of us are bound to make fools of ourselves before anything really happens, don't you?' Or

(iii) simply say: 'Yes, but that isn't really what we're discussing, is it?'

Regil and the Economics Ploy

Type Eight, REGIL,[1] is different from all the foregoing if only because he knows, if possible, less about the subject under discussion, and the business of the committee generally, than anybody else present. He is rather like Maidenhair, the First in Classics, except that the general impression is that Regil took a First in Economics.

Regil invariably creates an economics wicket by referring everything to the social or monetary sciences. He often speaks of 'structured behaviour' and uses the phrase 'inner directed', frequently mixing it, according to Whyte of Manhattan, with a colloquialism ('He's pretty much of an inner-directed guy').

Regil, however, certainly comes into his best on his own subject, economics – 'the plonking science', as Matthew Arnold called it; and it is generally agreed that almost any phrase from any chapter of this extraordinary subject will meet any emergency, if the sentences are spelt out sufficiently slowly and clearly.

Sometimes, of course, Regil, especially after a short snifter, enjoyed himself with a little wild incomprehensibility (*Economics Approach A*).

'If you want to influence the general liquidity situation of banks *and* public,' he would say, pretending to expect a reply. 'If you do,' he would go on, 'I think you're forgetting that the Bank of England's discretionary action on the cash basis took the shape of dealings in Treasury Bills, the market rate of discount on which could *and did* fluctuate.'

Regil would firm up his voice a good deal on 'did fluctuate'. But he was always at his best, I thought, on the more classical *Economics Approach B* (the 'Approach of Utter Obviousness').

This 'stupefaction of the exhaustingly clear' (Watertower) was used by Regil at moments of some crisis. 'I'm not going to tell you why most demand curves slope downwards,' he would begin, as a paralyser. Then he would become clear, in that frightful way of his. 'Unless something happens to change the state of demand,' he said, as if he was quoting, and incredibly enough he was, 'more will be bought at any given price than at any higher price.'

Another pause, before the next sentence, when his voice became so cuttingly audible it seemed to pass straight to the centre of my head

[1] These titles may have some religious or cosmographical significance, or they may be the names of the first eight losers backed by us in the Yeovil Handicap, Spring 1952.

and short-cut the organs of comprehension completely: 'Any rise in price WILL REDUCE THE VOLUME OF SALES.'

Suddenly he was quiet again, for the homely instance:

'When a child enters a shop to buy a pennorth of bull's-eyes, *by the mere fact of asking for the bull's-eyes it incurs a debt of one penny.* Look—'

I knew this 'look' of Regil's. It was the prelude to a sort of Economics Oration, which we were all too hypnotized to interrupt:

'Look, and what do you see?'

Generally I saw the ash-tray, steaming with unfinished cigarettes.

'You see the farm labourer in the fields, tending the cattle to be marketed. The factory workers controlling the machines, feeding them with raw materials which they *transform into manufactured produce.* The miner is extracting mineral deposits from the earth, the clerk is recording transactions in the office, transport workers are moving persons and goods from one place to another. By cable and wireless instructions are transmitted with amazing speed . . .'

And so it went on. The fact that most of us were always complaining of telephone delays, and that none of us had ever actually seen any of these things (except perhaps Rusper, the clerk), didn't stop Regil from having another of his recurrent successes, from flattening the committee into respectful silence, and from mounting, with one foot on 'produce' and another on 'goods', yet one more rung on Businessmanship's difficult ladder.

4

CORRESPONDENCE COLLEGE

DEPARTMENT OF ART

THE COMPLETE printed syllabus of our courses is available through the usual channels, but as the two schools I have so far described are both vocational, I am anxious to reassure readers that the Arts are not neglected at Yeovil. On the contrary, I doubt whether there is any department in which new ground is more obviously broken.

The Doing of the Doing

Whereas most universities teach the history, function, practice and criticism of drama, music and the plastic arts, no attention whatever is given 'to the doing of the doing' – i.e. to that natural one-upness which even the Lifeman visitor to theatre or concert can so unobtrusively suggest, and which the actual Life-artist, the creator, assumes as a natural right. How often do we not find, in the pre-Games lifemanship era, that the artist is actually one down?

De-Slading and Counter RADA-ship

Painters, writers and actors particularly find, to take one example, that our Corrective Course, for ex-students of the best establishments, is a blessing. 'Opens a new world in a fortnight,' wrote one.

Take a would-be writer who has just taken a First-class Honours in English Language and Literature at Oxford – Balliol, typically. What chance has he got of success in an author's career compared, say, to a tramp, a Lieutenant-General, or a photographer of East African animals?

Or take the RADA-man – the dramatic student. He may have been trained and passed with Honours in basic movement, including basic sitting-down, a silver medallist in basic door-shutting, basic speech,

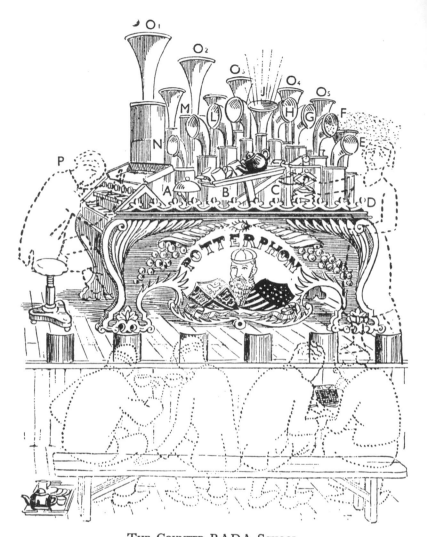

The Counter RADA School

This drawing of the Potterphon, evolved for our Founder by F. Wilson for teaching students to act the mad scene in *Hamlet* under conditions of mean average distraction, is self-explanatory. Students will note (A) bell for simulating fire-engines passing down Shaftesbury Avenue; (B) tea-tray rattler; (C) paper-bag crumpler; (D) student-actress speaking the line 'Here's rosemary, that's for remembrance'; (E) icy blast from wings; (F) dust from flies; (G) whiff of grease-paint; (H) whiff of beer; (J) tea attendants saying they haven't got change; (L) sweet-sucking; (M) orange-sucking, with whiff; (N) distant voice calling, 'Star News Standard'; (O 1–5) coughs, whispers, etc., controlled by mixer; (P) the Founder; (Q–T) inattentive audition-holders.

basic silence and basic basic. But these accomplishments can scarcely be said to put him in the one-up position or make a Chapter Two for the theatrical autobiography which we generally recommend should be written at the age of twenty-four.

Humble Startship

No. For genius-ship, a smooth beginning is fatal. In our Edmund Kean Wing we roughen these young actors, we put them through a course of Crummlesship. In the constant smell of grease-paint, sprayed through special nozzles powered by diesel fans, we let them mingle with the dust of a typical green-room (painted by the Brothers Harker). They learn to juggle, to walk the tight-rope, to wander about in the flies, to go without food for thirty-six hours, while they wait to fetch pints of beer for a drunken stage-manager who teaches them nothing except how to receive an oath and a cuff.[1] We teach the girls while still in the dingy lodgings and unhealthy surroundings which we provide, to step at one hour's notice, still rubbing embrocation on bruises pitifully redolent of stout, into some performance of, say, Beatrice in *Much Ado* or Bridget in *While The.*[2] Between the acts they eat dummy steak and onions and drink a pint of porter, then go home to the wretched apartment of the travelling mummer. They may be RADA-women up to golden goblet standards, but they will still be able to say, and feel, that once, in the beginning, they were struggling in the hardest school of all.

Counter-Slading

A basically similar though outwardly totally different course is given to young art students who have been Slading away for three years, admirably taught, of course, Antique and Life, who have spent the correct number of vacations in Paris and even enjoyed the fruits of a Prix de Rome, thereby shutting themselves off apparently irretrievably from contact with the people, humble startship, naïve-ship and spontaneous folk art.

Here again we supply the humble start and set them to work locally, in the signal-box at the level-crossing by the back of our garden, for instance, where they have no time, labouring fourteen

[1] The post of this 'stage-manager' is filled by Leonard Moppet of Buttermere.

[2] We encourage professionally abbreviated names of the plays of Shakespeare and Rattigan (*While the Sun Shines*). Actually, we shorten them even more, sometimes calling *Much Ado, Much.*

hours a day at the clerical duties of assistant-signalman, to think of easel and palette. Yet their art will begin to show itself in the decorations they will add, naïvely bold, painted on the gateposts of the level-crossing, or in chalk drawings of village wedding scenes rubbed on the back of the routine reports of changes in the railway time-table or dossiers of local goods trains. These we make a point of discovering after three months, whereupon, in little less than ten years, the new artist has slightly more chance of placing his work in Bond Street, or at any rate of being noticed in Park Crescent.

5

A NOTE ON EXHIBITIONSHIP[1]

The following paragraphs were issued at the request of the Arts Council on the occasion of the closing of the South Bank. We reprint them here unaltered.

'EXHIBITIONSHIP' IS the name for the various ploys and gambits connected with the art of being, or seeming to be, a visitor to an exhibition. It is not the art of exhibiting (Barryship).

The basic gambit is of course the achievement of the state of one-upness on the rest of the public. A word of advice, then, perhaps particularly to the foreigner – always welcomed to our country by the lifeman – on certain simple methods of visiting an exhibition.

Classical Wrong Approach

Though there are confusing exceptions to this rule, British visitors to London go to exhibitions as a duty, not a pleasure. Note at the Zoo the fixed smile of the mother, determined to get through with it good-humouredly. Note, in the Egyptian Room of the British Museum, how grim the father and how quivering the elder sister. 'Stand still, Frank,' she says. Or, 'You'll spoil everything,' to an innocent child who is quietly fermenting, having been fed on nothing but starch since they all left Colchester by bus at six in the morning.

This is classical Wrong Approach. To be out of the ruck, be gay. Come into the Egyptian Room, if necessary, with a smile and a wink. Roar with laughter as you approach the neolothic flints. If with a young child, it is possible to increase this effect and sustain your reputation for child management at the same time by occasionally feeding it with the special glucose sweets we supply – dashed with opium or some other not quite harmless somniferent. 'I think it's because we never say Don't, you say to a group of friends who are admiring the child's acquiescence. 'She is rather sweet, isn't she?'

[1] I am going to make no mention in this note of 'Bonding', as it is miscalled, because this is dealt with in a special pamphlet Y.16, 'Bonding for Beginners', which deals with what to say at the Redfern, what to say at the Lefevre and what to say at the Leicester, and other Bond Street Galleries not in Bond Street.

Practise on the Tate

It is as well to practise all gambits on the permanent museums and exhibits before approaching any special collections or centenary shows.

Practise in the Tate Gallery, for instance, not to shuffle grimly from picture to picture, not to hang one methodical minute before each exhibit. To achieve the one-up position, let it be known that you have 'come to see the Steers'. This refers of course to Steer the artist. Say that there is one particular Steer of a luminous seascape with a patch of elephant grey (do not say 'a small battleship') on the horizon and if it is not on view it must be in the vaults and can you please have access to them.

It is a fairly good gambit, certainly at the Tate, to be friendly with the attendants. At any rate, address them by some name such as 'Kemp', and say, 'Good morning, Kemp. Is Mr Laver in today?' 'Mr Laver' is what is called an 'OK exhibition name'. Or you can say, 'Good afternoon, McIndoe, have you seen Sir Kenneth?'

With pictures, and with art in general, it is rather a good thing not to go to the places where everybody else goes. E.g. avoid the air-conditioned room at the National Gallery unless you can say that you personally had a hand in mixing the air or advise on the mean warmed-upness. Change the subject and talk instead about something almost completely inaccessible.

'Have you ever seen that little collection at the Walthamstow Waterworks?' you can ask. 'Chiefly Saxon, of course, Saxon coins picked out of the King's Scholars' Pond Sewer. The design is debased Roman, and if you are as absurdly keen on debased Roman as I am, you won't grudge an hour or two at Walthamstow.'

Be fairly ruthless, I think, with opponents of 'modern' painting. If you are lucky enough to find a man who still says: 'I don't know about pictures, but I know what I like,' point out to him that because he does not know about pictures he does not know what he likes, and repeat this in a thundering voice. If he whimpers back something about it all being too advanced for him, point out exactly how many years Cézanne died before he was born, and the precise date of the exhibition of the first Modiglianis in London. Exaggerate both these dates and say, 'After all, Matisse and your great-grandmother are exact contemporaries.' If your man says of some picture, 'Yes, but what does it mean?' ask him, and keep on asking him, what his carpet means, or the circular patterns on his rubber shoe-soles. Make him lift up his foot to look at them.

The safest subject for criticism is the accuracy of the descriptive notice. At Kew Gardens it is no bad thing, when wandering through the shades of the collection of elm-tree species, to read out 'Ulmus flavescens' from the label and say, 'It's not, now, classified as a true elm at all,' Or with a display of musical instruments, better still, read out 'Violin by Armedio, 1760–1820,' and then say, '1760, or course, is complete and utter guesswork.'

It is always possible, when in doubt, to 'criticize the lack of information for ordinary simple people like myself'.

Another useful ploy is to criticize something for what it isn't, even if what it isn't isn't what it is trying to be.

For example, take an exhibition of beautiful books. The basic gambit (since the object of the exhibition is to demonstrate the æsthetic quality of the type, binding, etc.) is to say *plonkingly* that 'To me personally a book is something to be read.'

You can then pick up three books at random and say of No. 1 that 'you'd like to read it if you could see the wood for the trees'; of No. 2 that 'the binding is certainly expensive, but does the book fall open *easily and naturally?*' and of No. 3 (*Paradise Lost*, printed in italics) you can say, 'Of course, if you like reading poetry at an angle . . . but after ten pages I should be in italics myself.' You can raise a laugh by leaning sideways when saying this.[1]

In the same way, at the pottery part of an exhibition it is always possible to say, 'What a pity there is no example of Leeds glaze.'

When looking at plants or animals in any kind of Natural History show or zoo or gardens just say: 'Oh, but it is not the same . . . not the same behind bars.' You can say that all round the rock garden at Kew, for instance:

'Pyrenean Iris. Oh yes, yes, yes, but terrible. Terrible if one has ever been overcome by the miracle of this thing bravely clasping the crevice of the perpendicular cliff-face at Luchesse – terrible to see it here, tamed and humbled by man.'

I like and recommend this gambit.

Special Exhibition Play

For crowded buildings and special exhibitions remember, in general, that you are different from the crowd. For instance, if the

[1] Students must not be confused if, after reading this paragraph, they are left with a feeling that they are not quite certain which side they are meant to be on. If we are continually expected to take sides, that is the end of argument.

notice says 'TURN LEFT' instantly turn right. Do not trudge round in a crocodile. If there is an injunction to keep moving stand stock still, eyes fixed on the ceiling.

Again, to suggest that you have the artistically awakened eye and can form your own judgment which the lay-out and emphasis of the exhibition seem to demand, pause a long time before some object which has nothing to do with the exhibits – say a fire extinguisher or a grating in the floor through which warmed-up museum air rises – and say, 'The influence of William Morris, even here', or just, 'Now *that*, to me, is a beautiful object.'

The best way to praise the exhibition is to say, 'It's a great jaunt, a delightful affair and a huge success. Exhibitions always are a huge success.'

You can then criticize.

After showing that you yourself are a jolly and exhibition-minded person, and have enjoyed, in the old days at the White City, the model of the Astronomer Royal in margarine, you can then be generally nasty by complaining that this particular show lacks the indefinable something, the gaiety perhaps, of the Petit Palais Exhibition at Varence in 1931 (designed by Pompipier), or the feeling for Internationalism which one got frightfully from that wonderful Füldenbliegen Collection in the Rond Tor at Uppsala. Behaviouristically, one should be alert and clever, also an expert in exhibition technique. Know, especially if in the company of a varicose aunt, how to park your car three miles away and walk, because it saves time in the end. Know how to come in ten minutes before closing-time, because that is the only way to see the rooms in comfort, if rather quickly. Know how to avoid exhibition malaise, how to diet for exhibitions, and the importance of light salads with a touch of garlic, because the rooms will smell of garlic, anyhow. Know how to keep your mind off what you are looking at, and how to bring pass-the-time puzzles of the kind, for instance, where you separate two twisted nails.

Finally, remember that the best and most overwhelmingly one-up way to go to an exhibition with a person is to be in love with the person and for the person to be in love with you. It is no bad thing to hold hands with the person even if she is not in love with you, so long as she does not look grumpy. It is said, too, that people will instinctively make way for young, or fairly young, lovers. This also puts the exhibition to its right use, as a wooing ground. Experience will suggest how the permanent Exhibitions of London may be utilized.

MUSEUMSHIP: CLEARING THE CROWD
The 'All the World Makes Way for Lovers' ploy.

Use as guide Billington's OLD WICKET GATE list (Billington's Woo Aids) of Museum Meeting Grounds.

List entries include a brief description of the kind of girl whom it is suitable to arrange to meet in Room 6 (English Glass) at the V and A, or the quite different girl you meet by the Beaverbrook at the Tate. And the third type equally distinct in *climate of attraction*, the girl you will meet under the Epstein frieze at the St James's Park Tube Station.

Don't forget also that there is a fourth type of girl whom you will meet by the east entrance of the Zoological Gardens. You must use your own judgment whether to refer, jokingly, to the fact that the cages for the birds of prey adjoin the turnstile.

6

A NOTE ON LITMANSHIP

In a popular American biography of the Founder the following statement occurs: 'In tracing the evolution of Gamesmanship, too little stress is placed on Potter's early work The Muse in Chains *(? 1937). For the 'Eng. Lit.' described in the early chapters of this once-forgotten volume, prized item now in book sales, differs little from the Art of Knowing about English Literature Without Actually Reading Any Books – working definition of Litmanship as taught at Yeovil.'*

EVERY YEAR hundreds, nay thousands, of young lads and lasses pass through the English Literature courses in the universities of this island. How to help them?

Many students come to us when it is too late, their brains permanently damaged by the dread litticosis. 'But I have worked it, worked it out,' I once heard a lass of twenty continuously repeating. 'If I read all the books I am supposed to read, I shall be 187 years old before I . . . 187 . . .' The rest of the sentence was broken.[1]

Yet ten days later this lass was alert and happy, and was leaving our portals, a qualified Lifegirl, to face her Finals Year with new courage. I had noticed how different she looked after attending the first lecture by our Gorboduc Reader, on 'First Hand Knowledge My Foot'.

Before she left I asked, as she handed over her modest fee, what had particularly helped her.

'Textmanship,' she answered, with a shy smile.

Let us give you this one glimpse, then, of what had helped Josephine. Textmanship. How, that is, not only to write an essay[2] about,

---

[1] 'And what about Bandello?' I actually replied, with a grim smile, because we must suppose she was supposed to read the Italian Sources and the sources of the Sources too.

[2] Old Yeovillers will understand that in her first lecture Josephine will have been told how to talk about some classic novel – *Wuthering Heights* is taken as type of book student will have heard of but not read – and write

but to give detailed comments on the wording of an examination set book without having actually read it. This is known as Gobbetship.

Gobbetship

The gobbet, hitherto the bugbear of all examinations in English Literature, is a selection of quotations from a Set Book or Set Text. First we harden students, immunize them, against the intimidating wording of such examination questions. (*'State exactly what you know of the following, Do NOT answer more than SEVEN of the ASTER-ISKS.'*)

Then we teach them what to say. Specimen author, typically, Shakespeare. Specimen play, utterly typically, *Henry IV, Part Two*. Specimen orders: 'Annotate the following.' Specimen quotation for annotation might be, 'The slings and arrows of outrageous fortune', except that this is (*a*) miles too easy, and (*b*) from *Hamlet*. More probably a line like this purposely chosen to put you off:

WHO KEEPS THE GATE HERE, HO!

Faced with this ridiculous line, what is the examined Lifeboy to do? All that is necessary is to have read a précis of the plot. Then make use of

1. *The Character Ploy*, and write

One of Shakespeare's subtle touches. Note how even the request for a gate to be opened can reveal the impetuousness of the bluff speaker, the lordly peremptoriness of one accustomed to be obeyed.

Without even knowing the *name* of the speaker, it is possible to go on and on about character, e.g.

This play, full of warriors and their retainers, kings and lords, might be termed a study in the terminology of feudal modes of address.

(Students are recommended to learn above phrase by heart.)

2. *The Compression Ploy*

Quote from the Intro. to your school edition, starting 'This line';

This line is typical of Shakespeare's middle-to-late historical period in

---

about it (*a*) as if she had read all other possible novels of the same type ('Middle Period of the Novel of Passion') or (*b*) as if Brontë was a bit of a copy-cat ('she shows, in her rapid transition from the vast to the intimate, the influence, first, of the literary heirs of *Werther*, second, of the Burney school of domestic observation').

its compression (essence of poetry). Earlier, Shakespeare could well have written 'What ho!' instead of 'Ho!'

3. *Imagery Ploy*

Note how Shakespeare employs metaphors suitable to the soldier or the man 'in use of war's account'.[1] 'Keeps the gate – Keeps the watch' is the imagery of the military man.

4. *Ti-TUM Ti-TUM Ploy*

If you know that a regular blank-verse line is made up of five Ti-TUMS you can look for irregularities such as – here – the start with TUM-ti and say:

Note the reversed stress of the first foot, a rhythmic variation which Shakespeare allowed himself more and more frequently once he freed himself from the bonds of metre.

It is possible to intensify the effect of this rather thin comment by (*a*) being scholarly and referring to 18 per cent of TUM-ti openings and (*b*) by shooting off some OK prose. Thus:

With what gaiety Shakespeare shook off the chains of metre, drawing the fine Toledo blade of his poetic mastery from the rusty scabbard of rules.[2]

It is rather a good thing, in general, to be keen on Shakespeare's freedom from fetters, and when saying that he was not a thin-lipped scholar prying over books, to use

5. *The Essentially Theatre Ploy*

and say how bald and inexpressive the line books *read*, 'but speak it and the whole thing leaps to life. Sometimes we forget that *2 Henry IV* was a play, and to be acted.'

Less recommended and now definitely less OK, and in fact shelved for a few years, is

6. *The Voice of Shakespeare Ploy*

A pity, because it was always possible to say up to 1925 that any two consecutive words 'show Shakespeare's condition at this period'. Why, at this time, for instance, 'the reiterated suggestion of closed

---

[1] One can soon get the knack of making up Shakespearish quotations like above.

[2] Learn this by heart, too.

'Who Keeps the Gate Here, Ho!'
('Remember it's a play' section)
It was only when we began to act the line on our little stage that we realized
that the words should be spoken outside the door, not inside, as, wrongly,
here.

doors and castles, prisons and castellations? Is it not that impending
sense of claustrophobic doom and frustration which preceded
Shakespeare's tragic period?'

7. *'Shakespeare's Theatre' Ploy*

If by any miracle Lifeboy happens to know that this quotation is the
first line of the play, or even if not, he can nowadays do much better
than (6) by referring to early inn-yard theatres, upper and lower
stages, and the use made of them in such a line as this.

Finally 8. *Punctuation Ploy*

Point out that there is no proof that the punctuation is Shakespeare's and if it was (?) instead of (!) or especially (!!) at the end of
the line, the whole sense would be changed. This is good gambiting.
Super gambiting is to show you are

9. *Versed in the Language of Shakespeare and his Contemporaries*

and go on like this:

Who ... here, ho! 'Who' is here, I think, the indefinite (= 'He who'), and not the interrogative pronoun, as is implied, for instance, by the punctuation, 'Who keeps the gate here? ho!' (*Oxford Shakespeare*), and 'Who keeps the gate here, ho?' (*Cambridge Shakespeare*). 'Who keeps the gate' is a periphrasis (= 'Porter') of a kind usual in calling to servants or others, in attendance but out of sight. Cf. *Henry VIII*. V.ii.2, 3: '*Cran* . . . Ho! Who waits there!' Cf. also Beaumont and Fletcher, *Maid's Tragedy*, V.iii: '*Lys* . . . Summon him, Lord Cleon. *Cleon*. Ho, from the walls there!' and *Jack Straw* (Hazlitt's *Dodsley*, V.396): 'Neighbours, you that keep the gates.'

This last gambit, shortened by two-thirds from Lifemanship's Arden Edition of Shakespeare, needs training, even if every single reference is made up. It is not known whether the above are.

LCC POST-GRADUATE
Some Simple Uses of Litmanship
I. ARE YOU FOND OF READING?

I like to finish these sections with examples of our applied instruction for post-graduates.

What is the use, Litmen are often asked, of being able to read Chaucer's *Prologue* in the original if you don't know what to do with it in after life? It is precisely in such a Life-situation as this that we like to feel we can be of most use.

Well Readship

In a word, how to appear well read. How to make it appear, without giving books more than a casual glance, for surely there is not time, that no man is quicker than yourself off the mark with the latest thriller, newest white paper on the development of opencast tungsten mining, or most recent reminiscences of some unheard-of nephew of Dante Gabriel Rossetti.

Coad-Sanderson was always my model here, and it was I who created him our Longfellow Reader at LCC. He ate, drank and slept the new books. Wall-paper controller, with income of £720 p.a., and a mother and stepmother to support, as well as his stepmother's stepchildren, Coad could afford to buy very few books indeed. His methods were and are: (1) To collect book jackets from a peaceful reviewer, Horton, whom he knows and who helps him. These jackets he wraps round old books so that his library seems to be in a constantly refreshed and up-to-date state. He has also (2) beautifully developed the technique of Upright Reading – that is to say, perusing books in

bookshops without actually buying them.[1] He also (3) reads the kind of
review which enables you to criticize a book without having actually
read it, and finally (4) he keeps certain blocks of typewritten manuscript always on show and will sometimes say, 'Willie Maugham
allowed me to browse through this before he made the final corrections.
There was little I could say which was of any value to him, I fear.'

It might be supposed that Coad-Sanderson, in order to maintain
his gambit, would have to read fifteen books a week.

He was saved from this stupefying task by two strong sub-quali-
fications, as we call them. The first: Coad was an Old Reviewer himself. He knew that there are only six things which can under any
conceivable circumstances be said for, not more than eight to be
said against, any known book.[2]

[1] The fact that Coad hardly read the books he possessed or that these were
few in number was never revealed. Coad was himself deeply influenced by the
brilliant specializations of (Miss) S. Arnold-Forster on Marginaliaship and
the ! Ploy. Miss Arnold-Forster has perfected a means of suggesting to
borrowers of books that their reading is superficial and that they are impercep-
tive of the finer nuances. This is done by underlinings, comments, etc.,
written on the margins of the book at random *in ink*.

'Surely' ploy:

"At this time William Cowper had <u>at last</u> settled down with his old nurse
and six cats at <u>Bath</u>, in the house he had so recently bought."

[margin note: *surely he means Bristol—cf. Mayhew*]

Question-mark ploy:

"I might be said that Wordsworth's <u>childhood in the Lakes may</u> have
profoundly influenced his poetic development."

[margin note: ?]

Exclamation-mark ploy:

"Maria Edgeworth's early experiences in the Liverpool slums brought
home to her that drink is indeed an evil mocker, and <u>she remained a total
abstainer all her life</u>."

[margin note: !!!]

[2] Not only O K Literary Names, with Rilking (see *Lifemanship*, p. 126), are
taught at L C C, but basic O K critical phrases (with intonations) as well. No
matter if they tell us very little of the object to be criticized; the main function
is to imply ('I'm Rather Delightfulship') that you, the critic, are an extraordinarily nice chap. E.g.

O K critical lines:

(1) 'Thank goodness there's no mention of Freud'

or

'Personally I'm sick of the Oedipus complex' (there need not, of course,
be any reference to Freud or complexes in the work concerned).

(2) 'Delightfully fresh and spontaneous'.

Both (1) and (2) will suggest that the critic, in spite of his rather scruffy
appearance, *is himself pretty fresh and spontaneous.*

(3) 'A rewarding experience'.

('Rewarding' is the new O K word for 1952. 'Climate of thought' is still
O K, but only just. 'Rebarbative' is *finito*).

O K Attacks:

(4) 'Personally I found the love-scenes rather embarrassing.'

It is possible, within eleven minutes, to learn five words to quote (supposed to be a certain way of proving that you have read the book through). Remember that any five consecutive words taken out of *any dramatic* passage of a novel or *deeply passionate* section of a poem will sound both forced and absurd if repeated by you on the top of a tram, while mixing a drink, or while the person you are speaking to is filling up a form.

If by chance one happened actually to have read a book on the morning of publication, Coad could always go one better. I have myself rushed round to Coad with a copy of, say, T. D. Pontefract's *The Tea Party* at 11 o'clock – two hours after it was issued – to see if I could for once be one up on him over a new book. I do not remember what he said, but experience has taught me it must have been either (*a*) 'Let me lend you the American edition. It's beautifully printed and it hasn't got that stupid cut on page 163,' or (*b*) (more simply) 'Good old Pontefract – still churning them out.'

This answer (*b*) brings me to the second sub-qualification which made things more possible for Coad in his pursuit of Keeping Abreastmanship. There are latest books and latest books, he would imply; and after he reached the age of forty-four, when reading became even more difficult for him, he would make a tremendous point, though as up to date as ever, of only buying the books 'which interested him'.

'Look, I've got a prize,' he would say to me, 'I've got it too,' said I breathlessly, pointing to my new Julius Simon.

'Ah, good, good,' Coad says now. 'But I didn't actually mean that one. Where does the Mysterious Religious Character come in this time? Chapter XIV?'

This maddened me, (*a*) because I had in fact been rather moved by Chapter XIV, and (*b*) because I knew Coad was going to pull out some small, almost privately printed book and say, 'I meant this – John's new book on the architecture of lift shafts. It's most frightfully good.'

---

(5) 'There is a certain archness which I found displeasing.'

(4) and (5) mean '*Though sensitive and cultured, my peasant stock ensures that I am O K for passion.*'

(6) Quote misquotations of commas.

(7) Complainingly quote cliches, or at any rate say, 'Why must "blood" always be "congealed"?' as if it *was* a cliche.

(8) In criticizing any translation, take any five lines of the translation and then quote the original and say, 'Why not let's have the original, so much more force and point, etc.' If the original language is Syriac, so much the less chance of argument.

I have said sufficient, I think, to show Coad's gambit. And what, you will say, of the counter? For each ploy has its anti. Coad is counter-proof, but there is a way of making the average newbookman feel feeble. It is based on a remark made 125 years ago next March by that domineering Lifeman Charles Lamb.

Lamb said, when any of his friends bought a new book, he bought an old one. This, in my view, is difficult to beat, as a ploy. There is an answer to it. Play can be made with the period flavour of ivory-towership, as a gambit. Yet on the whole it is a reasonably disabling ploy, and the only reason we sometimes frown on it is that, containing as it does a grain of truth, the taste remaining in the mouth is scarcely a pleasant one.[1]

[1] *Wilson's Wile.*
We are working now on the counter to this ploy of J. Wilson of Oxford Street, i.e. the bookseller's ploy of knowing more about the subject than the author who has written the book on it.

'RECEIVING DAY'

A group of us ready to welcome the new batch of week-end 'guests'. On the left, Odoreida, with Cogg-Willoughby in characteristic pose. On the right, Ivy Spring and Gattling-Fenn.

PART TWO

THE HOUSE PARTY

ORIGIN OF THE HOUSE PARTY

The title 'Lifemaster' – what does it mean, what does it stand for?

In the old days it stood for a thorough course at the Lifemanship College, including such extras as Foreign Languaging and Manglo-Relations. These were not optional. The test was severe. Credits were necessary in eighteen of the twenty-two subjects, and the candidates must have satisfied the examiners in at least one of the papers of London Matriculation.

But there were many promising students who found this insistence on mere scholastic ability a permanent bar to high office. A profession where personality was so important needed a new test. It was for this purpose that the House Party was created. It is an institution copied now, I am glad to report, very honourably, we need not say by whom, and familiar throughout the British Army in the technique and counter-techniques of Wosbyship.

In essence our House Party is a friendly enough affair, in which young Lifemen visit us as guests (for list of fees see back page of pamphlet) and are made to feel uneasy, but not aggressively so, while they on their part make their student attempts to undermine our long-trained one-upness.

We watch our candidates, of course, without their knowing it, although they are all aware of this being watched without knowing it. As they drive the car or wield rod or gun, field-glass or wine-glass, qualities of Life-leadership and the reverse are quickly spotted. Few may there be to fail to be awarded the title, with its additional fee, of Lifemaster.

7

GODFREY PLASTE

SOMETIMES THE lifemaster candidate at the House Party is under inspection before he realizes it.

Take, for instance, the journey down, by train or car. Perhaps he will have some lifetutor as companion. If in a car, he is supposed to know something of car theory, and to have read our pamphlet, here reproduced in shortened form, on *Carmanship: or the art of stealing the crown of the road without being an absolute hog*.

Godfrey Plaste, our Differential Reader in Carmanship and for many years referee at our Gameslife Students' Sportsground, must have written nearly a third of a million words on the various Lifemanship gambits associated with his almost too passionate spare-time interest in car and driver play. Never satisfied, Plaste tore up sheet after sheet as he wrote, sometimes even before, until at last only four complete pages remained. These he handed over, with a rather fulsome dedication, to myself, expressing a hope that I would not publish.

As the 'wish' was obviously only a gambit, now that Plaste has passed on I am giving what I hope is the gist of Plaste's pages here, trying as it were to reconstruct from the fourth lumbar vertebra, the skeleton of a Plasteploy.

As is admitted, Godfrey's motor play evolved from one primary gambit which he perfected over many years. It is known – easy phrase to remember – as 'Plaste's Placid Salutation', and I am bound to say he brought this to a fine art.

A ferociously selfish driver, Plaste gloried in bringing approaching limousines to a dead stop by choosing the wrong moment to overtake. I have myself seen an oncoming quadruple tank-carrier forced by Plaste's carefully timed passing to mount the verge and melt through a concrete lamp-standard. Yet Plaste got away with it by this 'salutation'. In essence this was a simple raising of the hand, an inclination of the head, and a grave smile. Instead of the scream of rage one would expect from the oncomers, they would often *actually salute back.*

PLASTE'S PLACID SALUTATION

Why was this? The only time I met Plaste on the road head-on he was passing an ambulance. Noticing the ambulance bell, I had slowed down and pulled well over. It was one of the narrowest two-lane traffic sections of the notorious Great North Road. Suddenly the light blue nose of Plaste's battered little saloon, screaming in some low gear, crept out behind. I almost drove the brakes through the floor. As my head hit the windscreen, I saw the hand raised slowly in salute.

There was something so calm and dignified about this gesture that I can only say that instead of anger I was made to feel that I had somehow helped; that some message of urgency for the nation had passed that way, a second saved, a crisis averted. I am not sure that I didn't salute back. It was only afterwards, looking back and recognizing the honeycomb of dents on the mudguards of Plaste's wretched car, that I became angry, and slowly began to shout.

PLASTE AS PASSENGER
(from an X-ray photograph)

We were fortunate to obtain this record of the position of Plaste's right foot, made at the moment when, using the Lifeman's 'art which reveals art' (Morteroy), he 'instinctively' brakes as his driver approaches a roundabout. Note particularly the flexure – almost a flexion – of Distal and Middle Phalanges, to suggest that driver's speed is carelessly excessive.

It was the success of this gambit of his which set Plaste thinking in terms of carmanship.

Ever since he was a child he has been fascinated by Back-seat Drivership (the Beastly Passenger ploy), a palaeo-gambit which existed before Gamesmanship and Yeovil were thought of. Plaste's passenger technique was first to remain absolutely silent for five or six minutes. Then a long time before it was necessary for me to brake he would fidget with his feet, but slightly. Later, when it was known that I should have to turn left, he would stretch his left arm far out of the car, half a mile before the turning point; and for a right turn jig his extended hand up and down as if he were scrambling eggs, thus making a dangerous Highway Code error and at the same time suggesting that my hand signals were ineffective.

If we approached a child under the age of twelve walking quietly along the footpath, he would first wince, then draw up his knees, then say, 'Toot toot' quietly under his breath.

> PLASTE: Toot-toot.
> SELF: What did you say?
> PLASTE: Only 'toot-toot' . . . I wasn't quite sure whether you'd seen that child on the footpath.
> SELF (*pause*): But it's walking into the house.
> PLASTE: *Oo* – yes. All right now. Exquisite little thing.

But if the tables were turned and he was driving, Plaste had amazing powers of making his passengers feel beastly. If, after dashing at full speed across three dangerous crossings, he was about to emerge, as he once was, I remember, from Wallingford on to the main Oxford road in Henley Week, I did say, smiling, 'By the way, major road ahead.' Plaste stopped his car instantly, drawing it into the side.

'Look,' he said. 'Do you mind if I tell you something? I have been driving a car for twenty-five years, and if any passenger is going to tell me what to do he brings to the realm of the conscious the very thing which experience has happily made intuitive and natural. I do not mind bad manners, but I do mind death. Thank you.' Of course what he said was absolutely right, and as he dashed out into the Oxford road and tipped off his front wing against a beer lorry, I began to mumble apologies.

'Forget it,' he said to me.

Plaste has another method of 'softening' his passengers. He had in his locker a collection of out-of-date and crumpled maps made at very different dates to very different scales, and through long wear rubbed into illegibility round the creases. He would hand a bunch of these to me and say, 'How about a little map-reading?' After ten minutes finding the right map and another ten finding the right place, Plaste would say, 'I say, do you mind keeping that map in the right folds?'

'Yes,' I said – really slightly pulling his leg. Then after another two minutes:

'Well!' he would say.

'What do you mean, "Well?"?' I would say.

'Where are we?'

'Getting on,' I said. (I knew we were about half-way between Nettlebed and Henley.)

Plaste began to use his quiet voice: 'Yes, yes, but I mean where are we? I mean, it makes it so much more interesting.'

'We're not anywhere exactly.'

'What do you – I wonder what that rather jolly little wood over there is called?'

After about three minutes' twisting and turning of the map I reply, 'It says "Upper Common". '

Plaste would then irritate me by using the annoying word 'Folk-moot' and saying. 'Doesn't that touch your imagination? Perhaps on this Common Land the Folkmoot was once held; the clearing in the forest.'

With women map-readers Plaste was even quieter and more in-cisive. He would say very clearly and slowly, 'All set, my dear? Now look, we want the second third-class road to the left.'

'To the left on the map?' most women would reply. 'How do you mean?' Plaste would say, rather charmingly. Then: 'Are you orienta-ted?'

After a pause the woman might say, 'Won't there be a signpost?' To this Plaste replied, 'What?' Still smiling, he would make elaborate hand signals and draw in to the side. 'I expect we've overshot it, haven't we? Let's see if I can find the place.'

After four or five minutes of this, few women could tell the differ-ence between a railway line and a reservoir, and there would be one of those lapses into tearful silence which satisfied Plaste so much.

This, I hope, will give the student what may be called Plaste defini-tive. For the rest, it is a scribbled note here, a word-of-mouth tradition there. Godfrey ployed his last ploy three years ago sadly enough, self-gambited. A collision while driving in reverse.

How did this come about? One of Plaste's most feverishly irritating techniques, we are told, was his knowledge-of-Londonship. He would go a whole mile off route to wind his way through some goods yard because it was the 'only way of avoiding the Notting Hill traffic'. To complain that this would not affect your journey to Swiss Cottage, anyhow, would be to play into Plaste's hands. He would 'know some parking place' under a disused railway bridge only accessible by taxi. He would know 'definite spots in parks where there could be no speed trap' and use his information by speeding at 50 m.p.h. round and round the Victoria Monument outside Buckingham Palace, for instance – quite useless of course. Finally, and fatally, Plaste would always approach one-way streets from the wrong end and then go up them backwards. 'Saves time,' he said.[1] It was while performing this evolution that he reversed at 30 m.p.h. into a car which was approaching in the correct direction at a similar speed.

Too late, alas, for Plaste to leap out of his car, his usual practice when he hit somebody, and cry 'Did you get that man's number?' We have the Plaste car in our Yeovil museum, though it is not usually on show. Not of any make, it was originally put together from spare parts by C. Plaste, G. Plaste's nephew, son of V. Plaste, the iron-railing manufacturer. The bonnet looked feebler than nine horses, but beneath it was, in fact, an old 17-h.p. engine with six cylinders, noisy enough, but impressive when 'G.P.' slipped into third and said 'Not bad for nine horses.'

The engine pinked like a chime of bells. 'Must do,' said Plaste proudly, 'with this little tiger, built for hotted-up aviation spirit.' In the back of the car is the string of tin medals out of crackers which Plaste referred to as 'Médailles d'Honneur Club Belgique'. There on the back seat are the tyre chains with special spikes for 'for the Courboise Pass . . . Monte Carlo Rally'.[2] On the dash of his

---

[1] Having spent nine months' practice in backing, this one branch of his driving was good, and as a wooman Plaste managed to keep one girl faithful to him for 2½ years by constantly demonstrating his virtuosity in reverse.

[2] I have been asked in the preparation of this book to insert a footnote on the Monte Carlo Rally, or Rallyship,* as I prefer to call it. As I myself go in for a different type of dangerous driving, I am in process, through conversations, of stabilizing the rules of Rallyship with Carlo One (R. Walkerley) who is in close touch with many fellow drivers at the Carburettor Club, which maintains its delightful atmosphere of incomprehensibly technical gambiting. Thus (at random):

A: Last Saturday!—
B: What?
A: You were fairly streaking along at Bedtimber.
B: Oh, I don't know. We dropped 900 revs on the second lap – just as you passed me.

car, examine the starter button, which is a dummy. Plaste would press this useless button, and then say, 'Never mind, half a jiff.'

I can see him now, whisking out three adjustable spanners, and then his long pink bony wrists would disappear under the bonnet where the normal starter button was concealed. 'Got it,' he would say, as the engine miraculously leapt into action, while the female passenger exclaimed with admiration at what appeared to be a miracle of mechanical comprehension, deftness and male mastery. There is no Plaste Memorial, but the simple, common nettles along the west side of our sports ground have remained uncut. He would have wished it.

A: Did I pass you – no, you were Number Ten, weren't you? I'd got my eyes so glued on the tail of Farina . . .

Rallyman A wins, with his suggestion that he was only really concerned with super-ace rivals.

The Carburettor Club has its own set of ploys belonging to what they term the Dicing-with-Death group or Dicemanship. Here are the two basic approaches, nicknamed the Walkerley Talkerleys.

DICEMAN A: Actually I was petrified. No anchors whatever, after two laps, so I suppose I did go rather fast round those corners. Actually, I was a bit shaken.

DICEMAN B: I know. But for some unearthly reason it seems to go the other way with me. You know that little Silverpebble incident when I lost a wheel? I went sort of calm and rather cold. I seemed to have bags of time to pull up on the grass, get out and walk away. But, lord, was I scared, later, when I thought about it!

Here is a parlette of Drink-diceman, interesting if only because it gives a perfect example of the riposte or anti-counter:

A: Drink?

B: No thanks. Got to drive on Saturday.

A: Well, speaking absolutely personally, I'm scared to get into the car unless I'm practically completely stinkaroo. (*He roars with laughter.*)

This is good ploying, as everybody thinks that A, who has built up an atmosphere of never drinking anything but Coco-Cola, is amusing and decent. Everybody, that is, but B, who knows that A always uses private flask before race.

---

*This footnote is highly technical, and should be read only by those who have achieved some record time round some record track. We ourselves hold a record for Silverpebble, having lapped it at 14 m.p.h. in an unblown Bean.

8

THE CARTER-WILLIAMS

RAILWAY GAMBITS

'I KNOW Carter-Williams personally,' said a young House Party guest to me one Friday, hoping to impress as he stepped out not of a car but the third-class compartment of a railway carriage, holding a first-class ticket in his hand. I approved of his sound railway-ticket play, with its suggestion of affluence devoid of snobbery; but I had to pull him up on 'Carter-Williams'.

'*Which do you mean?*' I said, for of course B. Carter and J. Williams, though known to each other, are two totally distinct persons, young National Service men who as sergeants were expert in furloughship, as we used to call it, and studied railwayship over a prolonged period of leave-fiddling. Far apart in conveyed climate as each terminus is, the Eustonian and Paddingtonian approaches are basically similar at the deepest level.[1]

There is, of course, one essential railway gambit in which each student is supposed to perfect himself. But before reminding you of this, which always comes at the close of our railway pamphlet, a reminder of Cogg-Willoughby and his railway work.

Cogg has only one railway gambit, and it is simple. It is to use the railway.

'I never go by car,' he says. 'Goodness no.'

So even, say, between Redhill and Dorking, he will take the frightfully old-fashioned electrified rail system. Portsmouth to London by rail is typical Cogg. And his total effect, of course, is to be alone, to be clean, especially about the finger-nails, to be unruffled, to read,

---

[1] 'The Underground is the Great Leveller' was first said by the amazing John Stuart Mill *at the age of four*, only 2½ years after he first mastered the Greek alphabet. Some part of our Fifth Volume, 1956, will be devoted to precocityship and its counter, Miltoning, sometimes defined as the art of not writing *Paradise Lost* before fifty.

and to go first-class with a third-class ticket – the reverse of the procedure we normally recommend. He also uses a cigarette-holder – quite unlike his normal character this – but effective, I am bound to say, with his thin discriminating temples and the vulnerable effect of his prematurely bald head. He wears horn-rimmed glasses designed by Chermayeff and *gloves while reading*.

THE BASIC RAILWAYSHIP OF COGG

Note: the book is Ruskin's *Seven Lamps*. The names of other books can be supplied.

He is usually sitting alone, occasionally non-smoking in a smoker, nice touch. And always quite clean, and calm. All this is aimed, need we say, at the Gattling-Fenns of this world.

Gattling, door to door, can get there seven minutes faster, over the 2¼-hour journey, by plunging through wind and traffic in his white-and-green roadster. But whereas Gattling on arrival is nervy, dishevelled and half his normal size with the desire for drink, Cogg-Willoughby steps out of his taxi ironed and tidied, and poisedly asks for soda-water.

But to return to Carter-Williams. As young militiamen they made great game, on long-distance journeys with dining-cars, of pretending to have dinner on both the first and second service while really eating sandwiches or even nothing, and vice versa – a lot of horseplay, to my mind.

But they did pick up a surprising amount of railship lore, and made a few converts with their slap-dash slogan – BE TOP MAN – WIN THE JOURNEY.

Little Wootton Play

Superior knowledge of the route was one method.[1] ('Little Wootton Play' is the random naming of indecipherable stations after they have flashed by.) In the dark at speed I have myself found it possible

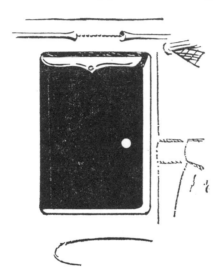

RAILWAYSHIP: LITTLE WOOTTON PLAY

During dark, nod towards any small lighted window as it passes and say, 'Ah, Tom's in—Tom Norris, head keeper of Lord Gravelstoke in the old days.'

to convince passengers that I know the position of the train *by sounds*. I say:

SELF: That loop of the Ouse is on our right now. (No need to say which of the fourteen Ouses you are referring to.)

PASSENGER: How on earth do you know?

[1] To describe Method Two I will quote direct from Carter:

'On the first reference by any of his travelling companions to the heat or stuffiness of the compartment J. Williams would leap to his feet, open all the windows and the door into the corridor, and *turn the heating off*. He would then put on coat, gloves and muffler, and wait.'

The counter-ploy to this, of course, is to take off your jacket, loosen your collar, and *appear to enjoy* the fresh air. But this move has never been used since *Healthman's Disaster*, when two determined Lifemen, travelling on the Flying Scotsman, arrived in Edinburgh frozen, almost incredibly, to death.

SELF: That rattle of points and then the rap as we went under the foot-bridge. Cobb's Corner.

Actually this patter was used against me by the dignified driver of the Coronation Scot. It was only afterwards that I discovered there was no footbridge and no Ouse.

TERMINUS PLAY
The seated figure is in the correct Eustonian position.
(*Sketch made while passing Watford on the up line*)

At the end of their pamphlet, Carter-Williams describe Rail Primary – the gambit we all practise yet never perfect. And how often in fact we fail in – what? In *Terminus Technique*.

There are still men, albeit the layest of the lay, who, coming into Euston, will begin fidgeting even before Watford, say 'Are we here?', begin to button some sort of dingy mackintosh, take down suitcase and remain standing, meaninglessly. 'New boy,' we all intone at him in a repeated plainsong – but are we always perfect ourselves?

Let me quote Carter:

If you are truly established as Top Man, your fellow-passengers will leave you to judge the correct moment.

There are two methods:

1. *The Eustonian.* If the line is well-known to you, as terminus approaches sit absorbed in a book, and make no preparations for disembarkation until *the very last minute.* Long practice in our Yeovil dummy railway carriage makes it possible to snap book shut and get out smoothly precisely as train stops.

2. *The Paddingtonian.* If you do not know line well enough to employ (1), act as follows. Prepare to leave the train *at least half an hour* before you are likely to reach your destination. Then leave compartment with word about 'getting opposite taxi.' Lay passengers are left feeling gloomy, apprehensive and feeble.

9

GAME BIRDSMANSHIP

DURING THE first day of our Yeovil week-end we encourage candidates to get out and about, either playing games according to methods recommended by us or taking part in sports, often called the 'shipless' sports because hitherto nothing has been printed by us on these themes.[1]

But now the time has come to get down on paper some basic code for shooting, fishing, etc., encouraging our Yeovil demonstrators[2] in each subject to say something of their technique.

Gifted Colonel F. Wilson, illustrator of our manuals, and often quite welcome when an extra beater is wanted, is Purdey Reader in Game Birdsmanship and avers that the whole craft needs a thorough spring-cleaning.

We are certainly cutting out, I hope, a good deal of dead wood. The man who trains his dog to go out quick after the drive and pick birds indiscriminately from all the way down the line – this man is no gamesman and should not so name himself.[3] And there is something,

---

[1] Nothing printed but plenty talked. For three years shooting men of all denominations, yes and fishermen too, have been sending in messages, 'advise' here, 'pronounce' there. 'Coarse Fishermen Expect a Lead from Yeovil' is a headline some may have seen in the journalism of this sport.

[2] These sporting-life demonstrators are not on the regular Yeovil staff nor are they permanent. The post is held for one year during which three lectures are given somewhere or other, often in the Off-Licence of some tavern. The office is known as Morning Dew Reader, although being able to read is neither essentially required nor an invariable acquirement.] There is no special interest in this.

[3] Away, too, with the man who says, 'Care to try my "Superstrike"? Knock over an elephant at a hundred yards' and hands his unsuspecting guest a cartridge filled not with normal charge but ordinary toy 'caps' for children.

too, like boasting even about Gattling-Fenn's reply to his host's complimentary 'You must have got over twenty birds there':

'No, only nineteen came.'

A good deal of Game-birding work has been done recently on the subject of luncheon in butt or by hedgerow.

GAME BIRDSMANSHIP: BECKETT'S BALK
M. Beckett's suggested technique for grouse shooting. Host sends guests to next line of butts in cars across bumpy track while he rides direct on old and sure-footed pony.

UNSTEADYING EFFECT OF BECKETT'S BALK
A. Guest.   B. Host.

Gattling and Cogg-Willoughby are contrasted here. Cogg goes in for especially luxurious luncheon-hampers, better than anybody else's, with special instruments, e.g. for cracking the shells of hard-boiled eggs. Gattling contrastingly produces a tin of hambones with only a few rags of ham left and some dog biscuits. His object (he tells students) is to show how absolutely at one he is with his dog. 'He is part of me,' says Gattling. Whenever his dog, Fossil, does anything (scratches, takes a left turn, etc.) Gattling will say at the same moment something like 'Huppah' and add 'You see', as if what the dog did was the result of his saying 'Huppah'. After opening the dog biscuits Gattling sometimes went off with Fossil to drink and even lap water at the same horse-trough. So much interest was soon aroused by these goings on that people on the fringe of our group would be offering Gattling chicken sandwiches or even inexpensive champagne, so that he always ended by getting a better lunch than anybody.

GATTLING-FENN DEVELOPING DOGMANSHIP TO THE POINT OF
ABSURDITY

'How do you do it?' I heard a Mrs Ems ask Gattling, admiring his dog's obedience.

'Just patience,' said Gattling. 'Patience. And being rather fond of the creatures.'

This annoyed me because I knew that Fossil privately loathed Gattling, and the only objects Fossil could and did pick up effectively were golf balls in play, usually from the first fairway of Huntercombe Golf Course.

One basic we can reveal as emerging in our Yeovil teaching, and that is that clothesmanship for game birdsmen *is perhaps more important than in any other sport.*

I do not wish to publish details of this yet, but would like to draw attention to a gambit of F. Wilson's own, with which we are all particularly wont to associate him personally here, although the 'official' name of the gambit is cumbersome ('Wilson's Wali of Swat-ship'). Its object is to suggest supershot one-upness by reference to first-hand knowledge of jungle sport, if not warfare.

'Nice bit of jungle,' is Wilson's opening line.

Wilson's next move is to handle his gun in a way which companion finds strange though not yet alarming.

WALIMAN: Sorry, I'm not used to this.

LAYMAN: Oh, well.

WALIMAN: I mean I'm not used to shooting with other people. I used to go out alone. Quite alone. Except of course for a few natives. It didn't matter if you peppered them.

LAYMAN: Of course.

WALIMAN: They liked it because I used to put an anna over each little skin puncture. Sometimes they used to *pretend* to be knocked out.

WILSON'S BLOOD-STAINED ANNA

It was in really cold weather that one saw the perhaps rather hateful side of this Far Eastern play. Wilson would wear a warm-looking sheepskin Afghanistan coat or poshteen. From the nice-chap approach Wilson would then offer other poshteens to fellow guns. 'Can't do anything with cold fingers.'

Wrongly fitted or put on, however, these coats have a trussing-up effect quite fatal, of course, to good shooting. By doing up a certain button, Wilson made wearers feel as if they had been skewered through the armpits. Then Wilson would say: 'The Wali of Swat gave me this. I don't know why . . . we sort of hit it off. He laid on a fifteen-gun salute for me. Frightful brigand of course. Here, let me pull this out of your eyes.'

'This' would refer to the Yarkandi hat which Wilson provided as an extra. With its wide, loose fur rim it would gradually settle on to the bridge of the nose.

Odoreida was such a bad shot that he could only get himself invited by some stratagem or forgery. Little to report on him, except this variation on the Striking Stranger gambit (see *Lifemanship*. p. 151).

GAME BIRDSMANSHIP IN OXON
The Wilson Strait-jacket.

I have always said that Odoreida was repulsive to women: but be that as it may, women were certainly repulsive to him, with the exception of his rather dolphin-breasted sister-in-law Paulette Odoreida, at whom he did once make a somewhat hectoring kind of pass. He even made ploy with this quite handsome woman and her two young friends, asking if he might bring them to a shoot. Once there, he would leave these youngish women embarrassingly alone, so that other guns would have to carry them over ditches or prize apart barbed-wire fences with a testy show of chivalry.

Odoreida trained Paulette to wear a gay light yellow scarf and then sit by the butt of a rival. Ocular reflexes caused the birds to turn aside out of range.

Remember, finally, the importance of the 'I'm not just a slayer'

GAME BIRDSMANSHIP
IN NORFOLK
Mrs Paulette Odoreida
distracting. The colour
of her scarf is canary.

approach to this subject, with the man who is interested in the natural history of the thing well in the foreground. But this subject needs a new chapter, and a new guide.

10

BIRD GAMESMANSHIP

THE ORIGIN of Bird Gamesing, or Bearded Titmanship, is easy to guess. The whole vast ornithoploy started as a natural-history gambit of ordinary game-bird shooting (see last chapter). It was Gilbert White, when out with his friend D. Barrington taking pot-shots at cuckoos, who first said, 'Yes, but how does it rear its young?' after which Barrington never hit a bird.

Our Zeiss Reader is B. Campbell, who, even if he was unlucky enough to be sacked from Selbourne, still writes actual bird notes in ornithological papers. The essence of this Birdsmanship he explains in a large work, which will be divided into three volumes.

The first volume will deal with *The Birdsman in Society* and the two basic ways of making the layman feel ill at ease. We have adapted these for Yeovil as follows:

1. In answer to Layman's respectful question to Birdsman, 'Do tell me, is this a good place for birds?' answer 'Well, no place is bad for birds really, is it?' This is said in an anti-plonking or softly sympathetic voice with a touch of substitute Richard Jefferies,[1] or at any rate a 'Let me be your Fabre' hint, always annoying.

2. A totally contrasted method can be used for Layman's 'Ah, you might be interested about my robin.' Without moving a muscle, say, 'Certainly, so long as you're not going to tell me that it (*a*) taps on your window or (*b*) really recognizes you.'

This completes the first volume.

'But what do you mean – a whole volume?' newcomers ask.

'Yes.'

'But isn't it rather meagre?'

The newcomer is ignorant of the scientific approach. The good

[1] Hence the term 'Jefferiesship' for this put-off.

birdsman can always fill up by saying whether or not pocket handker-
chiefs were worn by which speaker and if so was it used or if it wasn't
and other observations especially absolutely unselected because once
you start selecting and therefore expressing preferences the scientific
attitude and the whole value of the thing as evidence goes bang.
But Vol. II is certainly more important. The Birdsman in the Field.

Binocular Play

Basic Birdsman is of course to have the best pair of field-glasses in
any group. What we teach is the counter to this gambit, the familiarity
of which has bred contempt. Method A is to say, 'There comes a
point, I suppose, when if they're too big and cumbrous you can't
get them on the bird quickly enough.' Counter B is the man who
keeps a very small telescope up his trouser leg.

It is worth remembering, we think, that bad old binoculars fit
well into bird clothesmanship, which surely must consist, basically,
as Campbell suggests, in wearing the oldest remains of *two* plus-four
suits, bound or patched with leather in unusual places, and a hat
which before wearing has been left for a week in a chicken-run.

Bearded Titmanship

This is the name given to the art of being in essence one-up in the
art of spotting uncommon birds.[1] Rivalry in this kind of field-work
is intense and many a broken nose results, while the words 'bigot' or
'sewer-rat' are flung back and forth in the correspondence columns
of *The Times*. Campbell-recommended parlettes are as follows:

(*a*) In the case of a not readily identifiable bird that stays put, birdsman
must be the first to ask, 'Well, what do you think?' which gives him the
chance of trapping an unwary diagnosis from his rival. Should this agree
with his own private opinion, he jumps in with: 'Of course, but the superciliary stripe (or absence of superciliary stripe) was a bit unexpected, wasn't
it?'

Alternatively,

(*b*) 'I never think it's safe to diagnose at this time of year unless one can
see the wing-pattern.'

s quite good.

---

[1] Don't, for heaven's sake, say 'rare'. A bird is only rare if it was 'reported
over Sheppey in 1908 and one shot by Colonel Westrup in Mull in 1884'.
No, the rare birds you are looking for, such as the bearded tit, are either
'infrequent' or 'local'.

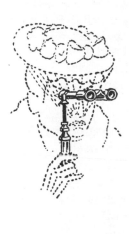

BIRD CLOTHESMANSHIP BASIC
Left: Classic type.   *Right:* Modern type, still
in experimental stages.

Tallyship has its own disciples and converts. It consists of keeping tally of the number of species observed in one garden, walk, week-end, or hovering over the funnel of the *Bournemouth Queen*. Adepts in this gambit have achieved high virtuosity (recommended method: walk through e.g. a wood head down and whenever some animal lets out some sort of squeak make mark in notebook and say e.g. 'nut-hatch'). But if tallymen can scarcely be outdone, they can sometimes be made to feel they are doing the wrong thing.

Play the opposite line. To undercut tallyman and bearded titman by one simple counterploy show a sudden liking for watching quite plain and ordinary birds.

'After all, it's only the common birds that really count, isnt it?' Continually hold up the party by calling their attention to robins or hedge-sparrows sitting in huddled attitudes on the vegetation. If after five minutes' observation the robin gives a perfunctory peck at its plumage, say, 'Nice – an intention movement!' and make notes.

Bird Committeeship
Campbell's third volume will be devoted to Bird Gamesmanship

committee meetings, to the use of a pipe[1] at meetings, and to the art of suddenly saying, without looking at anything or anybody very special, 'Do we know that?' quietly but definitely plonkingly. We are grateful to B. Campbell for many of his suggestions here and also for his ready scientific attitudeship when cornered in committee and asked genuine questions about birds. His answer is basically 'I don't know,' the Socrates ploy: and these replies are probably soundly worded and would, I expect, read like this, e.g.:

Q: *Do robins have spotted eggs?*
A: We shall all of us know more about that when we have a longer series to work on.

or

Well, that's really David Lack's speciality, isn't it, and it's a bit sort of – well, awkward – if I go barging in on his territory. Look, I know Lack . . . etc.,[2]

or

[1] Mention of the use of the pipe in scientific argument and indeed in committee work generally reminds me of the pioneer work on pipemanship of E. Sigsworth of Leeds University (*Yeovil Post-Graduate Research*, Vol. CIV, p. 86), 'If you have no advice to give, the pipe will do it for you' – how often has this been said: but Sigsworth, with his addition of the technique of spittlecraft to the pipeworthy situation, has put order into the chaos of 'intuitive' pipe behaviour.

To give an impression of dependable listening, it is essential to know *when* to puff smoke, when to go 'bup' or 'bp' with the lips, and when to take a long noisy wet-sounding blow through an extinguished pipe, to clear the passage.

We usually practise on some young woman who wishes to talk to us in confidence – usually about some love affair. Here is a timed table of pipe effects, with dialogue:

GIRL: . . . and I've often wondered whether I was right to make friends with him even. He would never, I think, think of me in this way. I'm sorry, but do I sound to you absurdly silly and pompous over all this?
PIPEMAN: (*puff*).
GIRL: What I should like to do would be to start all over again with him – get back to the mutual interest in work we've always had together . . .
PIPEMAN: (*bup-bup-bup*).
GIRL: What? Do you see what I mean? Because apart from any question of – well, falling in love really with each other there's always been this – something – between us which is quite outside love – not better or worse but outside it. I can't talk straight, but – do you see—
PIPEMAN: (*the long spittle effect*).
If these effects are rightly timed, the girl will feel not only that she has been talking well, but that she has never been given such sympathetic advice by such an intelligent listener.

[2] P. Scott is also decidedly an O K birdsman name. Which of the two is actually the robin specialist is not known.

Ask me in nine months' time. We've got a mass of facts – not yet in very good order.

or

You're taking a terrific lot for granted if you use the word 'spot', aren't you?

A Test Case

B. Campbell draws attention to the gambitous nature of the tendency of that very O K Birdsman M. Nicholson to call birds by somewhat archaic though of course perfectly authentic names. The wider O K-ness is involved in this difficult problem. Is it not fundamentally *correct* scientific attitude play to give the faintest possible pat on the head to the brightest jewels in the diadem of English verbal felicity? Anyhow, that is the Nicholsonian theory. The process, according to Campbell, is known as 'throstling' or 'dunnocking' ('dunnock' for 'hedge-sparrow', 'throstle' for *Turdus philomelos clarkei clarkei clarkei*[1]). But long ago during an abortive aeroplane trip I gave it the rank of ploy with the name 'smale foulesmanship' – and the name has stuck.

I have said enough, I hope, to show that Birdsmen are natural Lifemen. The kind of question we shall be dealing with in 1953 is Counter-birdsmanship, and it will certainly be one of our headaches. The W W W (Windermere Watcher Watchers) are a small Lakeland society who try to force ornithologists into the one-down position by observing them, taking little notes about them, publishing minute pamphlets about them, writing letters to the *Telegraph* about their first appearance, etc. I believe they have some slight success. For myself I prefer the Return to Nature Poetry approach, and write J. Fisher[2] letters about fledgling voices in the vocal grove. But looking back over the years, I have to admit that this has been only partially successful.

[1] Experts will note that Lifemanship rejoinder play is to use the Latin name, *but in a slightly out-of-date version* – 'for old times' sake'.

[2] Another O K bird name, though one is bound to admit that Fisher frequently broadcasts, and in programmes which are liked.

11

TROUTMANSHIP

WHAT A COMPLEX world is here! Yet in the relatively small province of our little Correspondence College we have made enormous headway and gained the thanks of all the fishership community by defining once and for all the two basic trout approaches, in one of which students are expected to satisfy the examiners.

Our Decontamination Reader in Trout, J. Hargreaves, is a pleasant teacher who plays the two-approach system admirably himself. With newcomers, he demonstrates this twoness with a pair of ordinary fishing-rods, one of which is new, the other old.

Rodmanship

This basic gambit is, basically, the art of being one-up with one's rod. Most commonly, the man who still keeps his old rod is pitted against the man who has just bought a new one. Old Rod makes first move:

OLD ROD (*looking at New Rod's new rod*): I like it. I like it. I like it. Of course I'm in my forties. I suppose my old one will see me through. Ought to. Ought to. Ought to.

NEW ROD (*countering implied criticism*): I was sorry to see my last rod go . . . But if one really *fishes* in water like this . . . you know . . . I suppose one kills about a rod a season? Mind you, if you don't go in for these acrobatic casts I'm always attempting rather unsuccessfully . . .

OLD ROD (*pretending to suspect origin of rod and holding it in his hand*): Tell me – where did you . . . (*our inflection for 'where did you' can imply not only that rod was mass produced, but stamped out of synthetic wood*).

NEW ROD: Well – you know – 'Jackie' Bampton happens to be rather a friend of mine. And my difficulty is that I'm not really comfy unless the action is, well, inches nearer the butt than normal—

OLD ROD (*out-gambited but fighting back*): Don't worry . . . don't worry

. . . it's like a woman. You get used to it. In a couple of years, anyhow, it will be part of you. Even if you don't catch any trout.

If New Rod's rod is longer, with a longer line, and if the river needs such a rod, Old Rod will be in difficulty. Spandrel's Underthwart can be used here.

SPANDREL (*old rodding*): Nice rod, but it isn't alive till you're fifteen yards out. I like to throw a shorter line myself.

With right inflection, OR can suggest that he is an ancient, almost neolithic, virtuoso of the trout-stream, a sort of Red Indian, really, belly to the ground, who finds no difficulty in trout work at ten yards.[1]

Troutmanship Basic

After practice in the two-approach system with rods, students may then start practising troutmanship proper.

This, too, is essentially an A *vs.* B situation. A the purist, the scholar of dry fly, *vs.* B the rough and ready, the ham, the hack.

Tell me frankly, says A the purist, *were you fishing the water or the rise?*

To counter this accusation of just chucking about, the student trained in Old Rodship should have no difficulty. I'm bound to say that Gattling-Fenn was at his best in this situation. Shirt open to the waist and apparently nut-brown to the navel (actually he wore a 'Suntan Gypsyvest'), Gattling was able to imply 'For Heaven's sake'.

'For Heaven's sake,' he said, and the gleam of his almost suspiciously white teeth suggested 'I'm just a hobo, son – a tramp. My father, and his father before him,[2] were born natural hunters to a man, like every Englishman born a mother's son.'

While suggesting every word of this, Gattling was at the same time able actually to say:

'I had him in a corner – and – yes, I'm bound to say the fly was a bit damp! Spam Special. Yes, I had to rob the sandwich . . .'

[1] Rodmanship Advanced for 1952. This year has seen New Rod placed in the one down position by Newer Rod Still. This instrument is made of molecularly reconstituted toilet soap. And though it is associated with wrong-clothesmanship (jacket and trousers clean, and matching) and wrong gadget-manship (fly-boxes made of perspex) the thing works. We are struggling with this embryonic counter:
NEWER ROD STILL: Yes, it's the first time these fish on the far side of the bend have had a fly decently presented to them.
COUNTERER: Well, I'm bound to admit it makes fishing easier.
NRS: It certainly does.
COUNTERER: I mean, you *could* use a Mills bomb, I suppose.
[2] This would be Gattling-Fenn's grandfather.

The following Hargreaves Hampers are worth study and are useful to others besides troutmen.

1. Do not cast in presence of other fishermen. Proved odds are 93 to 1 against anything happening. So if A says: 'Have a go at him,' you, B, should reply either: 'No – you. I had a good day yesterday,' *or:* 'Oh, that one? He's nearly had me once already. Ruddy great chub.'

2. For use against man who catches fish bigger than yours in same water. .

TROUTMAN: That's a good one. What does it weigh?
LAYMAN (*cool*): I don't carry scales.
TROUTMAN: I'll weigh it for you . . . 1¾ pounds. That's funny. How long is it?
LAYMAN: Frankly, I don't carry a tape measure either.
TROUTMAN: I do . . . Thought so. Nearly 16 inches. That's the trouble with this water, it won't stand fish this size. Ought to be two pounds. It's gone back.

Layman begins to realize he has caught a fish almost on his knees and practically fainting for want of food. He could have picked it out of the water with his bare hands.

3. Rub it in. If, for instance, rival makes clumsy cast, go on and on pointing it out. Thus:

TROUTMAN (*smiling through clenched teeth*): *Now* you've put him down. Now you *have* put him down. Crikey, were you trying to brain him? Doubt if he'll put his nose up for a week. Should think he'd rather drown. I'll move upstream a bit, I think. Happens to all of us.

Marshall's Mangler

This subject is still very 'young' as we call it at Yeovil – i.e. there is still a lot of loose fishing play within our orbit, and a dozen gambits not yet properly described. That is why I am glad to mention Marshall's 'Mangler' – a gambit invented by H. Marshall and needing a finesse and urbanity of execution which totally belie its sobriquet.

The general object is to express an enormous Upper Sixthism so devastating that practically no one else can ever speak about fishing again; and it is done in this way.

The catching of your specific fish is *a Problem*, and must be so approached, without fervour, without even enjoyment.

On one side of your equation is your possible fly, x: on the other, certain variables.

Let a = weather forecast.

   γ = weather.

   γ^i = flow of stream in relation to mean number of solid factory deposits and old cans.

   β = probable age of trout.

   σ = probable age of fisherman.

   π = distance of nearest active motor-bicycle or farm tractor.

   δ = temperature of fish.

Then by a simple calculation jotted down in a waterproof tent with unrunnable ink on unsmudgeable paper, Marshall would get some equation as this:

$$x = \frac{\delta^{16}\,\sigma\,\sqrt{a^3\gamma}\ \ \gamma^i - 8}{\beta^2\,\pi} = \text{Split's Indefatigable } or \text{ Aunt Mary's Special}$$

Hand this result with your rod to the ghillie and walk quite slowly away, leaving him to catch the actual fish. Marshall has learnt to intensify the effect of all this by turning up on the bank in a bowler hat and a dark pin-stripe and a pair of thin, blindingly well-polished, black shoes, in which he delicately picks his way back through pool and undergrowth.

12

THE ART OF

NOT ROCK-CLIMBING

Rock Play of Odoreida

'JUST-A-SCRAMBLESHIP', as Rockmanship is sometimes nicknamed, is actually taught in the grounds of our College where, between the croquet lawn and the putting-green, is an imitation concrete precipice, four feet high with a three-foot drop to a spring mattress. Believing that demonstration in the field is essential, students are here taught on the spot how to talk about 'holds', 'grips' and 'nice little problems', and how to come unstuck without actually mentioning it.

This art has a special interest for students of Gamesmanship and Lifemanship – not surprising when it is realized that it is the adopted relaxation of G. Odoreida. Some of Odoreida's gambits are objected to by the older members of our Council, but if Odoreida is the name on every rockman's lips, no less is he referred to as chief authority, by ourselves, in that aspect of this art which may be sub-titled: 'How to climb rocks without actually going up them.'

Our Matterhorn[1] Readers, K. Fitzgerald and B. Hilton-Jones, have described in a definitive conversation the technique of Odoreidaism, and from their comments this analysis is borrowed freely.

Students of Gameslife will be aware that in the actual playing of games Odoreida, though often seen on the edge of a cricket field, was a complete rabbit. The weight in his pear-shaped figure, although suggesting the attitude of one accustomed to standing at fairly deep mid-off, was so unusually distributed that genuine climbing looked to be, and was, almost impossible. Besides, it is known that on heights he once said he was 'frightened he might throw himself over'.

It was therefore plucky of Odoreida to life his way into this reputation of his as a skilled rockclimber.

How did he do it?

Odoreida Rock Basic is to be the Man Looking On. Older now, he is inclined, he tells us amusedly, for slippers. In that little place at Pen-y-gwryd, he is never very far from the fire.

There he will be knowledgeable about past climbs, or present routes. 'Yes,' he says. Odoreida is encouraging at first. 'I do consider the bottom pitch of Charity to be harder than anything on Cloggy.' He speculates. 'You know' (making the wet sucking noise on pipe (see p. 236)), 'I've always thought the wall on Craig Yr Ysfa would go.'

At this point an absolute stranger or complete new boy might begin to call Odoreida 'sir'.

'Would you, sir?'

'Well, one or two of us saw it the other day on a top rope. I think it would go. By the way, I see you are still using those nails.'

New Boy is made to feel the nails in his boots are unsafe, or out of date. Having by this and that prepared a Lifeman's wicket, Odoreida goes in to bat. Essentially his is climb avoidance play, while seeming to be eager. I know all Yeovil men will want to join me in emphasizing the importance of this gambit.

The H'm Tinge

Maybe he's not going to climb just now because it's the wrong time

[1] The original name remains, although the Matterhorn is no longer an OK mountain.

of year. In June, Odoreida says, 'I only like Great Gully at Christmastime when it's full of ice.' At Christmas, on the other hand, he recalls that everyone's done it every Christmas, and that everyone is doing it now. In fact it's pretty well got Stop-and-Go lighting.

Somebody else says something else is a difficult climb.

'Well – I seem to remember when Jack did it he did "Sunset" afterwards. After all, the Caldecott brothers took 140 pounds of photographic equipment along that ledge in 1903.'

A 'h'm' climate is built up.

'The Sceptre presents the same problem – only I suppose ten times more tricky. But I was rather surprised to find ironmongery all over the cliff – the whole place is getting bunged up with it. Bad as the Matterhorn. Look, I found this halfway up Great Slab the other day. Look.'

I knew that Odoreida always keeps a rusty piton, scarcely an OK climbing aid in this district, always in his pocket, and that he casts doubt on actual climbers by 'finding' it. Occasionally he has a rather technical way of saying a boot climb ought to be done in rubbers (or vice versa). Thus:

'No, I don't think so.'

So few climbs seem worth while to Mr Odoreida, thinks New Boy.

'No – I should have to take my rubbers. And it's essentially a boot climb. But the holds are so worn now. But you go, if you want a nice scamper in a pair of gym shoes. I've got my *War and Peace*.'

'Good old Wagger-Pagger,' replied Gattling-Fenn once, knowing that Odoreida had never read this book, though he was always being found with it in chimney corners.[1]

If really pressed, Odoreida would be quite frank about it. 'No,' he would say.

Frankly I'm frightened of it.

LAYMAN: Don't blame you. Hardly any holds of any kind, are there?

O: Well, the holds which do arrive, arrive well. Not holds perhaps – certain helpful rugosities ... But ... no, I've got my family, and I think if one's got a family ...[2] No. For me Pinnacle Wall is out of bounds.

[1] Odoreida's only genuine reading, besides the *Rockclimbers' Record*, which he memorized for its technical terms, was *Whitaker's Almanack*, in which he liked to check up on the salaries of his many acquaintances in the Civil Service.

[2] The only person this could possibly refer to is Odoreida's sister-in-law, bolster-thighed Paulette Odoreida, whom he only saw once a year when he took the Odoreida children to the annual opening of the Chelmsford roller-skating rink.

The danger of Odoreidaism was shown when he sometimes almost convinced *himself* that he was or had been an expert climber, and began talking himself dangerously near to having to make a climb himself. But he could always take refuge in the 'frankly I'm getting older' defence.

'The trouble is,' he might say, after dinner, 'I get so tired standing on one leg looking for the next hold. Coming down I wanted to smoke – but I was finger-jamming all the way . . .'

The New Boy may move in closer, now, to listen. 'Only the crook of a finger between Odoreida and eternity,' he thinks to himself.

Feeling himself in form, Odoreida might now develop the Other Interest move.

'No. This was in '36. I thought an off-day was about due . . . and I heard that that lovely little Alpine ranunculus mentioned in Butcher – a kingcup in miniature – had been seen on the Devil's Cliff in 1876 . . . and of course I knew that Hanging Garden Gully has been stripped to the bone by botanists, from the local High School I guess . . . so I thought I'd have a look at the Kitchen proper . . . and there it was, well, just inside the mouth. I think I shall always remember it. Seeing that flower.'

I heard this and of course was simply waiting for the laugh. Odoreida and spring flowers!

'How did you get *there*, Odoreida?' I said.

Somebody said 'Sh!' Odoreida turned smiling towards me.

'Oh, I went up the first couple of pitches of Advocate's Wall, then broke out to the Gut for about thirty feet . . .'

SELF: That's new surely? . . .

O: Well as a matter of fact I think it probably is . . . Having to finish up the wall was too sticky altogether for what I call good climbing.

NEW BOY: But that's one for the log, isn't it?

O: My days for logging climbs are over – that's for you younger people. But I'm afraid it is known, now, isn't it, as Odoreida's Rib? Of course, I wanted it called after Messinger, because he first saw it. And it was only chance that I found myself on it at all. The whole thing reminds me of the day I nearly got stuck in Lockwood's chimney.

I couldn't help joining, though for different reasons, in the respectful smiles which followed this, and made no use of my private knowledge that years ago Odoreida, lost in the mist when going to post a letter, really did get stuck near the foot of this climb, and insisted on

being pulled out by three lady members of the Pinnacle Club and a
Brownie.

13

CLUBMANSHIP

THAT so typical institution of this island, the Club, has aptly been described as the normal field of exercise, if not the happy hunting-ground, of the astute Lifeman. Knowledge of some Club play therefore is considered an essential qualification for Lifemanship.

I propose in this chapter first briefly to outline Club Basic and then to analyse only one, but a very important one, of the main gambits which are essentially Club and which *for that reason* (and because the particular is the only true general) have the wide application always implied in the local.[1]

I. CLUB BASIC

The Two Club Approach

Clubmanship proper consists, I always believe, in the continuous implication that you have Another Life, so that even if you dig into your club regularly at 11.45 a.m. every day and stay there till, dazed with smoke, you feel your way out at midnight, you can still give the impression that it is a question of dropping in for a moment's rest, quiet drink or chat in between violent spasms of key jobs or valuable social activity.

Certain coarse and obvious ways of trying to show your important independence we have denounced as Sloppy Lifemanship. It is quite wrong to bustle into the Club and tell the Hall Porter that if any messages come through you're 'not in'. The porter will know and may even say that there have been no messages, not even a postcard, for eight weeks. Unsubtle and vulnerable, this approach is termed by us *Lifecorny*.

Never make the mistake, either, of not remembering who your fellow clubmen are. On the contrary, know the names and, if possible, the salaries, of everybody, especially if they don't know who you are.

[1] The local referred to in this paragraph is, of course, the Black Lion, Hammersmith.

TWO CLUB FORCING APPROACH (1)
Hugo Coating at the Studio Arts dressed as a member of the Artillery.

Take an interest in their professions. Be actually extremely nice to any crotchety club servant there happens to be and to unusually old members, particularly if they are expiring. It is by such little gracious acts, combined with enquiries about 'that nephew of yours with chronic nosebleed' that one-upness is established. Then you can pounce.

Basic Club Play as we teach it is the Two Club Approach. In other words, it is essential to belong to two clubs if you belong to one club. It doesn't matter if your second club is a 5/– a-year sub. affair in Greek Street: the double membership enables you, when at your main or proper club, to speak often in terms of regretful discrimination about the advantages of your Other One.

But for those who play the genuine Two Club *Forcing* Approach, both clubs should be roughly of equal standing, and, if possible, OK. Then, if the two clubs are of sufficiently contrasted character, which they must be, a fascinating set of ploys can be brought into operation. The essence of the technique, of course, is to maintain the condition of being, as F. H. Bradley, genial old Mertonian, once wrote in a different context – 'the other in the other'.

I.e. supposing your two clubs are called, to use a thin disguise, the

THE TWO CLUB FORCING APPROACH (2)
The same man (Hugo Coating) at the Artillery dressed as a member of the
Studio Arts.

Artillery and the Studio Arts, basic play is to appear in the artistic
club very much a member of the military. Exhibit quite a light touch,
in the modern military manner, at the Studio, but maintain a basically
clipped appearance, hair short-looking, with bowler hat and the
correct clothes for the Eastern fringe of W.1. Ask somebody to
'explain' the work of H. Moore, and listen quietly attentive as if
knowing perhaps a bit more than you let on, but remain definitely
incisive and a well-disciplined clubman, silent in the silent room,
snookering quietly in the snooker-room, drinking soberly at the bar.

When, however, at the Artillery, be quite different, in fact the
opposite. Be enervated from your pottery designing at Chiswick, in
huge red corduroys and an indigo shirt. Early on, perhaps, you have
pointed yourself out by presenting a picture, a particularly abstract
abstract, Paris 1926, to the committee. Already it hangs, if in a very
dark corner, near the Lucy Kemp-Welch picture of the Omdurman
charge. In mien you are, perhaps, suffering, in accordance with the
view which you think Artillery holds of the way the artist behaves.
You are certainly abstract. Walking into the library, a man who has
specialized in this work, Hugo Coating, suddenly holds his hand
over his eyes and says, 'Oh, my God.' When he said it again at the

other end of the library a Lieut.-General Broax once said, 'What are
you "My Godding" about?'

'I think perhaps . . .' began a more sensitive member – a young
Captain in the Light Ack Ack.

'I'm sorry, but I praised something I thought was bad. Something
that I knew really was bad. Oh, God.'

'Oh yes,' said Broax.

'That is the only untruth.'

'How about a cordial?' said Broax, with a look of rough sympathy,
seeing that Coating had flung himself face downwards on the settee
and kept knocking the arm of it with the instep of his upturned foot.
And Coating was often being timidly offered drinks in this way, and
though he seldom offered the other half, before long he was able to do
what he liked in the Artillery and was a sort of authority, and it was
taken for granted that it was perfectly O K for Coating to sit in the
seat with arms at the head of the long table. Coating became as
respected at the Artillery for his Studio Arts background as he was at
the Arts for his 'in the services' tone.

2. A GAMBIT ANALYSED

The Affair at the Monosyllable

Queer aspects of Clubmanship, extraordinary instances, are often
brought to our notice by students, and their treatment becomes part
of our regular teaching. No harm, now, in revealing that G. Odoreida,
with his revolutionary but often coarsely effective Lifemanship of the
Left, has a brother, V. Odoreida (husband of rocking-horse-nostrilled
Paulette Odoreida) who, it is now well known, is still farther to the
Left than his brother G. Heaven knows we do not recommend the
ploys and gambits of this man for the use of genuine Lifemen, but
there is no sense in denying that they exist.

'The Monosyllable' is not the real name of a club. It stands nevertheless for one of the genuinely exclusive clubs the names of all of
which, Lifemen will have observed, are, lifishly enough, only one
syllable long. Only Cogg-Willoughby, of our staff, has succeeded in
making the membership of one of these. G. Odoreida, of course, scoffed
and V., his brother, was almost maddened by Cogg's success. He
determined on a counter. An incident occurred which we may as well
outline. As the members of the Monosyllable were trickling one by
one towards the dining-room, a message came for Cogg.

'Your guest has arrived, sir.'

Cogg stopped in midstream to look round. Had he forgotten? Who? A voice came.

'Hallo, Len, I'm sorry I'm late.'

Cogg turned like a shot at this hated abbreviation of a Christian name he had always tried to suppress. A dozen members must have turned with him to see V. Odoreida standing with a long coil of ticker tape paper held before steel-rimmed spectacles and wearing a shirt slightly soiled and *open at the neck, no tie*.

Cogg had just enough presence of mind left to blurt out 'Thank you. And could you clean the plugs as well?' But he felt few were deceived. He rushed from the scene, leaving by some servants' exit. But the damage to Cogg's confidence was lasting. It was at least three months before he next visited the Monosyllable.

14

WINESMANSHIP

Definitions

WINESMANSHIP WAS once listed as a department of Clubmanship. But although it is itself only a province, albeit a vast one, of the area roughly defined as the Gracious Living Gambit of Lifemanship, Winesmanship may play a big part, sooner or later, in the lives of all of us.

A schoolboy definition of Winesmanship is 'How to talk about wine without knowing a Hock from a Horses Neck'. But in fact Winesmanship is itself a philosophy if not an ethic, and can be used in Young Manship, in Jobmanship, even in wooing.

Winesmanship Basic

A few phrases and a ploy or two, to get our bearings. Consider the simplest first. If you are taking a girl, or even a former headmaster, out to lunch at a restaurant, it is WRONG to do what everybody else does – namely, to hold the wine list just out of sight, look for the second cheapest claret on the list, and say, 'Number 22, please.' Never say the number, anyhow, because it suggests that you are unable to pronounce the name of the wine you are ordering. Nominate the wine in English French, and make at the same time some comment which shows at least that you have heard of it before. Say, for instance:

'They vary, of course, but you seldom get a complete dud.'

Or simply:

'I wonder . . .'

A useful thing is to look at the wine list before the waiter comes and say, 'Amazing. Nothing here you can be sure of. Yet the food is quite good. But I've got an idea.'

Then, when the waiter comes, say to him, 'Look. You've got a Château Neon '45 somewhere secreted about the place, I know. Can you let us have a bottle?'

(You know he's got it because you have in fact read it off the wine list, cheapest but one.)

WINESMANSHIP: A LITTLE-KNOWN PLOY

After saying (not of course really having a cellar) 'I'll get it from the cellar,' enter any cupboard (preferably beneath stairs), *close door*, and make sound with feet as if descending to and (after pause) mounting from a wine-cellar.

When the waiter leaves, you can say, 'They keep a small cache for favoured customers.'

With a little trouble a really impressive effect, suitable for average city-man guest, can be made by arriving fifteen minutes early, choosing some cheap ordinaire, and getting waiter to warm and decant it. When guest comes, say, 'I know you'll like this. Should be all right. I got them to get it going at nine o'clock this morning. Not expensive but a perfectly honest wine – and a *good* wine if it's allowed to breathe for three or four hours.'

For Home Winesmanship, remember that your mainstay is hypnotic suggestion. Suggest that some rubbishy sherry, nine bob, is your special pride, and has a tremendously individual taste. Insist on getting it yourself 'from the cellar'. Take about four minutes uncorking it. Say, 'I think decanting destroys it,' if you have forgotten, or are too bored, to decant it. Keep staring at the bottle before you pour it. When you have drawn the cork, look particularly hard at the cork, and, of course, smell it.

For the first sip of the wine, here are some comments for Student Winesmen. Remember, if the wine is claret, 1920 St Emilion Château Cheval Blanc, that strangely enough absolutely everybody is supposed to know whether it is a claret or a burgundy. Remember also that practically absolutely everybody is supposed to recognize instantly the year. Practically almost absolutely everybody should be able to say 'St Emilion'. The only tiny shade of doubt which can enter your comment is about its being Château Cheval Blanc.

Don't say too much about the wine being 'sound' or 'pleasant': people will think you have simply been mugging up a wine-merchant's catalogue. It is a little better to talk in broken sentences and say 'It has . . . don't you think?' Or, 'It's a little bit cornery,' or something equally random like 'Too many tramlines'. I use this last phrase because it passes the test of the *boldly meaningless*.

An essential point to remember is that everybody is supposed to take it for granted that every wine has its *optimum year* up to which it progresses, and beyond which it falls about all over the place. E.g. you can give interest to your bottle of four-and-sixpenny British Russet by telling your guest that you 'wish he had been able to drink it with you when it was at the top of its form in forty-nine'.

Alternatively you can say, 'I'm beginning to like this. I believe it's just on the brink.' Or I rather like saying, 'I drink this now for sentimental reasons only . . . just a pleasant residue, an essence of sugar and water – but still with a hint of former glories. Keep it in your mouth for a minute or two . . . see what I mean?' Under this treatment, the definitive flavour of carbolic which has been surprising your guest will seem to him to acquire an interest if not a grace.

Alternatively you may admit, frankly, that your four-and-sixpenny is a failure. 'They were right,' you say. 'The twenty-fours should have been wonderful. Perfect grapes, perfect weather, and the *vestre* – the Dordogne wind. But for some reason or other they mostly sulked. Taste it and tell me what you think. You may like it.'

Or if your four-and-sixpenny is only two years old and unbearably acid, you can say, 'Let it rest in your mouth. Now swallow. There, Do you get it? That "squeeze of the lemon", as it's called . . .'

Then, if there is no hope of persuading Guest that what he is drinking has any merit whatever, you can talk of your bottle as an Academic Interest treat.

'Superb wine, but it has its periods of recession. Like a foot which goes to sleep, has pins and needles, and then recovers. I think that was

André's[1] explanation. At the moment it's BANG in the middle of one of its WORST OFF-COLOUR PERIODS.'

Watch your friend drink this wine, and if he shudders after it, and makes what we winesmen call 'the medicine face', you can say . . . 'Yes! You've got it? Let it linger a moment.'

'Why?' says Guest.

'Do you notice the after-sharpness, the point of asperity in the farewell, the hint of malevolence, even, in the *au revoir*?' If he says, 'Yes', as he will, look pleased.

Note on Tastingship

Many Yeovil Lifemen are so completely ignorant of wine of all kinds that in our small pamphlet AC/81 we have had to tell them that the red wines are red in colour and, confusing point, the white yellow. It may not be out of place if I remind general readers here, too, that *method of drinking* is an essential accompaniment to *method of comment*.

Before drinking, or rather sipping, the wine, you smell it for bouquet. *Not* with a noisy sniff but *silently and delicately*, perhaps making a funnel of your hands to concentrate the essence. G. Gibbs used to

THE BATH-MERITON POSITION
FOR DRINKING FROM FAR SIDE
OF GLASS

create some effect by smelling the stem of the glass as well, but there is no real point in this. A good general rule is to state that the bouquet is better than the taste, and vice versa.

In sipping, do not merely sip. Take a mouthful and chew it, making as much noise as you can. Having thus attracted attention, you can perform some of the evolutions favoured by that grand old Winesman Bath-Meriton. The most ordinary method he used was to lean his head forward so that his rather protuberant ears were extended like the wings of a monoplane and drink the wine from the far side of his glass. To get the bouquet he would smell it first with the left nostril, closing the other with his fore-finger, and then with the right. He

[1] André Simon, completely O K wine name.

would also hold it up to the light and then shine a small pocket torch containing what really looked like a miniature fog lamp through from the other side! He would dip the end of his handkerchief in the wine and then hold the dipped end up to the light. And remember, when it actually comes to the tasting, sip from the *far* side of the glass. Gattling-Fenn once said, 'Why not simply turn the glass the other way round?'

Winesmanship Advanced

The average guest, who knows no more about wine than the Winesman himself, can be easily impressed by such methods. But there are men who genuinely know something of this subject, and they are a very different problem.

I used to advise a simple and direct approach with such people, including an anglicizing of the simplest French words (e.g. call the Haut Brion the High Bryon). Gattling-Fenn at his first Saintsbury Club dinner realized that it was 1,000 to 1 the man on his left knew more about wine than he did. So he said (of an old burgundy, using the recommended Ordinary Approach):

'Like it?'

EXPERT: Yes.
GATTLING: It's good.
EXPERT: Yes, but you know what's happened?
GATTLING: Yes – in a way. What?
EXPERT: It's been poured through the same strainer that they used for the Madeira.

Gattling broke into a hearty laugh at this, which quickly froze as he realized from the puzzled faces round him that the expert was speaking seriously.

No – the only method with the true specialist is what we call Humble Studentship, mixed in with perhaps *two* carefully memorized genuine advanced facts.

There are, however, lesser specialists, semi-amateurs, perhaps trying a little amateur winesmanship on their own, for whom we recommended the following advanced methods.

1. *Beaded-bubbleship.* This obscurely-titled ploy is merely the art of speaking, and especially writing, about wine as if it was one of the OK Literary Things. Be vague by being literary. Talk of the 'imperial decay' of your invalid port. 'Its gracious withdrawal from

perfection, keeping a hint of former majesty withal, as it hovers between oblivion and the divine *Untergang* of infinite recession.'

Smiling references to invented female literary characters are allowed here. 'The sort of wine Miss Mitford's Emily would have offered Parson Square, sitting in the window-seat behind the chintz curtains.'

2. *Percentageship* is, of course, the opposite method, and designed to throw a different kind of haze, the figure fog, over the wine conversation. Remarks like 'The consumption of "treated" vermouth rose from 47.5 in 1924 to 58.9 in 1926 . . .' will impart a considerable degree of paralysis to any wine conversation. So will long lists of prices, or imaginary percentages of glucosity in contrasted champagnes, or remarks about the progress in the quality of cork trees, or the life-cycle of *Vinoferous demoliens*, little-known parasite now causing panic in the Haut-Baste.

It is always possible, if a wine completely stumps you, to talk in general terms about winemanly subjects.

If it is a warm summer day, say that 'dear old Cunoisier will be getting worried about the fermentation of his musts'.[1]

But if in real difficulties, remember that there are moments when the pickaxe is a more useful instrument than the most delicate surgeon's forceps. And I shall always remember Odoreida thrusting aside sixteen founder members of the Wine and Food Society with a 'Well, let's have a real drink,' and throwing together a mixture which left them breathless.

'Pop-skull, they called it in Nevada,'[2] he said, and poured two parts

[1] If you have reason to think that your guest is not particularly up in American madeiras, quote the following words in a plonking voice: 'There was an 1842 which Sohier took the trouble to bring all the way to London from Boston and gave us in 1938 (April 11th) at the Ritz; the voyage had upset it and it had not had time to recover from the shock.'

[2] A basic subdivision of Winesmanship is the US hard-drink gambit and the question of its counters. The US gambit is to be amused when anybody orders sherry, and to flock round and watch it being drunk, particularly in a club at six o'clock. It is an exaggeration to say that they expect the drinker to bring out knitting or start reading *Old Mother Goose*, but they are interested.

Nevertheless, the deliberate drinking of sherry will wear many US men down, particularly, of course, if it is mixed with a rather pi-faced lecture on the American 'inability to enjoy wine' and a richly exaggerated account of one's own national habits with drink, making your audience really believe that every typical British family serves a different wine at a different temperature with every course.

A wholly different counter to the US icy hard-drink gambit, based on our management of religious men, is to go one better. Serve drinks yourself so

of vodka into one of sherry and three of rum, adding a slice cut from
the disc of a sunflower.

---

cold that they are frozen to the glass and have to be filed out and chewed.
Let your Martinis be mixed in a much stronger proportion of gin to vermouth
than six to one, in fact, some counter-US experts pour vermouth into the
glass and then pour it out again, lightly mopping the sides with their hand-
kerchiefs, and then fill the glass with what is, of course, neat gin. Another
ploy is to invent some 'little drink' or name of a drink which 'everybody is
drinking in Nevada' (all Americans admire the suggestion that you have been
to Nevada). Call it not 'Frozen Larynx' or 'Surgeon's Knife', which is
1937–38, but Martini, mixing two absolute disparates as in the Odoreida Ice-
berg described above. Then peck at it and say, 'Oh for a real Martini – a big
Martini, one you can pull over your head like a jersey' (phrase of US Lifeman
46, reported to me in April 1952 by USI).

15

CHRISTMAS GIFTMANSHIP

A VISITOR to our College may be agreeably surprised to find a tiny room devoted to Present Giving and Good Cheer. Surprised, I say, because sometimes we are given the reputation of being spoilsports at Yeovil, or told that our Science is a dour one.

Not a bit of it. We have many laughs in and out of hours: and good nature and geniality, at the right season, are encouraged to reign – encouraged, of course, so long as the Lifeman retains his prior right of one-upness.

All of us think of Christmas, particularly, as a time when the spirit of friendliness, of being unusually nice to children especially, should prevail. Yet the alert Lifeman, even at this time of the year, apparently so unfavourable to basic gambiting, knows that he can make the recipient of his niceness feel unpleasant, if slightly.

It was Gattling-Fenn, good Lifeman and great Christmas expert, known for his Favourite Uncle play (see *Lifemanship*, p. 149) who first described the 'Remember Mrs Wilson' gambit (see the special edition of *Lifemanship* printed for the Vassar Foundation). Gattling, by exploding comic sausages, would rouse the children to a pitch of frenzy and then suddenly tell them not to make too much noise because of Mrs Wilson, a mythical invalid.

It was only last year, however, that I realized the delicacy of Gattling's actual technique with the actual giving of presents.

If I may summarize Gattling-Fenn, the object of Christmas Giftmanship is:

1. To make it seem to everybody present that the receiver is getting something better than he has given you.

2. To make the receiver feel that you have got away with a present that looks all right but which he knows isn't really.

3. To make the receiver feel there is some implied criticism about the present you have chosen.

To take the last section first because it is the simplest and the easiest to explain: a rather dowdy-looking and badly made-up woman who prides herself on 'not always dabbing herself with a powder-puff' can in certain tones of voice effectively be given the present of a beauty box. Conversely, a woman who is insidiously ostentatious about the flower-like and impersonal quality of her beauty can be given a hot-water bottle, a small biscuit-coloured Shetland shawl to wear in bed, or a tin of patent food which announces clearly on the front label that it has been specially treated to be made more easily digestible. Add a shopping bag (a group of friends may arrange together to give this lot as a set) and the effect is almost bound to be annoying over a long period and especially in retrospect. Particularly if, thrown in with the rest, somebody can give her one cheap lipstick smelling of lard.

Under this same head come special presents to men who fancy themselves remarkably young for their age. A spectacle case, for instance, for the man unwilling to disclose the fact that he wears glasses: or, best of all, a small 'YOU AND ME' sound amplifier 'which anybody over the age of twenty-five is bound to find useful when listening to conversation in a noisy crowded room'.[1]

For the going-one-better ploy, one must act quickly and buy the present for the giver immediately one has received the gift. If a man

---

[1] A good deal of work has been done on the dialogue for this particular item. This was demonstrated in the Fourth Lifemanship Lecture ('Sloppy Yuleship'). Here is the actual dialogue or parlette:

LIFEMAN (*handing small strangely shaped parcel*): Happy Christmas.
LAY RECEIVER: What?
L: I said 'Happy Christmas'. Something for you.
LR: Oh, I say . . . (*Paper unwrapping*) What on earth? . . .
L: Like it?
LR: Yes. What is it?
L: Try it. No . . . look . . . put this little thing in your ear. It's a sound amplifier.
LR: What for?
L: It amplifies sound. When it's difficult to listen – in a crowded room – put it in your ear and wear the battery in your buttonhole – do you see? Let me . . . it's not a real carnation, it's only a dummy – and if you have the least difficulty in hearing—
LR: But I'm not—
L: No, of course you're not. Of course you're not. Of course you're not. But – anyone over the age of 25, really, finds it difficult to hear in a crowded room. It's not that you're deaf. Here. Let me talk to you through it. (*Then recite some poem very loudly but with mouth well to side of microphone of machine*)
     There was a boy, ye knew him once,
     Ye cliffs and islands of Winander—
LR: Of what?
L: WINANDER. Wonderful, isn't it?
LR: Thanks very much.

gives you (if you are a woman) a handbag, you should give him a cigarette case *with initials on it* to hint that you have taken more care and he must do better next time. If somebody gives you one of those *de luxe* editions of Jane Austen in a stand-up cardboard case, you can immediately buy any old nineteenth-century copy of a George Eliot novel and make the Jane Austen giver feel he is merely a trier by telling him you have hunted four years for this example 'of the Bristol edition' (you can call it a 'Bristol first'), and that when you found it six months ago you knew he would be the person to appreciate it. At the same time, Jane Austen will half realize he is being fooled and that you have probably only paid half a dollar for it, anyhow.

In more advanced work, poor relations may be maddened by giving them useful presents, like scissors or bradawls. Eminent art critics can be given the World's Best Twenty Masterpieces in Oil, done in rather poor colour reproduction, with the dirty pinks merely brown and the browns merely dirty.

A jolly little poker-work doggie which pops in and out of a kennel shaped like a shoe is a splendid present to give to either (a) a zoologist, (b) a collector of Staffordshire glaze, or (c) a breeder of pedigree poodles. To one's wife, of course, one gives the present one wants oneself – a book on astronomy, for instance, or even one on golf, 'in the hope that she will really start to play, now'.

A keen gardener, who knows something about gardening, can be enormously irritated by being given a poetry anthology on the theme of garden flowers referring to flowers in the vaguest possible terms and quite often describing spring flowers and autumn flowers coming out at the same time, and vice versa. Golfers who pride themselves on the manly professionalism of their equipment can be given golf mittens embroidered with knitted nosegays.

It is rather a good thing to give expensive presents (a) to people who think they are helping you financially, or better still (b) to those whom you owe money.

Any man who prides himself on the period accuracy of his room decoration can be given a crinoline lady to fit over a telephone ('Grenfell's Good Turn').

If a hired servant, give your employer something better than he has given you. If you receive an obviously dud present, such as a cheap china sweet tray, when the giver next comes to the house to dine place her present ostentatiously in the middle, with your own sweet trays (silver, and of obviously better design) grouped round it.

If the boss, it is a good thing to give to your employees a calendar consisting of an owl with little numbers under it which have to be moved every day. They will have to be moved every day.

Wonders can be done with a genuinely old painted tray, one handle of which, however, has been broken off so many times that it consists entirely of glue and falls to the ground after half an hour by its own weight. After handle has come off twice, you can say fairly sharply to recipient: 'Yes, I'm afraid it was born in an age when mass-production was unknown.'

But Gattling is at his Christmas-ship best when it comes to the treatment of children. His basic gambit is to give them presents a couple of years below their age-group. If the child is continuously burying itself in a corner with *Lord Jim*, give it a book about a wild wolf dog which saves a baby from an eagle. If the boy is in the space-travel, space-ship phase, give him any book in which animals talk and hedgehogs wear a watch and chain. Or to any child over seven, just getting really interested in revolvers and sawn-off shotguns, Gattling may, with that genial twinkle, give a book printed on indestructible paper with special 'Childprufe' binding about Duckie and Cock and his adventures in Woollie-Woolla Land.

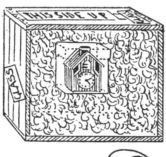

LIFEMANSHIP ACCESSORIES
LIMITED

F. Wilson has improvised this dummy 'Petit Chalet' cuckoo clock, with extra-loud cuckoo at quarters, and dustpan-and-brush-proof packing shavings with special ADHERO barb ensuring that each has to be removed from the carpet by manual torsion.

(Note ring on little finger of hand on left supplied by our Department of Foreign Amity with a small point on the inward side, for slightly pricking the grasped hand.)

16

HANDS-ACROSS-THE-SEAMANSHIP

It was once said of Yeovil, I think not unjustly, that 'the subject of Foreign Relations is neglected here'. Now each candidate is expected to show some proficiency in what, reduced to its simplest elements, may be represented as $k\lambda$ 3.26084, if 'k' is the factor of constant international difference[1] and 'λ' the vague desire to be pleasant.

It is not our policy continuously to try to be one-up, as a nation, on other nations; but it is our aim to rub in the fact that we are not trying to do this, otherwise what is the point of not trying to do this?

First lessons concentrate on the necessity of always using the same phrases, and using them again and again. No harm in the general reader memorizing one or two of them now:

We have a lot in common.
After all, we come from the same stock.
We have a lot to learn from each other.

[1] i.e. the tendency to be faintly irritated by foreigners.

Plasterman's Approach

The important thing of course is, when speaking to this man from overseas, to get in first. No one followed this rule more keenly than Gattling-Fenn's half-brother, who was not called Gattling-Fenn at all but Joe Plasterman – whence the whole gambit-sequence involving the use of those phrases sometimes called 'Plasterman's Approach'.

It is known that when Plasterman was a guest at the Monosyllable he saw two members standing at the bar. He was unknown to these members, *and they were at this time unknown to each other*. But Plasterman's host had happened to mention that one of them was an American.

Plasterman went up to these two men and placed his hands gently on their upper arms, standing between them. Quietly he said:

'The future happiness of the world is based on the friendship of the two peoples.'

Then, with a slight downward pressure of his hands on the shoulders of the two, he added: 'I won't say any more.'

'Do you know those two?' said his host, when Plasterman got back.

'Why not? They are my brothers, aren't they?' said Plasterman, still in the Approach position, but he noticed that his host looked as if he was trying to disappear into himself. Host began to whisper:

'But I mean that was Ed Murrow and Harold Nicolson. They can't both be your brothers. Besides—'

'However unworthy the sower of the seed . . .' began Plasterman; but his host was beginning to edge off, and Plasterman – fate of the Lifeman – was left alone with his one-upness.

Plasterman's work was quickly recognized, and it was not long before he was given a position of trust in the Goodwill Department of the Ministry. It was through Plasterman, actually, that a specifically US Problem came my way, no doubt because I know the States well myself, having lived there for close on thirty days. It was therefore as Founder of the American branch of Games-Life (Principal, J. Bryan III, of Wa.), in conjunction with the Office of American Enthusiasm, that it became my pleasant duty to greet American visitors to Britain in the Festival Year, and appear to be trying to make them feel at home while at the same time becoming one-up on them (GB-manship). My pamphlet on the subject has long been delivered to the department concerned and may be printed early in 1965.[1] Here, meanwhile, is the work of our collateral branch on US-manship.

[1] My summary will be published in 1953, Series IV, *Games-Life*.

US-MANSHIP

A note on how, when visiting Britain, to appear to be quite happy to be one-down, while actually remaining one-up.

General Rules

The basic gambit for all Lifemen, of course, is to praise. And the basic, because slightly annoying, thing for US-men to praise in Britain is its charm. This is sometimes called 'Cliffs of Dovership'. It can be done with most effect if you praise, and with politeness, the charm or quaintness of any of the following:

(*a*) Pseudo-Tudor, such as the thatched telephone kiosk on the London–Oxford road, or some frightful old barn which has been casting a shadow over your host's garden for years, shortening the lawn tennis court by two feet, yet incapable of being pulled down, removed or destroyed for lack of money, labour and the necessary pulling-down local government licence.

(*b*) Some bits of condemned and muddy farmland with neglected coppice and untended rivulet, which local residents are particularly ashamed of.

(*c*) Something which the British don't think charming at all but on the contrary particularly up to date and mechanized and modern. Stand, for instance, in front of the new London University building, one of the highest in London, and 'love it because it's quaint'. Watch one of our most renowned and actually streamlined engines, the Bournemouth Belle or the Coronation Scot, sliding out of its terminus, and say, 'I've always wanted to see a steam-engine again. Why, I remember when the Twentieth Century Limited used steam.' Or ask to be taken on a tour of the largest British film studios, at Denham, and say, 'Why, it's got everything, cameras, lights, and here's a little carpenter's shop too.'

Another good general ploy when in Britain is to take for granted absolute ignorance of anything American, and then be surprised, if not offended, if your British listener has not heard of some name of purely local interest. E.g. say, 'We have a magazine called the *New Yorker*' or 'There were two President Roosevelts, you know.' *Then* talk without any explanation but with a wealth of local detail about 'Lausche in the days when he was Mayor of Cleveland', and take it for granted that your British listener will not only be interested but informed.

There is a decidedly irritating way of 'being amused', very difficult to acquire, yet recommended to the advanced US-man. He will suggest to his British friend that like all Britons he thinks of American history as beginning with George Washington and the apple tree, leaping straight to the Boston Tea Party, jumping thence to Uncle Tom's Cabin via American Indians being shot down one by one as they circle round Gary Cooper, and a band of early settlers who succeeded in preserving America for Rockefeller and Harpo Marx.

This friendly teasing is irritating because it includes and subtends a basic gambit, 'Grain of truthship'.

Behaviour

In dress, be either (*a*) keenly American or (*b*) extremely English. But note to Bostonians: extreme Englishness is set off rather than spoilt if one Americanism creeps in: e.g. in day dress it is OK not to show cuffs: or (recommended American pronunciation inserted in perfected Bostonian English) retain the American '*mus*-tash' instead of the relatively feeble English 'mstarsh'.

It is slightly annoying to the English to be told that their English accent is 'perfect' or 'sweet' or 'cute', since the Englishman rightly believes that he alone has no accent whatever. It is also annoying to the English who pride themselves on being able to imitate the American accent to point out that in fact the accent they are trying to reproduce is a mixture of the dialects of six American states, all of which are not less than fifteen degrees south of the Maine accent to which, from its wording and references, the mimicry must belong.

Interest in Cricket

US visitors must, of course, go to Lord's – sacred-shrine-of-cricket, in an attitude of gentlemanly respect and alert anticipation. If they find while watching the game that for the first twenty minutes absolutely nothing happens, they should not comment on the fact that absolutely nothing happens, but they should suddenly turn to their host and say, 'You know, we have heard so much about Lord's in the States. Now I want you to analyse for me the wonderful atmosphere which they say pervades this place.' After forty minutes, if a batsman scores one run, it is coarse US-manship to say, 'Would Di Mag have powered that one!' Just say, 'Wow'.

Make some reference, suggesting that an effort is being made, to W. G. Grace, England's greatest genius of cricket, but get one initial wrong, perhaps the second.

Individual Ploys

When going to a British Railway station, do not *say* anything about the relative miseries of these spots, but bring galoshes, blankets, air cushion, packet of sandwiches and own coffee in a thermos. It is quite a good ploy in England to be seen constantly carrying about coffee in a Thermos.

Conversely, yet perhaps connected with this, it is rather a good thing, having arrived in Britain by air, to ignore Westminster Abbey, Parliament Square and the Tower of London when your host mumbles something about these places with vague pride, and say instead, 'I can't wait to get to see Waterloo Station.'

Carry with you any example of a recent British article criticizing America, broadmindedly and genially agree with it, and praise the British for having given such a good example to the Americans of what the Americans ought to have done. E.g. take a recent British *Architectural Review* attack on domestic architecture in the United States and read it out aloud to your British friend while standing amidst the housing accretions of any suburb of any large British town or in any recently built village, and say, 'Yes, you certainly have got a way with your domestic architecture which we can't touch over there.'

It is quite a good thing to read up bits of local history and literary association, then ask your British friend and guide questions about them. Henry VII's Chapel in Westminster Abbey makes a good background for such knowledgeable questions; or Dove Cottage, home of Wordsworth in the Lakes, with special reference to Coleridge's visits there. In both cases, of course, your British host will be unable to conceal his almost complete ignorance of the facts involved.

If your British friends fail to be put off or made to feel slightly awkward by these delicate little gambits, and mutual friendliness and goodwill insist on breaking through, it is always possible to fall back on Anglo-American relations. We at Yeovil are at present formalizing this splendid instrument of general dis-ease, gambits, counter gambits, and the one-up-one-down atmosphere. We are rather proud of our name for it – 'Manglo-Relations' – which has been formed syncretically from the two terms 'Anglo-American Relations' and 'mangled feelings'. The natural friendliness, the recognition of a home from home, the geniality and mutual admiration which exist between the two nations, can always be frustrated by anyone who uses the word Relations, with its disagreeable double meaning. This can be brought in indirectly, or insidiously, by expressions based on the phrases students should have memorized from the beginning of this chapter: 'The British are our best friends' or 'The freedom of the world depends on America and England keeping in close touch, pooling common knowledge and working eye to eye.' Whatever phrase you use, the Manglo-Relations Department can always be guaranteed to put temporarily out of joint the firmest and most lasting friendship in the world, and frustrate the un-Lifemanly habit, much in evidence recently between British and Americans, of just plain ordinary liking each other.

SUPERMANSHIP

or,
How to continue to top without actually
falling apart

PRELUDE

SIX YEARS have passed since we last issued a gamesmanhsip pamphlet (*One-Upmanship*). Yet these pages were the vanguard, merely, of newly co-ordinated research at the Lifemanship Correspondence College of One-Upness and Gameslifemastery.[1] Our endeavours, largely unpaid, have recently been intensified and extended to the political scene and the international sphere. These must remain secret. But feeling, naturally, that the extension of our orbit, called for a strengthening of our terminology, the introduction of a significant prefix became only a matter of time. We are no Supermen at Yeovil. But the term Supermanship, devised by our Creative Department, does convey, I hope not too pompously, the intercontinental grasp, the roots deep in human character, of what we have come to call, when we speak of the basis of our theory, the Contribution.

[1] The suffix 'manship', still used by our outside workers, is generally shortened by us, now, to ''ship', or even quite frequently merely ''p'.

1

FACES OLD AND FACES NEW

AN INTRODUCTORY MESSAGE FROM
THE FOUNDER

('*Something of Myself*')

IT IS pleasant to look back. In the evening of life, or at any rate the
tea-time, there are successes, and there have been things less successful.

My early volume on the great central section of Hove, wide though
its field, never really sold: the history of a famous pewter-maker, a
commissioned work, is not much read outside pewter circles. On the
lighter side, I told the story, valuably I think, of the sudden improve-
ment in my golf which followed my discovery of *artery-thinking*, as I
called it in my manual *Down to Sixteen or Less*. (This was illustrated
by action photographs of myself which I myself actually took, by
means of a simple device of ordinary pulleys and a piece of ordinary
tape.) But there are plenty left of the first printing.[1]

And then the queer accident. Philosophy I would have chosen, but
the public must decide otherwise. I browse in the realms of Behaviour-
isticism and Implied Anthropology, and behold the result. Gamesmanship and Lifemanship have had followers, though not always the
ones I expected. And when an alert student pointed out to me the other
day that it was now twenty-five years since the incident of 'Joad's
Request', as it has come to be called – since the day, that is, when Joad

---

[1] During the war, I wrote for the B B C's Overseas wavelength a series aimed
at the strengthening of morale – really dramatized biographies of British and
Dominion writers – Pope and Peacock, Blake, Milton and the rest. These
were twenty minutes apiece, and well packed moreover with material showing
the first struggles, early conflicts, later struggles, and last struggles – there
was scarcely a line of dialogue which was not the result of reading and research. I printed a collection, adding my suggestions for background music,
most of it from Elgar and Brahms. But *Airborne Heritage* sold, I think,
less well than any of them.

called across the lawn tennis court the words 'kindly say clearly, please, whether the ball is in or out'[1] – it seemed to all of us that notice should be taken, an occasion marked.

There was nothing sentimental – no 'gush'. One of the nicest things for me was that a special Lifemanship Literary Luncheon was organized for me by Miss Ivy Spring, Yeovil's sole female staffer. The small tables for onlookers were only partially filled (the date clashed by chance with the arrival of the Brazilian Commission) but the 'high' table was full of guests distinguished in many walks of life and included F. C. Littleman, the famous anthologist of bowls and (friend from the past) Anne Briar, water-colourist of broadcasting fame. We much enjoyed the *bons vins* and dishes provided by the *chef maître* of the Clapham Junction Hotel.[2]

CARRYING ON

Work is constantly in progress at Yeovil, though little of it sees the light of day. Only last month a stranger wrote asking for news in enthusiastic terms – though by the way it irritates me if my first name, is spelt with a v. We have continued to keep ourselves free of the old pernicious educational strangle-holds of 'test' and examination. Our diplomas, by no means expensive to buy, must, though, be signed by at least *one* other member of our staff besides myself.[3] If the IQ of our students is low, it is because we are keeping it so – because it is not in the parrot-like ability to write down the correct answers, in the unpleasant precocity which enables the student to be at his best in, of all places, the examination room, that we place our faith. Mere written work is on the whole discarded. We teach our students to make, to act – to 'get their hands dirty' as we say, and they succeed in this extraordinarily well.

Apropos, a question from Oxford! 'Yes, but how do you do that with the young economist?' asked once of me shyly R. Harrod, of Ch.Ch.

'By sending him into the coalmines, instead of bemusing him with fuel figures or supply and demand curves. By putting him into grubby overalls, to pick up a lump and question the miner, eager to teach him,

---

[1] See *Gamesmanship*, p. 11.

[2] Gattling-Fenn, the only member to make two speeches, gave me a clock, with a plate inset for an inscription (he insisted that if I chose the wording I could have it done myself). Odoreida gave me a very useful little upkeep set for my spectacles.

[3] This other member must never be G. Odoreida.

on the spot. A month in a drawing-pin factory bringing cups of tea to the men who mix nickel with brass is worth six months' study of the inverse demand curves of international alloys. Later we teach them to make real graphs out of pieces of wire; and the squared paper is ruled by a group of pretty dark-haired girls.'

Faces Old . . .

Gattling-Fenn and the rest are still with us, needless to say, at the prime of whatever age they are. 'Rattling Gattling' as we call him, Gattling the bit of a cadman, is still forceful and eager. After twenty-five years of being the oldest young man at Yeovil, he has now entered into a new lease of life as the youngest old one. When, in the summer, he addresses, in the open air, a small group of students sitting out of doors relaxed on the natural asphalt, he now concentrates on being amazing for his age. Owing to his exercises, which we hear something of before breakfast, he is definitely able to sit springily on his heels. He never now changes from the blazer and Old Wantage scarf which he wore on the occasion when he first applied for his post with us.

Cogg-Willoughby is now the internationally accepted scholar of Gameslife and spends his time codifying and rectifying. Every day through the Wild Garden between the roller and the greenhouse, both out of use, he delicately picks his way for twenty minutes and it is generally recognized that this is Cogg's relaxation, and no student is allowed, or wants, to speak to him.

G. Odoreida is still – Odoreida. He holds no actual Lectureship with us and has not for four years. We did allow him, when he advertised for pupils, to refer to himself as 'sometime Reader at the Lifemanship College': but by altering 'sometime' to 'sometimes', he managed to give the impression that he occasionally did us a good turn, and that it was he who had parted with us, instead of vice-versa.

In fact, for the moment – doubtless a very brief one – Odoreida is enjoying an extraordinary success. His evening seminars at home are really well attended – quite enough to fill the hateful little study of 'Wendyways'. He actually pretends to be selecting applicants, making students on their first appearance pore over intelligence-tests cribbed from job-suitability tests and of course quite beyond Odoreida, who scribbles 'neater work' or 'very fair' or 'mind sp.' at random on the top of some wooden hexagon, cut-out triangle of newspaper, or some other mysterious Test object completely incomprehensible to him.

WE ALSO HELD . . .

. . . A LIFEMANSHIP RALLY

Wert of our staff is returned to us. In my absence he was somehow 'cleared' of the charge of Unlifemanlike Activities. I mention him now because it was he who discovered an extraordinarily irritating thing about Odoreida; which was that in his private seminars he actually charges 15s 6d for a half-hour of 'instruction', during which of course he teaches those ploys and gambits of the very kind which we always try to keep out of the clean and straight-forward atmosphere of Yeovil. Gattling was particularly angry and once said to him in front of a student: 'How on earth do you get away with it, charging fifteen and six?'

I knew what Odoreida's answer would be. It was a ploy he was very keen on at that time. He stuck his little head against the back of his armchair, looked at the ceiling mildly, and held his arms out straight, palms down.

'I T' he said in a sing-song voice to the tune of the first two notes of the *War Song of the Priests*. 'Income Tax, my dear,' he continued to the girl, who annoyingly enough had rather elaborate dark eyes, and had been heard to refer to Odoreida as 'podge'. Money of any sort only had to be mentioned in any kind of big way for Odoreida to look at his finger-nails and say 'I T'.

'Fifteen and six is exactly fivepence three farthings after deduction.'

Gattling was much too annoyed to answer, though he later got Ivy Spring to work out what Odoreida's income would have to be if this remark were true. Answer: £216,750 p.a.

. . . and Faces New

But now for our big bit of news. What of the College Building itself, you will say? Is it true that it has been taken over by the National Trust? No. It has of course been visited unofficially by students of its particular periods, 1876 and 1891, which have been the subject of an article in our Journal by L. Brice and Veronica P. Hartridge; of the very few bricks of the original wall in the front garden which have been disturbed, all have been put back in the same order. Whether or not it will eventually be bought for the National Trust we want to know quickly: because the big news is that we have moved our headquarters from 681 Station Road to a new superheadquarters No 675, just the other side of the level-crossing.

This was an important decision for us. The new building is actually smaller, but it is infinitely preferable because it is infinitely more modern. In period houses such as 681, it is true, students drink in

OUR NEW HQ (This drawing was executed before the repairs to the left section of the outside wall were put into full operation.)

an enormous amount of history through the pores, even if they don't know the date of Trafalgar. But how much more in key with the new Lifemanship is 675. Totally untraditional, it is sheathed in concrete while one whole big side of it is half glass, or looks vaguely like it. Look at it from Siemann's the tobacconists and see how colour and atmosphere are given by reflection only, in the glass sheeting, of signals and telegraph poles, tautly upright, and as counterpoint the yellow smoke-plumes from the engine-funnels. Indoors you can say the atmosphere is controlled. The roof is wide open to the sun, and there are days when definite sun-bathing is possible, which will be more generally enjoyed when our plea for smokeless fuel in Essential Products Ltd. our nearby factory, has met with some response, or our letter is at any rate answered. The whole thing was created by Tackton in 1925 and partly derives from the Chapel of the Secondary School at Ausvierfleischenhültz. The window frames are by Slipton, the chimneys by Skipton, and the filling material, used to cover the cracks formed by the rather lovely weathering to which all concrete is subject, is by Odzon.

The new grounds are smaller too, but what do we have instead of the old-fashioned garden? An outdoor museum, a gallery open to sky

A CORNER OF OUR NEW COMMON ROOM

and wind, of Gameslife mementoes. Over there is the original internal-combustion engine with the device for starting the car from under the bonnet, invented by Godfrey Plaste to give the impression of mechanical aptitude; and close by, the actual processed cheese advertisement taken from the wall of Aldgate East Underground Station at the exact point where the Founder first thought of Potter's Opening at Chess. By the gate, the dusky white of a patch of viscid sneezewort has sown itself, gentle visitor, in our grounds.

C. Sticking

We were enormously helped in our decision to move, and in our choice of a home, by a welcome addition to our staff who must now be introduced. For a long time we had had the feeling that the atmosphere needed modernizing: and Cornelius – 'Corny' – Sticking was obviously the man. He was easy and big and wore thick sports coats.

'Such a wonderfully unfrightened head,' Effie Weeks said: and it was Gattling who pointed out that his up-to-dateness was proved by his courageous way of breaking fetters, even on buses or at tea time. Indeed he broke fetters on holiday, as I remembered on a week-end at the Maudesleys. The house was in the rather densely kitchen-farmed and thickly populated area of mid-Essex, and I always remember my introduction to a Sticking 'country walk'. No sooner did we get onto a road or even a path than he leapt or grubbed his way through a hedge in order to continue in a straight line if possible. This took much longer, but S. insisted on this straight line because he wanted to treat this chewed-over part of Essex as if it was as wild and empty as

C. STICKING

Winnipeg prairie, walking indiscriminately across back gardens, small fields made of a kind of glue, and the winter parking-quarters of caravanettes. How he enjoyed it – but what? He was completely blind to the quite pretty water-colour landscape, though he did once refer – at the world record unsuitable moment, I should have said – to something being 'typical Constable'. The whole point of his walks was this smashing through in big boots past NO ENTRY notices and anti-trespasser signs. And it took me quite a long time before I realized that when Sticking plunged straight across the corner of Mr Butt's orchard, disturbing the chickens, what he was saying was 'the land is for the people' as if in some way he was more people than old Mr Butts.

What was the secret of the Sticking gambit? For although in the end Cannery and the Other Man between them got Sticking down, we certainly learnt a lot from his basic approach.

The simplicity of Sticking's primary attack is what makes it so difficult to counter. In a way, it is simply Sticking's laugh, big and Falstaffian, blowing away cobwebs. A happy, guilt-free laugh – 'gloriously sane', little Effie Weeks called it.[1] Sometimes he went too far: but it was extraordinarily difficult to counter.

The Coming of the Lawrenceman

Or so, for a long time, we thought.

Sticking ruled the roost, with his wonderful gambit of driving home the out-of-dateness of a date so distant that most of his audience had never even heard of it. The Founder apart, Sticking for about fourteen months was top man in the lifeplay: and he was destined to play a useful part long after that. But after the coming of the Lawrenceman, his major power was gone.

When exactly did this tremendously new face first appear? There was this boy, my second cousin Ginger. He was playing Red Indians in a wood and 'found a funny man with a beard' who said, according to an observer, that 'the cool prying of the North child can never find the secret of Poplihotl'. This was the Lawrenceman. He was small, pale, intent, serious, with rather large plastic features in a small face, and a big dark beard, round and soft and soggy. The shadows on his face made me think, when I first saw him, that he was standing under a gas lamp, but of course he wasn't. When he spoke, which was seldom, it was in an undertone. Mrs Fenn, who rather liked him, said he had a very sensitive mouth, and everybody wondered how she had seen it, under this poultice of beard and hair. Whether he had ever actually read the works of D. H. Lawrence we could never prove; but he did look like a warmed-up version of this great man and he did get hold of a few phrases and he made good use of them. It took a long time, but under the Lawrenceman treatment Sticking's confidence began to seep away. I first noticed it when Sticking was in one of his disgusted moods being disgusted about some Somerset people, who 'put on their best clothes to go to morning service on Sundays'. 'Is that a badness?' said the Lawrenceman mildly. Stickers froze.

'Your question?' said Stickers, pretty crisp.

'I think it has something of good, or is a symbol of something good.'

[1] It could make people simply ache with indignation. 'What, frightened with false fires?' he would say to a brilliant young art critic who said that except for the Meistersingers he wasn't very keen on Wagner. 'He's worth a hundred of these jazz saxophonists.' There was something so absolutely inappropriate, on five levels simultaneously, about 'jazz saxophonists', that it seemed hopeless even to try to answer back.

You would never guess that the voice came from the motionless beard of the Lawrenceman.

'Remarkably little to do with Christianity,' said Sticking. I felt we were in for a dose of Golden Bough, but somehow the Lawrenceman checked him.

'Perhaps,' he said. There was something tip-top about the placid way this word was said. He went on:

'Yet there is a ceremony of departure, a sacrifice. On the hill they lit the wood fire to the morning.' Lawrenceman's eyes were wide open, but he wasn't looking at anybody.

'You don't make yourself clear,' said Sticking, in his most distinct voice.

'Can anybody *make* themselves clear?' Lawrenceman turned to Sticking for the first time.

'That is the general supposition.'

'I think a man can make his words clear, and even his thoughts. But himself . . .?' After this stunning and really first-class statement, Lawrenceman turned his back on us and walked to the window, and Sticking made a mistake. He tried to

THE LAWRENCEMAN

look clear. We realized even then that it was a beginning, and a portent. People began to say 'Poor Sticking'. For after all he was on the right side in the right arguments. He was a good Wolfenden man, a first-class don't say, 'don't' to children man. But even if he said something fairly unarguable, as he often did, sometimes over-doing it in fact, repeating for instance that the long-range H-bomb was madness, the Lawrenceman could somehow get him down with Slow Withdrawn Look and use some all-round-the-compass phrase like 'Does then the destroyer hate the destroyer?' Sticking would bury himself in a nest of galley proofs. After about twelve minutes he would get up and walk in a markedly open-air way to the Railway Station Buffet and order a small stout. 'You can't argue with a fog,' he said, 'or a marsh mallow.' But he never did get round to answering back the Lawrenceman, so in the end Sticking was forced to change places with him, officially, on the Lifemanship ladder.

The Mild Young Men and I. Cannery

For a long time it looked as if the Lawrenceman was to master us all. Of course I always knew what the counter to him was, but I wanted staff and students alike to find it out for themselves: besides I liked Lawrenceman, and wanted him to have his day. The end came simply and naturally, with yet one more new member of the staff, who in his simple manner was the master not only of Sticking but of Lawrenceman as well. It happened in rather a curious way.

Dealing with correspondence is always a problem. A whole bundle of letters was on our desk three years ago asking us What is the attitude of Yeovil to the Angry Young Man?

MILD YOUNG MEN
(The candidates' waiting-room at Yeovil has never before been shown to Anyone.)

In fact Yeovil as a whole did not care for this movement, since most of us, about thirty-three years ago on the average, had been angry young men ourselves, in fact much angrier, and this particular movement of our own had attracted no attention whatever. We took the obvious step of trying to engage, countering, an exceptionally mild young man for our staff, and I well remember the millions of cups of tea we had, interviewing candidates for this post, and the feeling as if one was trying to play squash rackets in a court whose walls were made of semolina pudding, when in answer to our hundredth impatient question, the fifteenth candidate said: 'Ah, but I see good in that too.'

In the end, as is well known, the post was allotted to the candidate who was easily the best mild young man we saw: the only fault, being that he was not exceptionally young. That is how we got Irwin Cannery.

We all liked Cannery, at first, anyhow. Not only was he mild, he was nice, and in spite of his mildness he was tremendously enthusiastic about his subject, which was the history of lift styles. That is how he got the Lawrenceman.

At first we were flattered by his interest in our old Yeovil HQ No. 681. 'Perfect 1892 . . . 1892 dead centre,' he said, literally rubbing his nose into the plaster work over the bell-push. But the amazing thing was that he subjected our fine modern concrete building to exactly the same treatment. 'Debased Bodzinsky,' he said, looking at our roof from the little sweetshop on the other side of the road. 'Delightfully wrong here. 1932 exactly.' Actually it was 1931, but we had to admire him – especially when he took exactly the same line with Sticking, as if Sticking was debased Bodzinsky too.

I. CANNERY

'Surely this is superior to your aspidistra and lace curtains,' Sticking said, progressively, pointing to a cactus on the window-sill.

'A-*ha*!'

Cannery turned on him a rapturously period-spotting eye.

'Aha, don't tell me you've got the complete works of Sidney and Beatrice Webb,' he said.

'No, I have not.' Sticking was pretty brusque. He was getting fed up with some aspects of his life at Yeovil.

'Ah, but how about *Progress and Poverty*? No . . . that wouldn't be right . . . *The Intelligent Woman's Guide to Socialism*?' Cannery added intently.

'I suppose you don't approve of such work ,' said Sticking, tentatively sheltering behind his basic gambit.

'Approve? I *adore* them,' said Cannery. 'And now about your name? Sticking? Isn't it actually a place-name in Essex? Essex would be too perfect, *too* Shawsy-Wellsy, isn't it.'

Sticking had a good idea. Pretending that he thought Cannery was really asking a question, he said: 'Perhaps the Lawrenceman can tell you.'

Lawrenceman was delicately putting a log on the fire, and watching the mystery of the smoke.

'Come on,' said Sticking, 'What do *you* make of Irwin Cannery?'

Lawrenceman didn't look up, 'I cannot "make" a man, I hope. If I could I would ask, when he enjoyed the fruits, the outerworks, why he did not let himself comprehend – know – the roots.'

'A-HAA!' Cannery turned on Lawrenceman more delighted than ever. 'I *love* you. Are you really a Blake man! So am I! And I bet you don't think much of Bertrand Russell.'

Then Cannery asked him a dozen questions, trying to place Lawrenceman, who became, in fact more and more silent. Later on our three new members, Sticking, the Lawrenceman and Cannery, used to sit round countering and cross-countering each other. 'Progress,' said Sticking in effect: 'In what sense . . .' said the Lawrenceman: 'Period,' said Cannery, 'it's dead right, for period.' Cannery always seemed to get the last word.

So much for our staff and headquarters. The pages which follow are a record of work accomplished, of researches in Supermanship.

At the beginning, the simple things; not less bold because the subjects are familiar.

2

YEOVIL JUBILEE PAMPHLETS

General Domestic and Sociological Problems with Special Reference to Inter-Family Superbehaviourism.

I. SUPERBABY

The Baby as Lifeman

Children! What a vast subject. Superchild is in all our lives: and in pamphlet and essay, many of them printed in earlier volumes, we have dealt with them, though not finally.

There still remains to be discussed, however, that much more important gambit-field, the infant or newborn baby. And let me say at once that we of LCC are against the ugly pictures, often showing them as debased ruffians, of our English children as drawn by many of our 'comic' artists today. It has been proved that in their facies, or general appearance, 53 per cent of the newly-born seem acceptable to their parents.

Indeed it is clear that babies are by nature one-up. Whatever they do it is your fault and your fault only. Babies cannot be, and are not supposed to be, good, reasonable or considerate. Further, they are completely unsusceptible to the normal life-attacks. The grieved look means nothing to them; the firm tone is something they know how to deal with. It is no good turning away from them with a supercilious curl of the lip. They cannot be patronized. Their reaction to such remarks as 'There's a clever little boy' is a long stare in the opposite direction.

Pre-Natal Lull

The target of Superbaby's gambits is its parents. During the pre-natal period the parents have a feeling of invulnerability, of being in charge. It is their conviction that they 'have decided to have it'. It is a hushed, OK period of 'baby's on the way', with very few premonitions at first of the fact that from the point of view of the approaching lifewave it is 'parents on the way', that it is you, the parent, who are about to meet for the first time the full shock of living. 'Of course I'm still playing tennis' is the brave, pathetic last flutter of the parental flag.

'We timed it so that we could go to Cornwall as usual.' Inside, gruff and grim is ominously silent.

Nevertheless, though between conception and birth parents may have an uneasy sensation that they are about to be taken charge of, yet there is no doubt that at first the mother is in a fine lifeposition, and even begins getting fond of the baby in anticipation.[1]

Indeed, the woman is a heroine and knows it. Certain fathers, as is well known, try to suggest that they are fairly heroic also. In fact at the other end of the scale, in the slums and dingy café society of border-lifemanship, there are some husbands who have succeeded in suggesting that it is they who need special attention, the extra drink brought to them, the cushion carried from another room for the small of *their* back. No one will be surprised to learn that Odoreida, for instance, during the last three months of his wife's pregnancy, used to take

ODOREIDA 'TELEPHONING'

[1] Corny Sticking will have his wet blanket even at this early stage, taking the anthropological approach, common-sensing right and left, and pointing out that the whole thing is as instinctive as an ants' nest and that it's simply due to millions of years of evolution, because mammals started as far back as Late Chalk.

every opportunity of sitting down in a collapsed sort of way and getting people to pass him things. In golf, if the match was going against him, he would walk in after the fourteenth, two down and four to play, 'because his muscles seemed to have lost all give'. And any time from seven months to go till two days before it was supposed to happen (when he should have been at home anyhow) Odoreida used to anger us (while gaining kudos from those who did not know him) by a 'half a minute' exit after the sixteenth hole, which happens to be near our clubhouse, 'to ring home'.

'I shan't be happy unless I know she's all right,' he would say. 'I think she'd rather like to hear the sound of my voice.'

We often had to wave through two singles and a fourball before he joined us: and the maddening thing is that I was never so placed as to be able to prove what I was inwardly certain of – that he never went near the telephone, but was simply standing and drinking, quite slowly, two Scotch and sodas.

The Primordial Protoployic Gambule[1]

But in truth the expectant parents are proud and happy people. Getting them down is no easy matter. Yet notice the powerful simplicity of the baby, the first act in whose life is a ploy.

He cries – to attract attention. But note – it is not just a call: apparently it is weeping. Imitation, you will say. Fake. But there are sobs, and a special kind of retractable tear. Yet when picked up the baby is relaxed, contented and thinking of something else; and quite often this big blob of tear has gone altogether, as if sucked back into the eye. This is no reasoned and deliberate plan – far deadlier, it is the result of instinctive lifemanship, at its purest and most powerful. That the instinct goes very deep is obvious in the many ways in which the baby can keep its parents and general entourage dangling on the wires. The skilled superbaby by a collapsed motion of the shoulders, for instance, and a swivellingly swerving motion of the neck, can suggest that its head is loose. A cunning baby can do this especially during those inter-suck pauses when the bottle is laid aside and the sun stops still in the heavens because the child is supposed to burp. The good burpman can keep a room full of friends, relations and casual business acquaintances in rigid and unnatural silence for perhaps a minute till the burp comes. Everybody's position becomes fixed

[1] Gambule. A new word for Gambit, it means precisely the same thing. Its use depends on usage – e.g. I am writing it here.

TCU–K

as if they were listening to the reading of a will. More deeply instinctive is the power to come out in a rash all over the scalp which, after the father has stood twenty minutes in a queue for a special baby ointment only to find that he has to go back to the doctor for a prescription, disappears completely one minute before he gets home. Some babies are able, in the cot, to seem to be breathing at three times the normal rate; others to be showing no sign of life whatsoever, so that they have to be taken up to make sure they are not stone-dead: others specialize in bizarre and puzzling symptoms which vanish completely while the doctor, urgently summoned, is actually ringing the door-bell, so that in time the doctor decides he is being hoaxed and refuses to come even when there is genuine cause to suspect scarlet fever. By practising some form of rigidity on the scales a few are able to show 'no increase'; but be sure that on the more expensive scales of Harley Street the weight will be exactly and completely average.

Besides this anxiety play of new-born infants, which is simple and strong, they have a set of effective little ploys which may be described as *Wrong Mood*. If its pretty and fastidious godmother is coming to see it in the afternoon, it will scratch its nose in the morning so that all she sees is a long diagonal scab. When she gives a gift – a valuable heirloom rattle, for instance – superbaby will get red on one side of its face only, go icy cold in the left hand, and eat the brown paper the thing was wrapped up in.

The Attack from Outside

Not only the baby itself, but external forces will soon be concentrated on the undermining of the parents. Baby Literature makes itself felt first, and Baby Instruction. Many prettily got-up booklets start with the dictum 'Enjoy Your Baby'.[1] This approach does well by repeating, first, that having a baby is as natural and jolly as a visit to the old Victoria Music Hall, and then going into very small print with graphs, diet charts, and measurements in 'c.c.'

Yet the 'c.c.' part of it is less dampening than the last section of the book, which always recommends that the baby should be surrounded by beautiful things, and beautiful sounds. Gattling-Fenn, the only time he stayed with us, made this an excuse for playing the piano, which we never normally allowed him to do. Every day he played a sort of psalmified version, with hymny chords, of 'Once you have

[1] Known at Yeovil as the Petrification of the Implied Opposite.

found her Never let her go', because, he said, the piano was just over the nursery.

Many of one's friends develop attacking gambits suitable to the baby situation. I quite admired Cannery's contribution though it takes time and trouble. It is a well-known fact that some fathers are rather clumsy about handling their own babies, especially their first babies, and pick them up as if they were made of pastry. They curve both arms underneath them, bowing low so that the babies have less far to fall if dropped; and if they walk it is with a wide-apart bow-legged gait to avoid tripping up. The baby cries. It was Cannery who had the good idea of learning this one thing, this lifting of babies. He had observed exactly the technique of one great clothes-horse of a monthly nurse who treated the baby as if it was a punch ball, humped it over while she was washing it as if she was basting a leg of mutton, shoved the bottle into its mouth like a dentist's gag, and could lift it up a circular staircase carrying a towel, a waste-paper basket and a bottle of disinfectant at the same time. It was this grip which Cannery practised. When some mother said 'Would you like to take him for just one second?' she would be horrified and then admiring to see him take hold of the baby with his safety lock on the child's thigh and swing it round in a way which gave satisfaction everywhere. 'It's always been instinctive with me,' he would say, holding the baby upside down.

Another Friend approach is exemplified by Zimmermann. As everybody knows, Zimmermann is Sticking's younger brother. Quite early in life he changed from Sticking to Zimmermann in the belief that this name was much more suitable for a research anthropologist. He is also, and here I rather envy him, one of those excellently lifeplaced individuals who have a degree in Medicine yet do something else. Surely it was worth it, this going to Port Despair University, off the coat of Greenland, Disko Island, where medical degrees are rather simple to get, in order to become MD and do something else. The something else he used to be an expert in varied, but with babies it was always anthropology.

'Well, who do you think he is like?' we would ask him – a fatal question when Zimmers is around because after talking about the 'factor of changing appearance in the newly born' he would scribble inheritance diagrams on the baby's weight chart proving that so far from taking after its parents, it was only by the merest stroke of luck that the baby, if a boy, was still alive. Zimmers could then pass easily to the sterilized approach, making you feel, in spite of all your

nursery scrubbing and boiling, that the baby might as well be eating
off the farmyard floor. Or he would switch to raised eyebrows at the
diet. 'Nowadays we are giving them the equivalent of sardines on
toast by week nine.' I must say that without being a complete cad

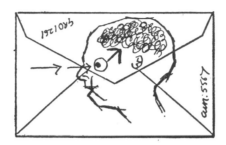

DIAGRAM BY ZIMMERS
Demonstrating that 'Look,
I think he recognized you',
must be nonsense, unless
the association centres of
the infant brain (marked in
fuzzy lines) are abnormally
developed or hypertro-
phied.

that old Ph D left us as miserable as most. He did not actually cast
doubts on the suitability of our doctor. I believe he once tried that on
Odoreida who, I am bound to say, did well by asking, in the same tone
of voice, who had been the doctor at Zimmers's birth and pretending
to be very interested because Zimmers couldn't answer.

Is There a Counter?

There is no doubt that there are parents capable of answering back.
Some mothers have a kind of school-matron approach with visitors,
telling them not to smoke, not to leave the door open, not to make sudden noises or movements, not to crackle paper, not to greet or touch

the child, not to be ingratiating, and not, above all, to breathe in the
infant's face. Mrs Coad-Sanderson had some fine successes with this

kind of toughness and once kept three brothers-in-law, all regular soldiers (gunners) – one a brigadier – in sterilized face-masks for nearly ninety minutes – men who had turned up under the impression that by coming to see her baby they were doing a nice thing.

But in general, once the child is born, the Lifemanship Force in array against the parent is strong, our techniques well studied and pursued unflinchingly. At the same time we are scientists and are equally glad to record, for the pleasure of adding one more brick to the pyramid of objective truth, that so far as discouraging parents from having children is concerned, our work has had no result of any kind whatsoever.

2. THE GREAT VICE VERSA
(*Town versus Country*)[1]

This primordial lifetheme has never yet been officially dealt with by us. Why? Because the opportunities for blast and counterblast are too dangerous; the one-downness of the subtended situation too potential. It is only after anxious discussion with a Ruridecane of York that we put forward this emasculated account of techniques permissible under this head. It has always been, and is here I hope, our aim to present our approach in terms deemed wise for family reading.

[1] These primary strictures were worked out by the Founder, F. Wilson, and the Leading Lifewoman. Surely the fact that their material was made use of is sufficient reward and acknowledgment. Any talk of 'two bob per point used' would be as ungracious as it is out of place.

What is this about? A major proportion of English people belong to one of two camps, Town or Country. Your home may be in what you are not naturally one of. There are small groups perhaps who, in the pursuit of supertaxmanship, have a foothold in each. But none of these modifications affects the primary type.

In order to disguise[1] the two contrasted characters we have in mind, we will call them Willie Westover and Edward Brick. Willie is Supercountry: Supertown is Edward.

Supertown in Supercountry

This is the basic situation: Town spends weekend with Country. Edward, Town, has strong feeling that on not less than seven weekends a year, he should leave his three rooms in Albany – he comes, fourth generation, from a strain of primitive flat-dwellers – and take the 4.10 east from Liverpool Street to Old Soking. He will enjoy the very smokiness of Liverpool Street; '4.10' has a magic, the waiting room of Mark's Tey Station is faery. He will arrive in a state of mild happiness, a placid expectation even a pleasure in Englishness not seriously scarred by the necessity of reading the *New Statesman*, which he had read up to the end of 'This Way Madness Lies' anyhow before reaching Ingatestone.

This sleepy contentment is precisely the state of mind which it is the business of Willie, Supercountry, to undermine. Willie will meet

W. WESTOVER (*right*) GREETS E. BRICK (*left*)
This record has been carefully drawn to demonstrate the Westover Wave, or minumum effusive greeting.

[1] Disguised against their will. But we are against giving publicity.

Edward, of course; but the train has moved off before Edward spots him waving over his shoulder from the other end of the platform. His back to Edward, who has two heavy bags, Willie is talking hard to the station master, complimenting him on having won second prize for growing the best vegetable garden on the Yeldham branch line. He takes Edward's new bag in strong grasp which strains handle. 'Good old Edward,' he says. 'Coming to pieces in several places at once.'

This is a good beginning because in fact it is Willie who is inclined to break apart: Edward never. Willie then pushes Edward into a Land Rover, first leaving Edward's white doeskin suitcase on the bonnet, thus giving it its first dose of bat-droppings. The back of the car is full of vague shapes, and there is a bundle reducing space in front, which means that Edward has to shut up like a jack-knife in order to get in.[1]

Edward will make mental note that next time it will be better, on the whole, to do the old dreary beat by car past Seven Sisters on to that kaleidoscope of gay scenery, A12, via Hangman's Corner and three single-line traffic-queues in the Brentwood area.[2]

The actual fifth-class track which Willie calls the Drive has a well made exhaust-winkler – i.e. a bump which claws off the silencer of any car less effectively high-slung than Willie's Land Rover. Willie then will make a tremendous point of having cleared out his 'berewick' (Willie must on no account be allowed to enlarge derivationally about the meaning of this word). However hard Edward will have made up his mind, driving down, to keep his new and glistening saloon away from one of Willie's 'garages' he will feel obliged to back the car to Willie's 'left hand hard down – no hard' routine, (specially simplified for Londoner) so that it is inevitably buried in the straw and sacking at the back, because Willie is absolutely determined that the door of this barn must shut, so that Edward's car (which Willie always refers to as 'the hearse') will be placed centrally beneath the nameless exudations, the bird and bat refuse, and the

---

[1] Edward guesses that the 'something' includes a large black sack, which occasionally moves slightly, and which he will have to help carry out: he is aware that there will be no drink.

[2] If Edward asks Willie to send him full directions somehow distinguishing which of the dozen *steep dip down to white gate, advise you approach it in first, and please shut gate again after you* it is which actually marks the gap leading to Willie's house, Willie will respond to this request warmly, sending sketch maps with quaint little jokes on them – e.g. 'here is Brick's Folly' (where Edward once twisted ankle) . . . 'Wood. Wylde beasties here.' The plan has twenty roads going off into nothing and is unorientated.

splashes of an acid substance which leave a stain long after the car has returned from its special cleaning.

As Edward clambers out over piles of pig-food his host warns him when he gets to the threshold: 'Sorry, we have a silly rule here. Shoes off. Brings mud in.'

If Supercountry's house happens to be large, enormous sections of it, the best, will be shut off and unheated. 'We only open these up when we have to put on our best bib and tucker.' If by any chance these unopened rooms have any kind of architectural merit, or are remotely Adam in design, or have more than a three-line mention in an *Ancient Monuments*, wife of host will early on cold morning ask guest his advice about moving furniture because 'Otto Carling is coming down, and I'm terrified of what he'll say. I hope you don't think William and Mary looks absurd in this little alcove.' The point of this question is to take no notice of guest's answer.

The undermining of guest's confidence by references to past and future guests whom 'we feel rather frightened of', was a gambit also employed by Willie Westover: and it must be said that he did well with his One Meal version of the Chief Guest approach. Willie would arrange the week-end meals so that they were exceptionally scratch and sardinified except for one, the Saturday luncheon, preparations for which, with full discussions, will have been apparently going on since mid-week. By Saturday morning every member of the household, including the usual guest (according to Edward, who was this 'ordinary' guest) is called into the kitchen to do amusing jobs, especially grinding or cutting things into very small pieces. By 11.30 there is a break for 'elevenses for the lunch workers'.[1] At 11.55 Willie blows a trumpet and puts on a chef's hat for some extraordinary sauce which is then put on the stove, and such a *pièce-de-résistance* atmosphere is built up round this sauce that Edward's spirits droop and dwindle at the thought of the congratulations and jokey French which will have to be dragged out for the 'success', when it is eventually served, of this sauce, the miraculous point of which will be that it contains some unheard of ingredient like hawthorn-leaf wine, the local name of which is cockroach claret.

'And then, and *then* who do you think the guest was after all this?' No need to ask me that question. 'Otto Carling, the Horrible.'[2]

[1] This, according to Edward, is the first decent meal of the week-end.

[2] Carling was best known as the man who had diddled the Meat Marketing Board in 1944, did a special trade in clothing coupons, and published a book illustrated by his own woodcuts on My Fayre Sussex.

'And how does O.C. do it?' What is the secret? For those interested in the Carling angle on this – for it wasn't only at the Willie Westovers that he managed to extract these specially prepared lunches – I can reveal Carling's method. It is to make absolutely no comment on the food, to be completely silent about the wine, and especially to say nothing whatever about the sauce. And never under any circumstances, to say Thank You.

Of all Willie's gambits this one of the Special Guest was the one which Edward found most difficult to endure. It is not necessary to say that with his very long nose and shapeless figure Carling had no vestige of charm nor goodness of looks; and this made his triumph all the more exasperating. Edward had ways of countering, as we shall see later. In the very throes of this luncheon he would amuse himself by planning a cocktail party in his Albany flat which he would arrange 'specially for Willie', when Willie came to visit. The carefully selected guests, quite well known in a slightly suspect way which would nevertheless appeal to Willie – the compère of Willie's favourite TV panel game, perhaps. While Willie was filling up Carling's glass, at least two and half times to every once for Edward, Edward would plan exactly how when Willie came bursting in to meet all these 'famous coves of yours', Willie would find himself stuck in a corner with Edward's aunt and never get nearer to Panel Game, or Everest as Far as Camp Four, than Edward's purposely generalized and untruthful 'You know everybody here don't you.'

On a cold Sunday morning, if Edward had put on a good but thin tweed suit, Willie would pat him chaffingly on the back, say he 'could see Edward was not a countryman' and take him out for a good walk, or perhaps simply to the church along a muddy 'short cut', lending Edward a pair of galoshes which were much too big for him and which kept sucking off. Edward would certainly be taken to church if Willie knew it was his turn to be sidesman. He would pass the plate personally to Edward, putting a new pound note in himself. Although Edward was practically certain that Willie would take this pound note out again afterwards, he felt constrained to look impersonal and fish for his only ten bob note, which would be scrunched up.

All this was not unsubtle on Willie's part, as it prepared for the visit to the pub between church and lunch. This was bound to be the low moment of Edward's day anyhow because the only drink available was pints of tremendously watered beer, any possible core of alcoholic content of which could not conceivably be retained in the body long enough to take effect.[1]

The object of the pound note ploy was to leave Edward short of money so that Edward embarrassingly could not stand his round of six pints. Needless to say Willie made the most of this business of standing Edward's round for him.

'Nonsense,' he would say. 'You're my guest from the very moment you set foot inside Hollyhock Lodge.'

Edward would quite have liked to have talked to one or two of the nice old men with amusing faces in this pub, and it seemed to him that quite a few of them weren't too mad on Willie Westover. But as soon as Edward made a move in their direction Willie would pull him aside by the elbow and in a sort of roaring whisper ask him 'why he didn't speak to them'.

'Talk to them. Mix with them. Old Cracky over there' – Willie would point a stubby finger at a man in the corner whose head was sunk so low that Edward could see a little way down his back.

'Old Cracky—'

Hearing what he knew Willie supposed to be his name, Cracky slowly turned his eyes, one yellow and one red, in their direction.

'Old Cracky, now he is a *real* person.'[2]

Counter-country

Many were the little counterplots and plans we discussed with Edward when he returned dim and baffled from a week with Super-country. What to do with Willie on his return visit. The 'you must meet' party was a sitter, but could scarcely be repeated. We were

---

[1] The alternative was a sherry, dark purple in colour, the taste of which rather pleasantly reminded Edward of the days when, kneeling in church in prayer at the age of six, he used to suck the varnish off the back of the pew in front.

[2] On the way back Willie tried to steer Edward past the Fullers' cottage because Rene, the little girl, usually said 'Good morning, sir,' to Willie. But instead of Rene it was Jeff who sarcastically said ''Ullo' and winked sadistically at Edward, looking straight past Willie. It was the only bit of luck Edward had that day.

even reduced to suggesting to Willie that for a theatre, he would like to 'see something French by the French Comedy people'. Long damped down in the fungoid undergrowth of Hollyhock Lodge, the libidinous spark in Willie's eye did flutter precariously to life for a moment: and Edward enjoyed watching it slowly fade through five acts of Racine and the Comédie Française. Any suggestion by Willie that he wanted to be taken somewhere 'off the beaten track' received a response of enthusiastic agreement from us. We took him to the little Latvian restaurant on the third floor of the tenement behind the Middlesex Hospital, which Willie well believed to be Soho because we drove through Soho to get to it. Here meals were served, swimming in oil, in the kitchen itself: and it was here, we felt, that we were really repaying Willie for those Hollyhock Lodge Sunday evening snack-and-wet-tomato feasts.

Willie countered rather finely by 'finding the whole thing tremendously entertaining', and by bringing his dog, a clumber spaniel, who was not only indescribably unsuitable for London but had an almost visible odour of her own which quietly outshone the rancours of Latvian oil. Edward's riposte was neat one.

'That dog needs exercise,' he said.

'Yes,' said Willie. 'But where are you going to get it, in the Brickyard?' This was Willie's name for W.1.

'Take it for a run on those lovely little stretches of grass alongside Mount Street,' said Edward. 'Tell the man in charge you're a friend of mine.'

He was referring of course to Cutts, the most feared Park Keeper in Southern England, who always stood motionless in the centre of these tiny public gardens, his cheek twitching. As is well known he allows no dog to pass him unless it has a muzzle and a lead of tested steel shackle. If the dog pauses in some trance or even slows down he will at once shout 'Keep that animal out of it', running the words together in one rasp.

Generalized Off-puts

G. Odoreida, who cannot be described as specifically town or specifically country,[1] has developed one or two putting-off ploys equally useful in opposition to either. There is his piano-playing

---

[1] In the country he gives the impression of being more naturally at home in London, and *vice versa*.

sequence, when he sits down and lets his fingers wander idly over the piano, according to a musical sequence (see later). If Supertown and Supercountry have one weakness in common it is that they become bewildered or uneasy if some average-looking guest starts playing an old piano which has only hitherto been used for some forlorn hope music lessons, which came to an end when she was nine, of the plainest of four daughters.

W. Westover (*left*) Secretly Prides himself on looking like his game-keeper (*right*). But in practice the result is *vice versa*.

Then again, Odoreida used to bring with him, in the country on walks, a disguised receptacle of the kind which we call a lifeprop. In it was a collection of deaf aids. No need to thrash out here the old question of whether there was really anything wrong with Odoreida's hearing. The fact is that he sometimes scored points in both camps with these aids. Supercountry might take him for Willie's muddy country walk through woods. O. would carry what seemed to be a large binocular case over his shoulder. This itself is good, because why does he bring it? Bird watching? But candidly this is never perfectly OK with Supercountry, because it suggests a slight reproof to the old huntsman, also a very faintly left-wing interest in Nat. Hist., and a suggestion that Supercountry, to whom all birds are some kind of target which he prides himself on being able to distinguish, without raising his eyes, by the sound of the wings, does not know his own job. Pressing the ornithological approach, Odoreida waits for the sound of some woodland bird. At the first 'pipple-pipple', he will slowly take out of his case not binoculars, but a small deaf-aid and a packet of sandwiches, will sit down on the newspaper the sandwiches are wrapped in. 'Sometimes we have to wait for hours.' If Supercountry says 'What for?' Odoreida has a special way of saying 'Sh'. Willie

TRY TO SUGGEST THAT YOUR PIANO IS IN CONSTANT USE

waits in agony, afraid of looking a fool in the eyes of Jack Minton, of point-to-point fame, who often walks this way.[1]

A Note on the Piano-playing of Odoreida

How to be good at the piano without being able to play much really. Here is a theme which has been so much part of my own life in music that I scarcely regard it, any longer, as a problem. It is an approach to musicianship which many senior students of Gameslife besides Odoreida have picked up, I suppose, from my own method. Yet the approach remains empirical. The technique has never been properly cleaned up by Yeovil Arts. The Post Free fifteen and sixpenny pamphlet, *You, Too. In Three Lessons*, was never published, owing to

[1] In London circles Odoreida would go in for small tremendously up-to-date deaf aids, suggesting for instance that his cuff button was a disguised microphone, and hold this practically against the lip of the speaker who is trying to tell the funny story which depends for its effect entirely on intonation.

Against somebody who starts off 'Look here Odoreida I'm never absolutely clear what it is you *do*. Civil Servant or something?' Odoreida is very good, especially with the big domineering man Adcock, a typically Supertown who says this sort of thing. He takes out a different instrument – actually an ordinary microphone with a wire attached – makes Adcock (who has a fibrosed knee) climb over a small couch crowded with people, and leads him to a dark corner where he plugs his microphone in and then says 'Would you mind saying that again more slowly – and rather more quietly please.'

the War; but my thoughts often returned to it, during the immediate post-war years.

Maybe this is a task for Canada. Meanwhile, to set the ball rolling, let me jot a hint, indicate a line of appropriate elaboration.

'Piano Tutors', and teachers in general, make the mistake of telling beginners how to play some rather feeble song or tune, some simple version of 'Tea for Two' or 'The Ash Grove' or even 'God Bless the Prince of Wales'. *What is the use of this?* How totally out of key it is with any conceivable lifesituation. No one, I said to myself when I started on my pilgrim's progress to pianohood, really wants, that is to say truly and deeply wants, to hear me play 'The Ash Grove'.[1]

What is wanted, if one can only do a tiny scrap, is the suggestion when doing the tiny scrap that one could do much more, if one was playing on the sort of piano which appeals to one but one can't, and to the kind of people one likes, which one isn't.

No need to detail the sixty different ways of making sure, if there is a piano in the room, that somebody will say, 'Do you play?'

'No' is *wrong* answer to this question. *Right* is 'Yes – far too much I'm afraid. But never in public. The point is that I learn music that way. It's the only way I can learn – by letting it soak in through the fingers.' The expert pianoman, holding out his fingers flabbily as if they were made of blotting-paper, can then show that he is pretty adept in almost every known branch of music.

First of all, while still standing, play three quick chords, very firm and staccato, like a piano tuner.[2] Then while sitting down do a short trill on the note B (month's practice). Then go from this trill into the first ten chords of the Siegfried Idyll. Why the Siegfried Idyll? First, because, although to those who happen to know it, 1 in a 1000, it is by no means particularly O K, to the rest it sounds mysterious and poetical: second, because it is possible by playing this an octave higher or lower, and then again by playing it with the left hand coming down after the right, to suggest that you are extemporizing variations on this theme.

Next, to show that you can't simply just play chords but must have technique as well, you must play something with a run in it. This is always the difficulty, but if you really can only just play one scale with

[1] Nor even the Chopin Prelude which is short and quick and slow and potty and keeps repeating the phrase Ma *Ma* Ma-ma Ma Ma.

[2] Some knowledge of the notes up to late kindergarten standard is essential. It is not enough to be able to spot middle C just because it is opposite the key-lock which fastens the lid.

the right hand, the scale of C, do it and say, 'Do you remember that lyrical Juliet theme in the Prokoviev – and Ulanova seeming scarcely to touch the ground?'

For modern music, I play any small tune, with simple harmony, but the bass note always the same. Try this with 'Au Clair de la Lune'. Finally, when audience begin to look stuffy and depressed it is essential to suggest that you can do jazz as well. I used to play, and keep on playing, the basic bass of boogiewoogie with the left hand, then twice rhythmically but bangingly bring down the flat of my right hand on some patch in the treble.

3

LIT

Recent Work in Litero Creato-Critical Fields

I. HOW STANDS REVIEWMANSHIP TODAY?

IT IS said, and we hope it is true, that it is in creation more than critic-ism that our ambitions lie. But Reviewmanhsip is an old Lifestudy, constantly being improved and re-codified. A few recent develop-ments may be worth recording.

The actual definition of reviewmanship is now, I think, stabilized. In its shortest form it is 'How to Be One Up on the Author Without Actually Tampering With the Text'. In other words, how, as critic, to show that it is really you yourself who should have written the book, if you had had the time, and since you hadn't, you are glad that some-one has, although obviously it might have been done better.

New Wording for the Special Subject Review
Suppose the book is on a specialist's subject like Rhododendron Hunting in the Andes. No known reviewerman will have been to the Andes; few will understand the meaning of the word 'Rhododendron'. But only the novice will take refuge in vague praise, will speak of the 'real contribution to our knowledge of the peaks in the Opeepopee district' or the 'debt we owe to Dr Preissberger, the author'. Much better to take the 'yes-but' approach, look up in any botanical manual the Latin name of any Rhododendron not listed in Preissberger's index, and say, 'Dr Preissberger leaves the problem of *Azalea phipps-rowbothamii* entirely unanswered'. Or start, 'It is surprising that so eminent a scholar as Dr Preissberger . . .' and then let him have it.

New Novels
That is the rough pattern for reviewing any specialist's book.

Reviewing novels is a more difficult problem and may even entail actual reading of the first and last chapters. If you don't know what it's all about by Page 12, it is perfectly fair to say that the book is 'slow getting started' and that the 'plot is involved'. Always quote something from the middle pages to show that you've thoroughly studied the book.

I was amazed by the sheer power . . .

A sound general gambit, if there is a love interest, is to single out words and phrases like 'sensual', 'full lips' or 'soft arms', string these together with little dots in between, and then go into a tremendously open-air early morning mood, pervade your article with the atmosphere of putting a big pipe in your mouth and say you are longing for a breath of fresh air. 'Thank goodness this is not typical of our younger generation,' you say, as if spraying disinfectant, and talk, in general, as if ordinary physical love was only gone in for by irregularly developed persons living in basements. But remember when reviewing novels, that you are always ready to give a helping hand to the young. The general rule here is to praise, even overpraise, any first novel, reserving to yourself the right, which you will invariably exercise, to pitch into No. 2 ('which shows little of the promise of . . .')

I was staggered that so eminent a scholar as Dr Whitefeet . . .

I was moved by this simple tale of young love . . .

Hamlet is a Lousy Farce

In other words, place one mood in the irrelevant context of a totally disconnected one. This ploy goes for both fiction and non-fiction. Say, for instance, of a treatise on infant mortality in nineteenth-century debtors' prisons, that you 'are afraid the author takes himself very seriously'. But if the subject is the Game of Badminton or the

What a pity . . we miss the true *saeva indignatio* . . .

... it leaves an exceptionally nasty taste in the mouth.

... I found myself unable to put the book down.

History of the Light Programme, do not fail to regret the jocular tone, not to be surprised that, in this context, the author should be so anxious to indulge his facility for humour.

Jeffrey was a rotter, but . . .

Certainly the reviewer must remember his status as a Friend of Literature, so let him be careful not to pitch into poets, particularly good ones. When he does, he must show not only that he regrets it, but that he could have eliminated a few of the more important of the author's errors if only he had taken the obvious course of confiding in the reviewer before publication and shown him the manuscript. We can't all be Yeatses. For criticism, it is a good thing to take any three consecutive words at random, and say you have studied this passage and that, and that when you were first led into the mysteries of language, you were taught that words have meaning. Then, warmheartedly, talk of Yeats as if he was a sort of simplified Macaulay, and that every word he wrote was clear to the merest schoolboy, and none the worse for that.

When discussing translations of poetry, the Critic is on surer ground. If (1) the poetry is translated from French or German, it is easy to suggest that as everybody is completely at home with French and German anyhow, why translate it at all? If, on the other hand, (2) the original language is rather less well known, Hungarian or Syriac, it is still possible to say: 'In the second stanza Mr Snyder is in deep waters. In his version the "brown flurry of wings" hastens "the thickening twilight". Let us turn to the original for a moment. How much more beautiful and, of course, more Syriac in spirit, is . . .' Translations from the Chinese (3) are inclined to be rather successful and difficult to criticize. S. Spender well says that it is always possible to suggest that 'one needs the Chinese calligraphy for full appreciation'.

2. THE MANSHIP OF MEMOIRS

'Anybody can criticize' – how often have I said this, not for students,

to whom I rarely speak, but to Staff. 'But how few do.' 'I mean *do*,'
I said, walking up and down the Common Room, while they sat
wondering. 'Do, DO.'

They looked at me queerly. We had just been working on this
critical section. 'We too should not be afraid of criticism.'

'Do what?' asked Cogg stickily. Cogg kept a diary which a publisher had once asked to see, and felt several points up so far as 'do' was
concerned.

'Yes, what?' said Sticking, who did oil paintings on wooden boards,
absolutely untaught, in his bedroom.

'We should write ourselves,' I said. 'Stick our necks out.'

'What!' said Gattling, heartily.

'Of course we could always write our autobiographies,' said Cannery. 'That would be dead right for 1958.'

I wanted the suggestion to come from them. After all G. Wert and
Effie Scudamore had written their autobiographies, and so had Sticking Minor, as we called Sticking's nephew, and he had had his
published, perhaps because he was only seventeen.

I did not make it an order but soon pencils were out, and I had
them all sitting round the Common-room table, making a start.

Before long Autobiography Hour was an institution on alternate
evenings. I sat in a corner stimulating the laggards; but on the whole
they went to it with a will. The Lawrenceman was the most difficult.
'My life – what *is* my life,' he was always saying; and he strode to the
window to stare at the low sun over the corner of the gasometer. 'To
write it in a room – behind glass?' he said. 'Perhaps, when saxifrage
grows on the walls, and the roof is open to sky and stars – perhaps
then.' But the greatest difficulty was Gattling-Fenn, who rather
surprisingly sat hunched up over his blank paper and could think of
nothing to say, not even with the help of an occasional gin and tonic.

The strange thing was that Gattling started better than any of us.
His idea was to begin with a sort of it-was-fun-while-the-going-was-
good book.

I applauded this until I read the following passage. I don't think
people who know us well would say that Gattling had travelled more
than myself. In fact we neither have. With this in mind, let us examine the following passages from his first chapter:

Over the desert the African wind plays queer tricks, and our tiny single-
engined Kalaad, flying much too low I thought, began to buck and slide

AUTOBIOGRAPHY HOUR

Left to right: Lawrenceman, Cannery (taking mint ball from desk), Odoreida, Sticking, Cogg-Willoughby, Gattling-Fenn. Although we did not know it at the time, Odoreida is simply copying long bits from the *Journals* of André Gide.

alarmingly in the surface eddies. Passengers were on the verge of panic and it was a nice decision whether to go forward to try and cajole our dark-skinned pilot (of the voluble gestures) to climb the obvious 6,000 feet, or to sit back and try to look bored as if everything was alright. I decided on the latter course. If 'Engleesh thinks O K' then, by some mysterious Law of the Tribes, everybody can feel safe.

Now I took the trouble to check back on this page because this was the first I'd ever heard of G. flying dangerously anywhere. He would have mentioned this about a million times if he'd ever done it. Of course we all knew that he had once taken this sea voyage to Gibraltar – the longest of his life – and had stayed there for a week at the small Stratford Hotel run by this Mrs Fenwick. What I did not realize was that on the Tuesday of this week he had taken one of the little Taylor Bros air-buses on the day-trip to Algiers and that this did involve, if you counted the very dried up little playground behind the Algiers-Astor where they had failed to make the golf course, flying over something which might be called a desert.

I took G. to task for this, and I am sorry now that I did so; because from that moment his inspiration faded and he never really got back his confidence. There were times when the spark returned, and he said that the only question was whether his was going to be the sort of life which would be serialized by the *Sunday Times* or the *Sunday Express*. He thought he could make great use of 1940, and the fact that at that time the Home Guard at Hale (a place just outside Manchester where he had been platoon commander) had been asked to man, in their exercises, a line from Hale Golf Course starting at the old eighteenth tee and ending at the branching of A56. He said that he expressed an opinion, in a mock exercise against Moodhams Enamel Company Home Guard (Moodhams Enamel Company being supposed to be the enemy), that the line should extend as far as The Grapes, Moberley. Well whether they had agreed with him or not, and this he couldn't remember, Gattling became possessed with the phrase 'I Disagree with High Command', and kept repeating it to himself: whereas we thought that even to suggest such a chapter-heading might put the *Sunday Times*'s back up, and no good could come of that. If he could have a hint of physical danger in his life, we said to Gattling, who was a shade too young for War No. 1, and hopelessly too old for No. 2, it would be better. But he hadn't. In the end we invented 'three years of his life, 1938–41, of which he could neither speak not write', and he 'must crave the reader's pardon for this gap in my brief story'. This idea was the best thing that happened to Gattling-Fenn, because it bridged over the time when he was being public relations officer in a firm which specialized in disinfectants – an unsuccessful episode in Gattling's career.

Another suggestion we had for Gattling, talking it over among ourselves, was that he should make use of the very fact of this bad luck of nothing ever happening. Coad-Sanderson had read some life of some quite good essayist who was also in the Home Office. There was a splendidly long passage in this autobiography taken up in a completely O K way by a youthful experience which for some reason 'meant' something to this man. It was about standing by some lock and watching the lock gates being worked, so that the flooding in of the water, and the punts and an old barge floating up underneath him started a new chapter in his life, and that the old floating bits of straw and one empty packet of ten Players 'shone with hidden gold'. Everybody agreed that this section was so good that Gattling could use something, pretty well anything, like this and that it ought to fill up about eight pages. The great question was what. We all chewed this over. 'The first thing I remember was being frightened of the knife-cleaning machine: it made me cry, and the smell of knife-powder made me sick,' Gattling said. That was good, but we all believed Gattling could do something better. The youthful visual experience which we chose in the end for Gattling was the soda-water syphon on the small

sideboard in the corner of the Fenns' living room which Gattling's father used to visit about ten times an evening. We explained to Gattling how to say that he suddenly really saw what it looked like.

'I should think I did really see it,' said G.

'No, we mean see,' we said, making a very slight pause before the word 'see', and slightly narrowing our eyes – all very annoying to Gattling, but we were of course helping him, and we took over for him, describing the spot of light gleaming and sliding on the spout on the syphon, as the bottle was tipped and retracted, tipped and retracted, and the impulsive plunge of the soda into the glass, making a gimlet-hole in the shallow pond of honey-coloured whisky.

'Shallow?' said Gattling, boringly still not seeing the point. 'To my recollection the whisky was at least the equivalent of a pub treble.'

This ran to six pages but we were still badly short of things to say. By the time we had got Gattling to his thirty-fifth year we were only on p. 19 – ridiculous. Really up against it, I exercised my right of issuing a circular letter to Lifemen overseas, explaining our difficulty and asking for suggestions. Samarkand (Idaho) wrote back at once. 'The usual thing in our autobiogs,' they said, 'is to have the hero get repeated to him some wise old remark made by some tremendous old character: but the remark must be really thunderously obvious – so much so that even hero understands it. The ideal is for the thing to have the words "root" or "soil".' Thank you, Samarkand, but it's space-filling, not half a page, that we want. Very much better was the  suggestion from Florida that though outwardly things were pretty smooth with Gattling, he was in fact slowly dwindling away from some obscure complaint, and that nobody was to know what this was, not even Gattling, though in retrospect it becomes obvious in a hundred ways. The Florida people had made a small study of this

important gambit, and though they were not able to help much with
our immediate problem, it became a stock subject, last Christmas, for
discussion groups (Christmas 1957). Memoirmanship apart, to what
extent is it possible to concentrate attention on oneself by looking
poorly? To what extent does it depend on the profile? Look carefully
at the drawing above, part of a local collection made by the Florida
branch of Gameslife Research American. Study the deflection of
the delicate head of the reclining girl. How she assumes a wan cheerfulness, to avoid giving sufferings to others. Even the game of croquet
is stopped, so that the visitors can gather solicitously round. Lopsy
MacGregor, the little black boy, is miserable. Even the dog feels that
there is something wrong with his beloved mistress.

Yet in fact the picture is a perfect illustration of our theme, pro-
visionally described as the inverse equilibrium of the slight headache
and the well-shaped nose. True, the name of this reclining person
is Dora de la Foissette Gastervil, but study the picture again, more
carefully. The croquet players, the solicitous guests, are the victims.
Genuinely worried, they are dupes. But the coloured boy obviously
knows something. The relations, in the distance, have their back to
the scene. Is the dog concerned, or merely recognized a familiar

odour? Why has the garden gone to ruin, the chickens running wild?
TB? No. Dora is suffering from the most appalling hangover, and is
still on an eight-day jag. The cooling drink Lopsy has been bribed to
bring her is nine-tenths rye – Old Grandma, double proof. And the
time is ten o'clock on a Sunday morning.

In other words, the guests are deceived because the profile is more
significant than the complaint. So far as Gattling is concerned, of
course, the only thing wrong with him is that he suffers from
eczema between the shoulder-blades in spring. But whatever was
wrong with him, Gattling's vaguely rugger look would stop this
suffering episode from being, autobiographically, of any use to him.[1]

The curious thing about Cogg-Willoughby was that so far as his
autobiography was concerned his difficulty was almost exactly the
same as Gattling-Fenn's – very little happened to him. To begin with
he was far more diffident about this than Gattling. He did make some
notes under the heading of 'Chapters out of Childhood' – an excellent
title we all thought, and a good theme; because although his childhood was unusually uneventful, it was a Micky Spillane thriller compared to his early manhood and middle age, when the most important
thing that happened to him was the death, in Canada, of a half-sister
whom he had not seen since he was six. Everybody agreed that if
Cogg's autobiography was worth doing at all, it must depend entirely
on the quality of the writing, and indeed Cogg was so conscious of this
fact that he took nearly a fortnight writing the first two hundred
words, although we were all around, on tap to help him with this
business of the quality of the writing. One of Cogg's difficulties was
that he had an extremely bad memory. 'An absolute must is your prep
school,' we said. There are only two things he could think of: one was
that he was once top of his form for parsing, and the other was a boy
whose nickname was 'Uncle' to whom during the autumn term Cogg
used to give an expensive firework once a week to bribe him out of
throwing Cogg into a furze bush. There was an obvious chance here
of building up Cogg as a man whose whole character was warped by

[1] To decide which members of staff or students reached 'mean inverse
profile requirement' of invalid ploy we had life-size reproduction of this
drawing pasted on three-ply, with a hole cut out in place of Dora's face
through which volunteer could place head. Rather an interesting example
this of our care for detail. It is also of interest, showing the difficulties of the
total ploy, that no member of the staff when tested produced a positive result.
This is an instructive experiment for the week-end shooting party or Boys'
Club, and will break the ice indeed at any sticky gathering.

being bullied; although there is a smaller group which remembers Cogg's rather horrid treatment of Mather, at Tidworth OTC camp. It is they who say that it was Cogg who was the bully, and that this is the fact which tainted his later life and left the trauma.

Later we went over this ability of Cogg's to win a prize: but it was not so fruitful as it at first seemed. 'You never had any difficulty with languages of course,' we suggested; and an interesting point came up here. Because Cogg's mother was half French, it was always regarded as absolute gospel that Cogg was bi-lingual. Actually this was far from the case, though he did evolve a series of valuable ploys to support this idea. If ever French had to be spoken he would always shut up dead or start reading a book, somehow suggesting that the sort of French we were using would fall to pieces instantly if he introduced the real thing. Occasionally people would ask him questions about French, and he managed these extraordinarily well. 'Now Cogg, what's the French for a "boarding house"?'

Cogg would not look up. 'There is really no word, interestingly enough.'

I wasn't going to let him get away with this so I said, 'But what about *pension*.' Cogg looked expressionless for a second; then he said:

'That is the vocabulary-book word, but – danger. *Pension* suggests a whole tribe of associations which simply do not exist in England.' As Cogg's vocabulary was only about fifty words he did well I think at this point by saying, 'Actually one should use a phrase. If you wanted to be colloquial you could say *coup de maison*.'[1]

Fowlering Up

Sometimes I am quite proud of my little band of 'Merry Memoirists', as I call them – we have plenty of chaff during break. But when we were in the midst of our difficulties with Gattling, I could not help noticing the change in Cogg-Willoughby, who to start with had been a good deal slower even than Gattling. When we were all sitting round at the autobiography-writing-table, scratching our heads, it began to be annoying to see Cogg scribbling away without a moment's pause. Now

[1] Cogg made endless use of this *coup de*. There was another thing he thought he knew about French, and he built a tremendous lot of his language life round it. And that was that the accent in French words 'always comes on the last syllable'. He would bring in half-Anglicized proper names like Avignon and hit the last syllable with an 'ong' like *Queen Mary*'s hooter. In a restaurant he would always ask, as his first thing, for Pâté Maison, partly because he had learnt how to accent these syllables like the opening phrase of the Fifth Symphony.

this is a fine ploy in the examination room. I have used it myself. Nervous candidates, unable to make a single movement of their pen, sit watching you, transfixed.

Cogg was annoying us. It became essential to 'stop flow', as we used to say in the crude but happy days of early Gamesmanship. It is essential in a corporate community to discourage the disagreeably outstanding. As I explained to my good friends, *we were a team* of autobiog. writers. With my more or less commissioned *Literary Guide to the Thames Valley* on the stocks I felt justified in checking Cogg myself; and I did it by a very simple method which I have used for about thirty years which I call Fowlering Up. You look over the shoulder of the writer and make a yes-but comment on something minutely verbal. Start smoothly by saying, 'I shall like this, I know. Yes, you're using the word "cathedral" in the right sense, I think.' That was the word Cogg was writing. He seemed to take no notice.

Later I said 'Yes ... "the monks intone" ... ' Then I twirled round quickly with my face practically touching Cogg's and said 'Why not say "chant"?'

'Why should I?' said Cogg.

'Shorter – simpler.'

'It's only a letter shorter,' said Cogg.

'More English?' I said. But you can never trust Cogg. Feeling that he was going to prove the word was Dutch or something, I tried to be more general, and quickly. I read again, over his shoulder.

' "The lights came on one by one" – isn't that rather a coincidence?' I was trying to appear to be appearing to try not to be patronizing. Cogg did slow down a little, when I said this.

'I mean aren't you a tiny bit bemused by the phraseology of your own pet phrases ... a little bit pen-proud ... what you-know-who would call a Grace?' Sure enough Cogg's pen did begin to drag a little bit – a little bit as if he was writing in treacle.

I had expected Sticking to have little difficulty with his own memoirs: but although he speaks so readily in his clear way and has more wit in his talk than most of us, as soon as he started to write the blood seemed to ebb from the expressive centres of his brain and all that was left by the falling tide was a lot of verbal old iron. Words like 'federation', 'workers', 'natural evolutionary processes', 'produce' and even 'proletariat' kept turning up. 'You must be more personal,' I said, looking over his shoulder. 'Detail. For Heaven's sake look at

this: My part in the development of the
Workers' Educational movement in East
Anglia . . .'

'Pure heaven,' said Cannery.

'What did you actually *do*?' I kept urging.
Sticking became uneasy.

By a series of cross-questions it turned
out that Sticking's only concrete memory
of this was bicycling along a muddy lane
near Hay Tor with one of his students, a
girl with a long fair pigtail. He had been
lecturing on Town Planning to the Colchester
Borough Council Management Summer
School.

In the end, curiously, we found it better
to make Sticking concentrate on his spare-
time fondness for the arts. 'Music is my
real life', became the start of chapter six. He
had a complete collection of Elgar, *The Ring*,
and any works by the Big Six of the great
Germans which were called on the label, whatever the facts, 'post-
humous'. Sticking always wanted an audience for his music, and
because we all liked him we stuck to a secret rota so that there were
always two detailed to listen. But as he kept his gramophone in his
bedder, and as it was of rather an old-fashioned make and would only
take 78s, which were lying all over everything everywhere, it was
difficult to move a step without making a sound like the delicate
crunching of sea-shells.

But those who expected bold attacks from Sticking were disappoin-
ted. If he wrote things about 'the uniform of convention', it would
mean that he had seen a lot of people wearing white ties at a performance of *Fidelio* at Covent Garden in 1936. He actually seemed to
prefer, when he went to the theatre, going up the back stairs to a
converted schoolroom in a district north of Camden Town with an
unheard-of postal number. Later in his book he did rather well by
describing a radio talk which he had suggested and which was 'mys-
teriously turned down' by the BBC.

Odoreida presented a different problem. 'Frankness is everything
in autobiography,' I had told my little band. 'Right,' said Odoreida
and began a series of recollections almost all of which, in spite of what

I had said, simply had to be cut out. For instance few people know that he was nearly two terms at Oxford University before he was asked to leave. How did Odoreida get to Oxford? As a 1923 equivalent of a Displaced Person? Displaced from what? Did he himself invent the name of the 'University of the Jamaican Dutch' which he represented as part of the special student exchange Peace Across the Waters agreement, something which 'embodied surely one of the best of the Liberal movements floated after Oners[1]'? Or did Odoreida invent this phrase himself? Was Professor Gilbert Murray, who 'was so gracious to me', really Odoreida's dupe? And even if not, does this make good autobiographical reading? Anyhow most of us agreed that he couldn't possibly say he was sent down for the thing he was sent down for, because however frank the self-revelation, no one could ever possibly put that particular thing in a book, discreditable as it was in a way so uniquely combining the unpleasant and the uninteresting. After a lot of discussion it was decided to suggest that the disciplining should follow some incident, which though true was less derogatorily vapid. In the end, pointless as even this was, we advised Odoreida to record those days in Eights Week when he used to wear an Oxford 'Blue' tie, though he was never a Blue not the least fraction of one. This act was so astonishing to some that they could not bring themselves to look squarely at the woolly dark-blue tie and scarf Odoreida put on. When he was challenged Odoreida would not defend himself. He would say that he had always wanted to be able to wear the tie or ties: so as he was not given it, he bought one. We decided Odoreida should put this in his chapter on Oxford – 'I Wake up the Spires'. 'No doubt the authorities,' it ran, 'no doubt the powers that be found it difficult to stomach this affront to tradition and "correct" behaviour. They cut me out of their friendly activities, particularly their boating dinners. My attitude hardened. Had one of them come forward with one genuinely friendly gesture, one hand-shake which was really warm . . .'

In the end we had to veto so many of Odoreida's suggestions, including three complete chapters, that he became huffy and said he'd scrap the whole thing, which he did. Instead he wrote a long autobiographical novel, solely in order to introduce a character whom he called Querula Minge, quite obviously meant to be Eva Plimm, so that he could go for this girl as hard as he could and simply tear her to

[1] Odoreida likes making little jokes, but these are always about totally unfunny subjects – e.g. calling World War I and II 'Oners' and 'Twoers'.

pieces. All this was because she had told Odoreida, when he tried to kiss her during some long train ride they had to take together down to HQ, that his ears smelt like tarpaulin.

3. TO WHAT EXTENT IS THERE A VIRTUAL SUPERLECTURE?

The other day I was thumbing through one of the early volumes of my 600-page folio notebooks,[1] repository of all the first sketches and miscellaneous thoughts of Lifemanship, quarries out of which, from such obscure jottings as 'how about antisepsis' ... 'REN 6382' ... '6 South African Sherry' are built what are to become the completed chapter. I found an entry with Lecturemanship written beside it in blue pencil. I had obviously given some lecture where there had been a few empty back rows. I began scribbling notes. Here is the result.

Chairman Play

Let me give a little shape to these jottings. One of the best ways of being one up in a lecture is not to lecture but be chairman. Chairmaning – the art of being one-up on the lecturer – has been independently well described by J. Priestley.[2] It is the art by which the Chairman can *break flow* of lecturer with such basic and even dramatic ploys as having little notes passed up to him and then making tiny 'unobserved' signals to people in the audience.[3]

Simpler methods do not need less practice. The Chairman who remains on the platform for the lecture should certainly have something distracting about him – he may cross his right leg over his left and reveal the fact that right sock is so shrunk that it scarcely comes above the shoe at all. Audience will watch this large white naked ankle. If his hands are rather red and puffy naturally, he may let one hand hang by his side with an inert look as if he had some deformity, slight, and possibly recent, but certainly growing worse. Occasionally I have seen a Chairman do well by coming on to the platform with three large books of his own, one obviously actually written by him

---

[1] Naturally a large proportion of the pages are blank, and will be kept so, I hope, in the eventual printing by the Facsimile Society, since surely this very blankness is indicative of a significant mood, of a pause in process, a change of direction even, though the order and the placing of the blank pages may be sometimes in doubt.

[2] *Delight.*

[3] Odoreida, when Chairman, was able to suggest that the note contained rather bad news of a derogatory personal nature.

(name big on dust jacket), and keeping these under his arm during the lecture as if he was just popping in, between two really important lecture engagements of his own, in order to give a hand to old Layman. He can establish this point in his opening speech by making two jokes of intensely local reference, about some unpopular fire drill, which he knows his audience will laugh at, though the point will be completely incomprehensible to the visiting lecturer, who will look uneasy.

Longer practice is required for what I call the off-beat laugh. This is really a slow chuckle developed during some serious part of the lecture as if Chairman was trying to lead the audience into the realization that there really was, after all, some grain of amusement in what Lecturer was saying. While thus smiling or giving a relishing chuckle, Chairman may turn, not his head, but his whole torso, in the direction of the clock, suggesting that he wants to know how the time is going in as unobvious a way as possible. Another way to do this is to 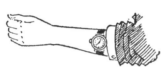 take a quick glance at the wrist-watch, but to have this strapped so high up that forearm that it takes a lot of covert arm-extension to get there.

At the end of the lecture the Chairman can get up after a short pause with a start, so as to suggest 'Why has he suddenly left off talking?' He may then say, 'Well, I am sure there will be lots and lots of you'll be wanting to ask questions and I am very glad Dr Layman has agreed to do this. Now then . . .' It is perfectly easy by the intonation to discourage the asking of any questions whatever.

After no pause at all Chairman can then say, 'Well, if you won't I will. I am going to sail right into it. Now Doctor, what exact evidence have you of your interesting suggestion about the IQ of Scottish children being higher north of Glasgow?'

Needless to say Dr Layman will stammer, if only because he never mentioned IQs at all; while the impression remains that Chairman has gone rather more deeply into the subject than the lecturer.

Gattling-Fenn

Gattling always interested me on the platform. He once studied a book called *How to Think Fluently On Your Feet*. One rule was 'Be economic of gesture'. Taking an occasional glance at his feet Gattling used to stand to attention through his whole lecture until he came to a bit where he said 'the whole edifice of modern civilization is beginning to sway, before it crashes to the ground in flames'. When he got to 'sway' he would use one of the gestures illustrated by a diagram in the book but not in my view the right one – a quick zig-zag movement of the right hand ending in a loop 'to suggest some phase of the argument was finished' – and *invariably* he barked his knuckles on the rostrum. Our audience of young people warmly applauded but I am not certain that he had really what we call 'got' his audience.

Later, Gattling changed styles to a kind of higher chatmanship, or speaking easily without notes, which was a bad choice because unless he had everything written out in full, he could never think of anything to say after about four minutes, and so had to use a lot of ploys to fill up time. One of these was to read out of a book. Realizing quite rightly that it is a bad thing to come in with a book stuffed full of paper-markers like feathers, and that this suggested careful preparation which is unsuitable for chat specialists, he would pretend to find the passage in his book by riffling through the pages, really getting there almost at once because of a piece of chewing gum he stuck in the page he wanted – typical Gattlingism, because more often than not he had to tear the pages apart with both hands. But I must say he had a wonderful way of closing the book after reading. I remember him once, badly stuck, opening at random a book left over from the last lecture, something about the History of Chartered Accountancy. After he'd finished it he looked deeply at the audience, while at the same time closing the book very slowly, almost with a faint suggestion, as it were that it was practically the Bible, a ploy which once nipped in the bud a slow handclap.[1]

In later life Gattling only gave one lecture – on the contrast between English and American humour – whatever the announced subject. He would pull out his dog-eared notebook and begin: 'Today, if I am interpreting your Chairman's wishes correctly, in speaking about the "Gothic in Art", I will approach it specially from the standpoint of the contrast between English and American humour.'

The danger here, of course, is that by some curious law, if you do

[1] For after-dinner speeches Gattling would write hundreds of words of notes on the back of old menus which he used to collect for this purpose, pretending, on the night, that this was the menu for this dinner, to suggest that if he was using notes, they were scribbled during the speech of the previous speaker. His next-door neighbours were always getting hold of Gattling's old menu by mistake, and it was amusing to see a man who thought he was going to get lobster *thermidor* being served with pressed duck.

this, you will see sitting in the middle of the front row somebody who listened to your lecture last week on Ralph Waldo Emerson, and who is going to be tremendously surprised to find that your Gothic in Art piece is precisely the same. This calls for bold gamesplay. You must say that you are 'delighted to see somebody in the audience who can confirm the difficulty we had in defining these principles in terms of Emerson', and 'wonder if they will approve of this new formula'. Say also, if necessary, that this person 'asked a very interesting and profound question' which although, of course untrue, will confuse and at the same time compliment this prospective enemy and the chances are he will string along.[1]

Cogg-Willoughby and the Distinction Ploy

Of all the basic techniques of this art the one I most admire and the most difficult to perform is the Distinction Ploy. I am not in fact referring to the effortless superiority of the man who combines knowledge with understanding, wisdom with learning, and clearness of aim joined to integrity of social purpose. One may have a little of that oneself; though even then one sometimes spoils it if, for instance, one misses the first step mounting the platform. No – I am referring to the art of creating the illusion of distinction. Actually our Cogg-Willoughby with his hollowed-out, hankering sort of face made a good shot at it especially if he stood under a top light, and increased this effect by the usual methods of thirty seconds' silence before starting, gazing at his manuscript and slightly shifting it around, with about two very slight coughs. He would sometimes get people really quiet, by taking one small tablet out of a green glass bottle from which a very long tail of cotton-wool had to be pulled before the tablet

[1] Gattling's attempts at gesture were tremendously developed by our Dramaship Instructor, G. Wert, who was a great sight on the platform. He used hundreds of gestures but they were all somehow like a repertory production of *The Beggars' Opera*. We could never understand why he had never been asked to speak on the BBC television, particularly as 'How to speak on Television' was one of the courses he most specialized in. I can see him now saying 'The atomic bomb can destroy a city the size of Wallingford like puffing out a candle—' (he said Wallingford because, although it isn't a city, that was the place the Chairman came from). Then he would turn full on the Chairman, hold out his closed fist and say, 'But it cannot make a flower grow.' As he said this he opened his fist one finger at a time, about a foot in front of the Chairman's chin, as if it were a flower growing. Privately this amused us because Wert spent hours every winter with an old bag of bulbs, hyacinths, and nothing ever came out of them, except slimy looking leaves about two feet long.

would come out, and then be stuffed back after. He was able to suggest by this that his stomach was only held in place by one frayed piece of catgut, that he was plucky to be there at all, and that it was only the inly burning fire of the spirit that gave him the strength to raise the chalk to the blackboard.

Mind you, some outside help is of great value to this whole Distinction gambit, and the Chairman must somehow be persuaded, or bribed with a Rover ticket of a Test match, to inform the audience beforehand, if you are lecturing say, on Blenheim (a theme which unless you are careful will need a good deal of mugging up), that you are not only a scholar of the Marlborough campaigns, but that you are so morbidly distinguished that not much information can be expected on such a well-known thing as the Battle of Blenheim from a lecturer who is such a tremendous scholar of his subject that he has spent the last two years studying the commissariat chits, 1704, of the 48th Worcester Horse, a regiment once reviewed by the Duke of Marlborough before the Battle of Oudenarde.

Counter-Inspector Play

No one boasting the name of Lectureman can leave out Tutorial Classmanship and Extension Lecture Play, if only because it is here that we find, essentially, the fine gambit field surrounding that passionate madcap of the Extension Lecture room, the Inspector. This great bird is by no means universal. It is fairly safe to say that that very fine lifeman, W. Auden, delivering his Oxford lecture on Poetry, will not be casting a dozen worried glances at the door in case the Inspector turns up. All the same, when one is lesser, and younger, Inspectors are pretty well inclined to swarm. Now the basic gambit against Inspectors is to be promising, and for that the 'background necessity' is to be (a) relatively much younger than the inspector whatever the facts and (b) gauche. *Never try to be distinguished and gauche at the same time.* Change over from the Distinguished as soon as the Inspector comes in. In the old days I nurtured my gaucheness for the good start it gave me against the Inspector. This Inspector used to arrive about every tenth lecture.[1] He would sit surrounded by frost in the foreground, not too pleased with his evening journey in his chilly

---

[1] But of course no good inspectorman would arrive the day he was expected. In later, more experienced days, I used to ring up Inspectors and say 'I think you'll enjoy the discussion tonight'. Amazingly, it worked. Tipped-off class would respond brilliantly to rehearsed inspector-lecture.

Austin Seven to my Tutorial Class in East Croydon. After listening, bolt upright, for ten minutes, he would put on his glasses and study the printed syllabus of the course, which I had written nine months before and crammed full of stimulating discussion points which I hoped would catch the eye of Mrs Hobchild, the Director, but which yet had a solid backbone of knowledgeable continuity for Mr Coldharbor, the Inspector, to approve of. In practice, of course, I never followed my syllabus, nor looked at it even if I could find it.

It was my personal custom, a good one, to talk about whatever book I happened to have been reading the week-end before the lecture.

Mr Coldharbor, after listening for eight minutes, then put on his glasses and had a look at my syllabus. He found Week Ten, February 4th, 1938, and began reading it, in order to discover what I was supposed to be talking about. A glance over his shoulder told me that he read 'Scandinavian Drama and its Influence on the Twentieth Century Renaissance of our Theatre'. What I had in fact been talking about when he came in was, because it happened to be the book I was reading on Sunday, the new Life of Isadora Duncan – the part where she renounces marriage bonds as a priest-ridden concept, antagonistic to the fuller life.

I owe so much to the hard schooling, the cut and thrust, of those early days. Looking back I very much doubt whether, now, I could with three swift and easy transitions show the obvious relationship between the first impact of Ibsen's *The Pretenders* and Isadora Duncan's renunciation of her second husband.

Prop Management

Although I myself wear glasses for reading off hidden notes, I have never fully developed Lens Drill. It is rather a good thing and, of course, common practice, when you have at last started a laugh which is liable to stagger on for a moment or two, to take off your glasses slowly and sadly and rub fingers into the tired marks under your eyes. Of course the real expert, making a particularly boring or pointless remark, can sometimes succeed in hypnotizing the audience into thinking he has said something effective by speeding up, rapidly diminishing the volume of his voice and dashing his spectacles on to the desk, looking at his audience with corkscrew intentness.

One of the shortest of our lecture experts was 'Winkie' Green, who lectured under the name of W. L. St G. Lauterberg Green. He was for some years very successful with a prop-gambit some have found worth

trying. When he first came on to the platform all you could see behind
the desk, owing to this shortness, was his hair, upright yet twisted,
like sticks of barley sugar. Winkie would then make considerable play
of his being too short, sending people to fetch something for him to
stand on and pretending to be embarrassed by this, gaining sympathy
at the start, though in fact his disability was one of his strongest
weapons, and he wore shoes without heels.[1] His prop he used about
half-way through the lecture. He once told me that it was a small
segment cut out of the top of a discarded hat rack. Anyhow from it
seemed to sprout a miniature arrangement of chimney-shaped
prongs, of different heights. Whether he was lecturing about Persian
rugs or bird-migration, Keats or the meaning of the Primary in the
Presidential Election, he would always bring out this old bit of hat
rack in the fortieth minute, place it, delicately and precisely, on the

table in front of him, take out a very
long pencil from the other pocket, and
point to some bit of this thing about
half-way up one of the chimneys. The
audience grew as still as death. 'This
model gives a very rough idea of relative
positions,' he would say, stroking the
top half of it delicately with the tip of
his pencil. 'Do you see that this "reaction" counterpart is much shorter
than is commonly imagined?' There
was not a soul in the audience, except,
of course, trained Lifemen, who did
not feel that this demonstration proved
that Winkie was a born lecturer, and
that, unlike some, he could give you
something to bite on.

Counter Chairman

At the beginning of these notes I emphasized the danger, for the
lectureman, from his Chairman. Here are a few hints from the best
Chairman-squasher I ever knew – Willy Jack:

'In style, be the opposite.' If your Chairman is a practised official
speaker he probably knows how to stand still and keep his arms
folded or relaxed by his sides. Suggest at once that personally you are

[1] Borrowed from an oldish male Ballerina.

not that kind of speaker (even if that technique suits the paid agent of some local political club) by allowing your hands to wander aimlessly, sloppily stroking the back of your head or fidgeting with your collar.

Arouse sporting instincts of audience by having slight tremor if you are unfortunate enough to have Chairman who is popular games hero. It may make Chairman hover nervously if you fiddle crossly with the lighting arrangements one minute before starting. If he happens to be enfeebled through age, it may be a good thing to ask him to move a heavy lectern a foot to the right. In general one should be reasonably severe to the Chairman. I have rarely encountered an audience who was not glad to see Chairman snubbed, unless he is an old war-hero or professional ball-game player. Never, on any occasion, make the hackneyed mistake of laughing and shaking your head when Chairman makes his joke or compliment. Always, including and especially when he pays his compliment to you, show no reaction whatever but let your eyes roam coldly yet intently over the faces of your audience, as if you were surprised and interested in something about their physical appearance or nationality. When audience applauds after his introduction of you, clap your own hands twice in a dangling way as if you wanted to make Chairman feel that for once in a while a tiny little bit of the applause was for him.

If Chairman sits on platform it is rather a good thing to turn suddenly full on him, bending your body right towards him, and say, 'But I wonder if Dr Riemann agrees with me?' This will make Dr Riemann look nervy and mystified and guiltily aware of the fact that he hasn't been attending; and it will suggest to your audience that you wonder privately whether Dr Riemann is quite the man for his present job.

When the Chairman makes his speech of thanks afterwards still pay no attention. You may smile, but smile half to yourself while busily

TYPICAL ODOREIDAISM

Asked to substitute for speaker at Yeovil Union, and faced by a house three quarters empty, he steps out and puts up this board.

picking up your papers, packing your glasses, etc., suggesting that for goodness' sake we all of us want to get on with the job, don't we. There are tremendous possibilities in after-the-lecture play. If there is a sort of sandwich-and-coffee period afterwards, mix freely with the young students and talk naturally to them in a light tone. Say very little to the Principal, be coldly courteous to his wife, and say nothing whatever to the man who was your Chairman. Do not even look at him. This will give him the impression, not too brutally I hope, that he has somehow put his foot in it.

4. THE OLD QUOTESMAN

Good Lifemen, returning from abroad, bring back lifeworthy objects for their friends. A dollar forged north of the Arctic Circle, a Highway Patrol identification badge. F. Wilson brought me a sheet of paper with some Chinese printed on it with, as I thought then, the excellent suggestion that I should pin it up in a thin gold frame near the projection on the mantelpiece on which I hang my old rowing cap, and that I should look at it occasionally and say, 'Don't you love those lines?' Guest should hesitate. He will probably say:

'What, do you mean you can read that?'

'Give me time – give me time,' I reply. 'Yes I can read it, I suppose, but don't ask me to translate because I don't think it's translatable.'

Then you stare at it and say: 'Well, let's have a shot,' and you start: 'The secret beauty-bird sings – chants – in the magnolia tree – the water buffalo strides in the brown waters of our . . . water margins . . . village pond, I suppose we might say. The scholar sharpens his nails: the sun is setting over the western hills – long shadows creep across the – the City of Exclusion – the Forbidden City, sort of . . . That's very roughly it.' The whole thing certainly has a mildly depressing effect on the visitor. But I must mention this incident. The 1000 to 1 chance happened to me, incredibly, the third time I tried this. H. Howse was my guest; and who would guess that such an expert amateur cricketer had taken a First in Oriental languages? 'I like your translation,' he said; 'but isn't that actually a warning against pick-pockets?' I turned slowly round. I remembered now that Wilson had told me. He had pulled this thing off the wall of the waiting room of a railway station. If I had been alone with Guest I should have said, 'Do you know you're the first person that spotted that?' and tried to create a leg-pull atmosphere. But Withers and Miss Plimm were there,

THE OLD QUOTESMAN

イェイツ「イニスフリイ湖島」

を写し出して、それを讃美するよりも、自分の心の瞬間の望みをここに結晶させたのである。しかしそれだけならば、表現は易しいのである。そして、それのみの表現をしてあれば、その詩は我々に訴える力が薄くなるであろう。イェイツは、この詩の中に、内奥の感情を歌って、人間一般の心に宿っている望みを表わしている。我々はすべて煩わしい現実を離れて、静かな心の安らいを追うという、理想をもつのである。しかもこの詩は、理想を表現するのみではなくして、一種の強い光をきらめかせて、人間の心の中に横わる根本的

so I had to try a less familiar counter. 'Yes,' I said delightedly. 'Isn't it a marvellous language? Against pickpockets or "hand-flickers", isn't it? But of course being Oriental it's all in terms of the "secret bird", the long shadows and the "forbidden city" or citadel of private possession.' H. Howse made no comment, except to say that if the text was really being reproduced in a book it should be stated that the Chinese was not Chinese at all but a comment, in Japanese, on *The Lake-Isle of Innisfree*.

4

RECENT WORK

IN ESTABLISHED GAMBITFIELDS

1. NEW NOTES ON BRITISH CAR PLAY

ONE OF the best-known chapters of *One-Upmanship* was, I think, miscalled 'The Carmanship of Godfrey Plaste'. The ploy of Plaste's Placid Salutation spread through the country: but the impetus came much more from the rich gambitfield of *driving* the car, in elaboration of my original definition of carmanship – 'How to steal the crown of the road without being an absolute hog'. I first formulated it, I remember, when I was alone sitting over the precipice at Cape Wrath, with nothing but kittiwakes and Dr Longstaff for companions.[1]

Nowadays Plaste and his work are in disrepute. He has spent the last three years fiddling about with impracticable car gambit inventions, the £250 horn (for his £50 car) which can be adjusted by finger-tip control to suggest, by its tone, not only such ordinary sounds as the raucous YAH and the ladylike BOO, but more complex ones like 'Keep to the left, rescue squad passing' or 'Pardon me, madam, but if you would do me the privilege of reading the road signs you would realize, I think, that this is my road. All I ask you to do is to keep your car stock still.'

Modern car research chooses different fields. Let us ask ourselves 'What is the perfect One-Up situation?' Undoubtedly when the car which has just passed you, owing to superior driving or engine power, is copped for speeding while still in view, and, even better, grazes a lamp post as well.

'Be one thing or the other'

But this ideal situation is beyond our control. Not so the car itself.

[1] See my *Short List of Places Where it is O K for things to come to you first at.*

This should be either (1) Old or (2) New. Nothing between. The
fading three-year-old model, desperately polished up till the chromium begins to wear off, is dubious, unless your ploy is the marvellous
something you can't buy now about your wonderful old bus. The-
very-good-quality gambit, suggesting money without a trace of
ostentation, is certainly difficult to counter, although I have one
useful recommendation here, I think, which is to say (glancing at
friend's black and unobtrusive but fairly powerful 1953 Bentley):
'Yes, but cars are basically made of tin anyway, aren't they. Why try
and pretend it's eighteenth-century Chippendale?' If your own car is
cheap and showy, coloured in alternate panels of ginger and rasp-
berry, you can look at it affectionately and say: 'I quite like old
Toothpaste Tube here.' But in most cases my advice is 'Be really new
or really old'.

If the car is fresh and gleaming, dress the part. Always put on
leather gloves (never buttoning them) while driving. Make a tremendous fuss about not leaving day-old newspapers in the back of the
car. Let your personality conform. Be inclined, now if never before,
to use a masculine but expensive cigarette holder. Clean and empty
the ash tray every day. Let it be known that you are of the opinion that
'mud unless instantly removed, rots the underside of mudguards'.
It may even be worth while having your car driven to your house by
your garage, for no especial reason. Peter Blond, the racing driver
(of Peter Blond Ploys, Inc.) has been a great help to me here. He
recommends that if there is a ledge inside below the real window, let
there be put one object only, carefully chosen – perhaps the large
long leather of a case of binoculars (unnecessary to buy the binoculars as well). Do not, he says, make the mistake of *gilding*. That is, do
not have any accessories whatever (patent fog lamps, offside distance-
markers, unusual extra reflectors). 'It spoils the line.' Practise saying 'It spoils the line'.

Old Car play is very different in some respects. There is a definite
time when new car becomes old car (point of no return to the dealer)
– when making a ploy of looking after it changes into making a ploy
of not looking after it. A new gash in the wing and you laugh. 'It's
only hanging by a thread anyway,' you say. In fact your whole
character alters. Instead of being dependable, husbanding, poised and
cleanly, you are now slapdash, open-air, good old Freddie. Change
your Christian name if necessary. Be generous in gesture when driving. Leave piles of strongly contrasted objects in the back which yet

give a favourable impression of the extraordinary variety of your interests. Squash racket ... micrometer ... *Stories of the Great Operas*. Old car should if possible be big. If it is very small as well as old, and unpleasantly refined as well, it may be necessary, on chosen occasions, to have it driven up by a chauffeur, which suggests big new car as well, somewhere in the background.

A sports car is a splendidly one-up possession, and the carman play is to leave it at that. Above all, for instance, do not cover the front with badges and arms of automobile clubs. 'There is only one badge which interests me,' say. 'That little bit of tin which means you've

For New Miniature Cars:
Effect can be heightened by sitting hired chauffeur on two telephone directories.

lapped Silverstone at a hundred.' If you don't actually have one, use a 98.8 voice here. Then: 'They cost about twenty pounds extra, but some think it worth while to buy tyres with RACING stamped on them.' Ignorant women and a few men can be impressed by the hot-rod approach, which is basically to let it leak out that the car 'isn't quite what it looks'. That you've had a Bosch ignition put in, and Frog lighting. Valves ground in Padua. 'I had to have this old Vauxhall body to take the $2\frac{1}{2}$ litre.'

Of course the skilful passenger can answer back this kind of thing. In the sports car he can say, 'I bet she'd really move with the right petrol.' Driving smoothly and silently along in his friend's gleaming new solid-worth type model he can say, 'I should have that little bbbrrp noise put right at once, tiny as it is.'

We most certainly offer people lifts

From time to time new Notes for Driver occur to us. Here are a few.

When you see a friend who obviously wants a lift, offer him a lift. But drive well *past* him before you stop, shouting in a drill-sergeant voice: 'Want a lift?' This will cause him to take an anxious little run to catch you up. Ram home this advantage by leaning over him, after he has got in and shut the door, so as to open the door and shut it again yourself, suggesting that passenger can't even shut a door, especially if he has in fact done so.[1] Ask him if he'd mind moving a little over to the side as he's in the way of the hand brake, as if the hand brake worked; speak again about the door, telling him to be careful

CORRECT POSITION FOR SUGGESTING:
'I don't in the least mind stopping to pick you up, but if you *could* get a move on . . .'

not to touch the door handle. Take corners more swingingly than usual, as you have the steering wheel to hang on to, he hasn't. If he is smoking, develop car pride and indicate that he should use the ash tray. You will point patiently to where it is. If he uses the electric cigarette lighter – has the effrontery, that is, to do so without asking – tell him you'd rather he didn't as it uses up a lot of current. If he fiddles about with matches, light his cigarette with lighter yourself, while passing lorry at crest of bridge. If passenger is made to sit in back seat it is always possible to make him feel inferior not only to yourself but to any other passenger in the front seat, and actually it often works well to put your own adjustable driving seat back to the full extent of its runners. As back passenger bends up his knees,

[1] The driver is the only effective person by historical right of assumption. Passenger can not only do nothing; rightly handled he can know nothing either.

ask him to be careful not to squash the greengages. Somehow ignore him, as if he were a hanger-on. Suddenly bring him into the conversation with some such phrase, half shouted, as: 'I'm speaking of Browning *the poet*', suggesting that you are in a half doubt whether he realizes that Browning is a poet.

After half an hour stop at a pub suggesting drinks all round in a way which implies that now, surely to goodness, passenger will be relieved to be able to make this slight repayment of your kindness to him. After twenty minutes further driving, do this again.

Cheeseney is now experimenting with holding the right hand of his girl, while driving, with *both* hands while steering *with his knee-caps*, which he presses up against the lower rim of his steering wheel. Some progress has been made.

Of course there are frequent occasions when the carman wants to impress his passenger, especially if she is a woman.[1] R. Cheeseney, the mushroom grower, who fancies himself as one of the 'ugly as sin yet a great charmer' boys, prides himself on the ease with which he makes his left-hand gear-change with his right hand while continuing with his left hand to hold the right hand of his lady passenger, or even to stroke her knee. Cheeseney is always theorizing about car-parking, when taking a girl to the theatre. He has a complicated graph showing exactly how far you can ask what kind of girl to walk from the car to the theatre in what kind of weather when she is wearing what degree of paper-thin-ness of shoe-sole, plus peep-bo big-toe-

---

[1] Godfrey Plaste, naturally cumbersome in a car, and never having possessed one which went more than forty miles an hour, was yet able to impress, some readers may remember, because he had the good idea of practising, for half an hour a day, the difficult trick of reversing. A Worcester girl, Daisy Hopper, is said to have been successfully wooed by Plaste, entirely by this speed in reverse.

holes. I have seen this graph, which I am bound to say seems to be designed by Cheeseney to prove the power of Cheeseney over girls in general.

Why I Admired Godfrey Plaste

I admired him, though I never liked him. How many times have I heard it said: 'Now he's a good driver.' Well of course he is and so are

all of us, who have been driving our car for donkeys' years, ten thousand miles per annum plus an occasional trip as far as Avignon or Aberdeen. We never think about it. We do it unconsciously. We are all the same. He is the same. Yet somehow he has made a thing of being a good driver.

He does not do this in the stupid obvious way of dropping hints about earlier experience 'on the circuit', though – smart ploy – he often speaks of parts of cars by the French or Italian names for them. I have seen him memorizing these, off a chart. Out of a car he is rather a vague man, but inside he suddenly becomes neat. His profile becomes definite and exact. In the car he wears a carefully placed hat. He takes hold of the wheel precisely, with gloved hands. I had a fine old aunt who though perfectly *compos mentis* wouldn't drive with me at the wheel, she would only go with Plaste. I once had to make Plaste drive my car, because we all had to go to some funeral. I watched his methods. Plaste started almost ridiculously slowly, while my aunt sat on the edge of the seat leaning forward and bracing herself as if she were on a scenic railway. Then Plaste said slowly, 'I hope you're not going to ask me to drive fast.' A moment later my aunt said: 'Thank goodness you're not one of those scorchers.' Plaste answered quietly: 'Can't afford to be, with all these Sunday School drivers about.' This meant nothing at all, as far as I could see. But the black flowers in Aunt's hat

wobbled. She was laughing. Plaste waved on a van packed with full milk-bottles. 'See that fellow?' he said (the speedometer said eighteen), 'though I expect you like to move a bit when the road's clear, you old serpent!' 'Oh, if it's safe,' Aunt said, pursing up her mouth and then suddenly smiling. 'So long as I'm with a good driver.' Quite soon Plaste was taking bends at fifty and once passed a car on a corner, typical mistake. Immediately he was explaining to Aunt the danger of passing on a corner, and she sat back relaxed, smiling and nodding. When his speed made it necessary for him to brake sharply he would always say '*Wow* – did you see that fellow?'

For more sophisticated passengers he would use different methods. For the boy who confuses good driving with good acceleration he would spend a lot of time, and make a good deal of noise, in second gear. With some people he found that a tremendous and to me quite ludicrous amount of hand-signalling created a good impression. Plaste had an instinct for this type, and would play up. With others, the lightly spoken technical word was a success, which reminds me that even in his little smashes, and he was by no means accident-free, Godfrey hardly ever lost face.[1] For instance I have known him, three times running stopped by lights, mistake reverse for first gear when moving forward on green. The third time he bumped back quite hard

[1] With accidents generally we have gone I think beyond the primitive rules which advised the basic techniques (i) to start shouting first (ii) to take out a notebook and write, saying nothing. As we have never been personally involved yet in any contretemps where any words of our prepared repartee have been of the slightest use or even heard, let me quote (because I admire them and because I want to say something positive) remarks made to me by a foreigner as he got out of his car to greet me, having run lightly into my side from a by-road when my car was stationary, outside the Sweet Nell & Co. Lipstick factory on the Great West Road. He simply smiled and said, 'Well, it eez good? There are no corpse?' I was much struck with the untutored skill. It may be the basis of a new school.

into the car which had been following him, and when the driver came
round to expostulate, he said: 'You realize what's happened of
course. The malden rod must have leapt its pressure rim. One is
helpless, I'm afraid. Look – can you give me a hand?' It may interest
Maida readers to know that Plaste now lives not very far from Acacia
Road, NW.

2. FURTHER NOTES ON PIPE PLAY

Is Pipemanship on the decline? There is no doubt that this subject
is profoundly historical. I think it is true to say that except with men
in remote country rectories, boys between the age of eight and fifteen,
the *nouveau feudal*, and a few somewhat older girls, the pipe in 1958
fails to impress.

Lifemanship's earlier annals record that we used to do a good deal
of work, some of it published, on the use of the pipe in its role of
Silent Conversationalist. If a young man wants to describe to you
exactly why it is that he is totally unable to work, or a young girl wants
to tell you how happy she is because she is in love with someone else,
who is in love with someone else, it is useful, it may be essential, to
have a pipe in your hand, and, if possible, smoke it. To look, during
a pause, very hard at the mouthpiece, turning the pipe upside down.
And we have explained how the prolonged bubbling blow through
the stem of a rather wet pipe can give the effect not only that you are
deeply sympathetic but are absolutely clear on the right course to
pursue.

In addition to this tried basic, there are lesser uses of the pipe as a
spreader of dis-ease.[1] At a party of the dinner-jacket order, for instance, the technique is to come not in a dinner jacket but in tails,
rather loosely worn, and then as soon as possible put a pipe with a very
large bowl and a very short stem in your mouth. Place your hands
in your pockets, and walk slowly up and down on the outskirts. This
suggests that there is not much difference to you between tails and
bedroom slippers and that dressing up is absurd anyhow and that you
are not to be influenced by it.

The main complaint of women against pipes is that the pipe person-

---

[1] A good modern approach, if asked whether you are really a pipe-smoker,
is to say that you have been asked to do so by the British Medical Association
as a control. This means that somebody exactly the same as you is smoking
cigarettes, which are known to be more harmful. By this means it is proved
that they are more harmful.

ality is boring and produces boredom. A rather confusing counter-effect can occasionally be made, therefore, by unpipelike people with an unpipelike pipe, small and straight, held horizontally in the mouth while speaking, in this strained position, quickly and wittily, yet with a certain amount of temperament and moodiness.

In spite of the great cigarette scare, only the most brilliant and advanced pipeman can succeed with the suggestion that the pipe is a symbol of Health, that the going for a walk with a pipe is as natural as, and difficult to distinguish from, going for a walk with a dog. But indoors, controlled practised pipe smoking is capable of making a a cigarette smoker seem flustered and untidy, particularly if the cigarette smoker is ashy and scruffy, can never laugh for fear of coughing, and maintains a long worm of ash messily drooping from his cigarette.[1]

Possible Slips

These may be serious. We ourselves have made mistakes. Early in life I made the primal pipe-fumble. Ostensibly to ask his advice, in reality to impress him with my talents, I called on a celebrated pipe-smoking author. I thought it would be a good thing if I myself had a pipe. After an hour's practice, I fancied I was perfect. It is not necessary to add that after a few minutes of my spitting and prodding and pecking, he asked me if I would like a cigarette, eventually (after much irritated difficulty) finding one for me at the bottom of his wife's handbag – a Turk, tasting of Valse Bleu, a medium-priced scent of the period.

Remember, always, that it is a grave mistake for the insignificant-looking man of no personality to buy a documentary film-producer's outfit and go about in sea boots, coarsely cut mackintosh, no hat and huge carved pipes sticking out of the mouth and pockets like candelabra. If your personality is small, be small in a delicate way and use, for instance, unusually thin cigarettes and tiny lighters.

Long practice and deep knowledge is the key to successful pipe control.

If you are going to possess a pipe, you must have the accoutrements and side effects which include, for instance, massive matches, and

[1] The best defence from the unkindness of being called 'a cigaretty old thing' is to have a good deal of cigarette-holder work and plenty of crisp clicking and exact handling about your method of smoking them. It is not enough simply not to dribble.

raw slices of unusual vegetables to preserve humidity in the pouch. If you are a pipe-is-my-best-friend man, it is advisable to study pipes as if they were pieces of rare porcelain, and know about pipe history. A sound gambit here is to show that everything is ever so much more early than anybody thought. So far, for instance, from Raleigh having introduced the primitive leaf to England, it is no exaggeration to say that what he brought back was in everything, perhaps, but the exact name and appearance, a packet of *Camels*. Try referring to neolithic times, mention Orkney excavations, and say something of the *Cigarro* casts of the mesolithic boulder and delta folk.

Tomorrow, at noon, in spite of the fact that they have been proved to kill you more quickly, I shall give up cigs and shall be once more slowly and carefully preparing the pipe which is going to be my friend, and watch the miniature wilderness of delicate tobacco fronds at the top of the bowl rot and moulder as they always do when I smoke them, to a damp and sticky block of seaweed.

5

PLOYS IN PROGRESS

Our purpose in this chapter is twofold. Its first object is to give some impression of the continuity, the multiplicity, and the ubiquity of lifesearch and life-contributions. Its second is to give encouragement to those many workers, by sea and land, who have contributed their own ploy or ploylet, and passed it on to Yeovil, where, after vetting and polishing, we establish it as something of our own, occasionally mentioning the actual author in a footnote.

I. AIRCRAFT PASSENGERCRAFT
F. Wilson, Nettlebed

F. WILSON, basic collaborator in and illustrator of Gameslife, has a circle of admirers only less wide than that of the Founder. Holding a high place in the hierarchy (Nettlebed 2a) he is most generally known for the gambit in which he so majestically majors – the Secret Mission which takes him to Singapore for tea and Beirut for elevenses. It should not be publicly revealed that secret mission is cover for private research: the reader must guess to what extent the development of certain ployfields owes its origin to the unconscious collaboration of HM Govt.

How to be top passenger is one of Wilson's flight studies. Although genuinely VIP, he has found it necessary, owing to the intermittent failure of a somewhat fluctuating personality, to establish this fact. Here are some of his recommendations. Only the grammar, punctuation, and vocabulary have been altered by us.

1. Sometimes the most obvious is the most effective. On the walk across the tarmac, lean for support on the air hostess who has come to take over. The quiet word 'Invalid' will be heard. A seat, perhaps even two, will be found for you away from the engine, near the air hostess, and right opposite the entrance to the bar. Remember to walk up steps one at a time. Many passengers will feel uneasy, and a few will think they have a Jonah on board. Murmurs of 'Captain Ahab'.

2. Once the best seat has been secured, invalid atmosphere can be

dropped. During take-off, if novice air traveller in next seat is a little tense, mark correct approach by quietly relaxed attitude. Keep on right-hand glove and start reading. (Suggestions: Proust translated into Spanish – 'much funnier': or take out a few wreaths of newspaper cuttings and say 'Do you ever *read* your newspaper cuttings? – rather amusing.') If novice stares in strained way at airstrip offer him the piece of barley sugar you have been given.[1]

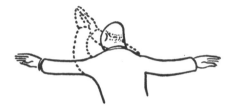

As soon as aircraft is well over ocean, Odoreida goes through the motions with his arms, of the breast-stroke.

3. When plane begins to sway in bumpy patch, say: 'I *thought* I noticed a change in note and a momentary splutter. Have you ever thought how sensitive these vast flying machines are – how human, like you and me? Almost a comfort to know that they, too, can err.' This is an Odoreida speciality. During the demonstration by air hostess of Life Jacket drill, Odereida always says: 'I bet the rubber's perished.'

[1] Beware of possible counters. 'Novice' may be Lifeman who says (*a*) 'Take-off still gives me a kick ... the sense of uncoiling energy ...' Or (*b*) 'An airfield is the place to see partridges. At Praha last month, I saw 7½ brace, plus four hares and six leverets.'

2. THE LIGHT PUT-OFF, OR CLUB STABILIZER
Staff, London

Armstrong Walter was in our Club, the Sequoia. He was better dressed than myself, and his luncheon guest was better dressed than either of us. This would not do, so I said to him while walking to the bar: 'Extremely sorry I couldn't get to your party the other day. I meant to write you a note. I didn't get away from my meeting till nearly midnight.'

As A.W. has never asked me to a party, and almost certainly has never thought of doing so, this microscopically *broke flow*, or at any rate led to explanations *which I could hurry apologetically away from.*

3. 'DONT'S LET'S HAVE TOO MUCH CHRISTIAN-NAMING'
Staff

Here is a crisp lifeplay, and this is its sequence. For years Mr Black has been calling Mr White 'White' – i.e. by his surname. Then one day he, Black, on some relaxed occasion, will call White 'Arthur'. This is a trap. White, encouraged by this, will call Black 'Nevill' next time he meets him. This is what Black has been waiting for. He instantly calls White 'White' like a sledge-hammer, repeating this with a strong suggestion of reproof, and more than a hint that he for one is not going to indulge in a forced matiness reminiscent of the Light Programme.

4. LET ME READ YOUR HANDS
J. Bryan III, Florida

Last week in Florida, I had an evening with Robert Frost. The conversation turned to fortune telling, and he told me about a hostess who insisted that Mrs S. read his palm: 'My dear, she's too marvellous and everything she tells you ... well!' Mrs S. was eager to read great poet's palm, so he held it out, first right then left. She bent over it, scrutinized it with knotted brows. Then shoving his hand aside, said 'Sorry, but I'm all out of practice,' and walked off. Frost says that ever since, when he walks down the street, he looks over his shoulder.

5. CHRISTMAS FEELING
G. Odoreida, Yeovil

Odoreida sends as Christmas card a twopenny postcard of Llandudno railway station with 'My. Xmas from Mr & Mrs G. Odoreida' stamped on in mauve ink, the ink very faint and the stamp much worn.

6. WHEN TO USE THIN SPIDERY HANDWRITING
J. Bryan III

Yesterday, I stopped in to see a friend of mine, and parked my car beside B's house, just in front of a gate marked DO NOT BLOCK THIS DRIVEWAY. I knew that it wasn't really a driveway at all, but B's system of reserving a parking space for himself. When my visit ended, I found a note on the seat of my car, 'Please do not block my driveway again. E.B.' (This was B's wife.) So I borrowed some stationery from a friend of mine named Buffington (a perfect name for this ploy), persuaded a lady with a spidery handwriting to follow my copy, and sent this letter.

Sir:

I was carrying some jelly to an *invalid* in your neighbourhood yesterday morning, and since my hip does not permit me to walk more than a few yards, I parked my car nearby, in front of what turned out to be *your* house. Only then did I notice your sign, *ordering* the *public* to stay away! I rang your doorbell, to *beg* five minutes of *grace*, and waited and waited, but *no one* answered. My hip was beginning to pain me, so I *peeked* through your gate and discovered that your 'driveway' (!) was nothing more than a *narrow walk*, impassable by any vehicle wider than a child's *express wagon* or '*Irish mail*'! You should be *ashamed* of yourself for trying to label this *path* a *driveway*! I propose to park there *whenever* I wish, and I would welcome an opportunity to defend my *right* to do so in a court of law.

My uncle, the late Major Wyndham Buffington, *died* for his convictions, on the bloody field of Sharpsburg. If necessary, *I* am prepared to do *no less*.

I remain, Sir,

(Miss) SALLY LOU BUFFINGTON

P.S. I would have communicated with you *at once*, but this experience upset me so that my doctor made me spend yesterday afternoon with the *blinds drawn*!

6

SUPERYULE

How to be Top Christmas

LET US first define the Basic Christmas Gambit. It is: to seem to be more truly Christmas than other people; to be top man, for geniality; to be one up in general Christmas kindliness; to be so managingly unobtrusive in the background that background becomes foreground.

Our early work on this subject, some of it published, may now look primitive and formless, but it was basically sound. It was constructed, students may remember, on the teaching of Arthur Meriton, chosen for his fine Christmas name, and developed by him as Good Old Uncle Arthurship. He was expert in inducing a suggestion that he was Top Uncle at Christmas Parties. If he found children disliked his hearty voice, and they often loathed it, he would immediately switch to an extremely quiet tone, crouch down on his knees so that his face was dead level with that of the smallest child in the room, speak to it so quietly and naturally as to be inaudible, and thereby achieve a kind of one-upness. Being nice to the smallest child present is unassailably correct Christmas play. Speaking to children absolutely naturally impresses grown ups; and Meriton made a speciality of this. If the child started to scream, Meriton used to say, 'Somebody's been made to feel a little out of it lately, haven't they?' as if it was somebody else's fault.

This sort of thing was rather in Meriton's family. He had a brother, Sebastian, who created a great Christmas reputation for himself by specializing in one ploy, and one only, which we have listed as How to Make Parents Feel Awkward about whether they make their children believe in Santa Claus.

To Santa-Claus-is-Real parents Sebatian would say: 'You let them believe?'

PARENT: Sort of.
SEB: And then, later, when they find out the truth—

PARENT: Oh, well.

SEB: Do you realize that to Charlie you are a king, an emperor, a god who can do no wrong, much less suggest a falsehood?

PARENT: You mean . . . sort of . . . oh, I don't know.

SEB: A child's mind is like a new leaf, as perfect as a spring shoot. But the caterpillar is not far away.

I have heard Seb go on like this for five minutes and then trot off to the garden to challenge a Santa-Claus-is-*not*-real father and start on him like this.

SEB: Hygienic.

FATHER: I beg your pardon?

SEB: No nonsense about you, and 'no such person as Santa Claus'. Good luck to you.

FATHER: Well, thanks.

SEB: I was brought up in that tradition too – calm, rational, very modern pictures, food sterilized to the last drop.

FATHER: Oh, I don't know.

SEB: Of *course* Santa Claus is not real: and of *course* not one atom of romance, nor the warmth of make-believe, must stain the black and white of the mind of the child of the rationalist.

Pre-Christmas Technique

All this may be described as basic Christmas play. Recently we have been devoting more time to what we call Counter-Christmassing. In this the expert prepares his lifefield by taking the Christmas out of Christmas for other people before it starts. This is obviously sound lifemanship in general: in particular it makes it easier for the lifeman, by judicious timing, to be top geniality at the right moment.

'*Thank Goodness That's Over*'

Coad-Sanderson has always been my model here. He was in advertising, and to be in advertising is to be naturally one up on everything except perhaps advertising itself. It is impossible for an advertising man not to know the inside facts about anything essential which can conceivably be bought, like boots and electric toothbrushes, and a lot of things which can't conceivably be bought as well, like Christmas.

Coad's small pale face was so ordinary that it was only just possible to distinguish him from other people by the small pale moustache, which seemed fixed by a tin-tack, as it were, in the middle of it. His face hadn't got a line on it because he didn't go in for expression, as he spent his life not reacting to anything in any way whatever, much less showing surprise. Round about the beginning of December, when we began to get a bit warmed up and prospective about Christmas, and started mentioning it, he would say:

'Well, thank God that's over.'

'How do you mean?' we would say.

'Well, of course, this Christmas started for me in February.'

'How February?'

'Frightful flare-up deciding on an entirely new lay-out for Shortt & Weitz's street level window-display for Christmas 1958. As you can imagine our client is on the conservative side. A tremendous robin-and-mistletoe man, but it wasn't until March that I convinced him that festooning them with holly wasn't the best way to sell ladies girdles – indeed that it was definitely *Resistens* advertising.'

Coad made really an extremely good story of these Christmas advertising meetings, but of course it had a very sapping effect on the thrill of holly and mistletoe which normally we wouldn't have thought of till rather late, and suddenly, two days before Christmas. Round about May if you went to Coad's office for a drink, you would find him shouting down the telephone about colour ads behind schedule for the Christmas number. Commuting in America on some cool beach in Maine, he would be writing letters to a comic artist in Georgetown briefed to invent, during a humid spell in Washington DC, a comic picture of a St Bernard dog in a snowy frozen waste. In fact not only in his work but in his life Coad was an out-of-season man, so that one had the feeling that whatever week of the year was the the actual week it was an out-of-date week so far as Coad was concerned, Christmas, of course, especially.

Office Partyship

Coad was brilliant in his way. But the nigglingness of Coad did limit his effectivess, and just where you would expect an advertising man to shine he was not really at his best. I mean, of course, in the important Christmas activity of his partyship. The art of office Christmas Partyship is the art of taking the opportunity to get one up on your rivals at that very time when surely to goodness all ranks are level and all thoughts of self-promotion, and indeed any business thoughts of any kind whatever, at that one time of the year when everybody should be perfectly natural together, shall and must be in abeyance.

This of course is a great time for the go-ahead mid-ranking executive. Coad's ordinariness stood him in bad stead here as few people
could remember who he was outside his office. What one wants here
is the sitting-on-the-corner-of-the-table approach, one foot on the
ground, listening extremely hard, smilingly but intently, to whatever
anybody is saying to you. I must say dear old Gattling used to do very
well here before he began to go bald in that curious way in which he
went bald. These are his notes.

One must mix of course; said Gattling, but at the same time let it be
seen that you are the one who even at the party keeps his essential

GATTLING BEING RATHER WONDERFUL
with Junior Stenographer.

finger on the remorseless pulse of business events and e.g. takes one
or two squints at the tape machine.

Simultaneously, and connected with this, you must make use of the
opportunity to show that you are in the secret confidence of the
managing director by accidentally revealing, twice, that you are on
much more familiar terms with him than your official ranking might
suggest, and that you are much better at talking to him easily than
Old W. who has been his Number Three for 22 years, and in fact
you have only just got to take a glance at me, now, to observe that
rather pleasant relationship which has grown up between me and the

managing director, who really, in a way, regards me as a sort of son.

But above all Gattling did this tremendous mixing at the Party. He was extremely good too at being perfectly natural, without of course a trace of flirtation, to the two prettiest office secretaries simultaneously, and then at looking just as intently and interestedly at Miss Heason, who was easily the plainest woman in the building. Gattling would also amusingly take part in the fun, do good imitations of X and Y, but essentially kindly ones, and show that he was essentially more youthful than many younger members of the staff and that that helped him to understand them.

Finally, he was also able, and this needed great care, to show that he was the one who could thoroughly mix and yet never get in the least bit tight. If Gattling had a fault, it was that he sometimes overdid this business of demonstrating that he was not in the least bit tight, though sometimes, afterwards, Gattling did well by being 'a tiny bit sorry that "J.G." rather overdid it at that party'.

I would like to add this note of my own.

(1) If you are the mad-ideas man with a flair, it is O K to get pretty gay and mad: and it is possible in the midst of the party to have mad salesmanship ideas and be brilliant about work to show how your real interests lie, revealed *in vino*.

(2) If you are the smart wife of director or chief executive, you must first find out what kind of clothes all the other women are going to be supposed to wear and then dress in the exact opposite manner. For instance, if the juniors are going to come low, be yourself buttoned up to the neck.

Not Being Sure About Dickens

My final example of advanced Christmas lifemanship I owe largely to the work of one woman, Angela Nethersole. The active part of her career belongs to a tremendously place-name-y village under the North Downs much visited by myself during Christmas holidays since the war.

Angela is neither pretty nor plain, but she is quite genuinely jolly, and likes fun; and she likes Christmas. Yet as soon as Angela is around at that time of year, one longs passionately for Christmas to be over, and nobody knows quite how she has done it.

One point she makes is that Christmas to be truly jolly must be spontaneous, and yet the way she says this is one of the most dampening things she does. She used to be very fond of Charles Dickens until she read the long life of him by Stebb-Nutting, which of course is very psycho and casts such a completely new light on *A Christmas Carol*. It was soon after this revelation that Angela began to be down on Christmassy Christmas cards. Last year she sent me a picture of the mummy of an ancient Christian found in Rome with 'Via Appia' on it. This was obviously anti-Dickensy.

Near Christmas, Angela starts referring to the 'Santa Claus figure'. She says that about three-quarters of our Christmas customs are pagan, and that our own perfectly straightforward way of always putting stuffing in our turkey is Bronze Age, and that you still find it in the disembowelling rites of Bush culture.

THE 'MUCH-BETTER-WITHOUT-AN-ACCOMPANIMENT' PLOY IN ACTION

I always like to play a few carols on the piano just about Christmas time, and I like it when other people join in, which is what generally happens. Gattling can put in quite a good bass to anything I play. But last year Angela Nethersole drifted in and almost at once I was conscious of a climatic change. Suddenly, while I was playing not untunefully, she said: 'Don't you think those lovely carols sound much better unaccompanied?' Gattling agreed, like a fool. But in less than two minutes it was clear that what Angela really meant was that it was better if *she* were to be in charge of the singing. 'It is a fifteenth century carol, "Icyle holde thee strait",' she was saying in her extraordinarily clear voice, which seemed also to suggest that the spelling was funny. She then *took out a tuning fork, and struck it*, made two or three quick passes with her hands, and started to sing this tune with four other people who seemed suddenly to have appeared from nowhere. They must have been practising it for days; and perhaps the most annoying thing was the way they stood absolutely still for pauses between verses. A lot of people sheepishly clapped.

Still there is no doubt that this one-up attitude to carols was a fine Christmas gambit, much better than such old-fashioned Christmas Day ploys as making the shyest and most nondescript member of the party dress up to take the part of Santa Claus, or, during the present-giving, making sure that you give Freddy exactly the same sort of present that Freddy gives you, but making it obvious, if it is given in public, that yours is the better quality, or, if given in private, worse. Against the expert Christmas man there is no sure defence, and it is better to fall back on the general suggestion that all this being tremendously nice at Christmas is redolent of Somebody covering up a tendency to be tremendously nasty all the rest of the year. Suggest that for you, personally, it makes no difference. Say almost anything, because whatever you say, at this time of year especially, no one will pay any attention.

ENVOI

Now Superman says farewell – indeed Superman is already on the way to a new assignment. International Lifemanship has enlisted his services: counter-Marxmanship absorbs his waning powers. His broadcast to the American nation on April 20th was badly jammed, but certain sentences were heard, a few phrases recorded:

. . . would start by saying that Lifemanship is exactly as old as the very words diplomacy and foreign policy. The utter unsuitability of the term 'foreign policy' in the context of friendship between people – what a fine gambit in itself. And the root meaning of diplomacy is of course 'double' – diplous, duplicity . . .

Khrushchev says, 'Let us end atomic experiment.' Think for a moment of historical Summit ploys. No need to remind you of Trojan Horsemanship, which perfectly describes the basic Khrushchev gambit. It is a type of all the doubleness of diplomacy. In the very act of making a friendly gesture – you can see the European headlines (GENEROUS GESTURE BY GREEK GOVERNMENT) and the attack is already starting . . .

. . . notice the splendid lifeword of the Greeks – they were *liberating* Helen of Troy.

. . . the perpetual one-upness of Marxmanship . . . that the Suez incident occupied five times the space of the Hungarian massacre when the United Nations met to register moral disapproval. One-downness by nature . . . of Eden.

Why is the one-upness of Khrushchev always intact? Is it an example of Beyond the Palemanship, which can use the very words 'we have no further territorial ambitions' as the code phrase for an unprovoked attack? . . .

Brinkmanship is a clever way of describing the Dulles attitude: but like all Americans, through some fatal streak of reasonableness or human feeling he falls short as complete International Lifeman.[1]

[1] Occasionally the US Government can deliver itself of a basic lifespeech, made for instance by Eisenhower more effective by the fact that he believes it himself. It was at the time of Suez that we heard him say: 'America has no financial ambitions in the Middle East.'

Khrushchev is the true Brinkman: his existence depending, as Russian rule has depended for thirty years, on enemy-at-the-gate-manship . . . diverting attention from the making of lethal weapons by sidelines made to please the public . . . the satellite gambit or Sputnik ploy. This is part of National Geophysical Yearmanship, and typically Marxian.

But Khrushchev must always be one-up because he is more words-of-one-syllable. 'End the bomb' can be understood by three-quarters of the world: 'Organize a committee for international inspection and mutual restraint' can only be understood by less than one-twentieth of it. 'Summit Conference' is easy to understand: 'Exploratory committees to ensure that a conference is effective' is a one-down phrase because it needs thought to understand what it means.

In the words of R. Abernethy, International Lifemanship is lifemanship carried to a point which stops short only at deathmanship, or the art of winning the world without actually blowing it up. (*The rest of the discourse was lost in a succession of buzzes and pings.*)

'A HELPING HAND'